SERIES IN GUIDANCE AND STUDENT PERSONNEL ADMINISTRATION
ESTHER LLOYD-JONES, EDITOR

No Longer Deprived

**The Use of
Minority Cultures and Languages
in the Education of
Disadvantaged Children
and Their Teachers**

Ruth Fedder
and
Jacqueline Gabaldon

Teachers College Press

**Teachers College, Columbia University
New York, New York**

© 1970 by Teachers College, Columbia University
Library of Congress Catalog Card Number: 78-76318
SBN No. 8077-1312

Manufactured in the United States of America

Contents

Not only professional and volunteer social workers, but all of us who work in public or private schools, have to work today with people, both young and old, from social and cultural backgrounds very different from our own. Somehow we just can't communicate, and the other "different," "deprived" ones don't respond to our efforts to help them as we would like them to do.

In describing several such situations, the really remarkable contribution that this book makes is to show exactly how a number of professionals went about communicating with and teaching children who were very different and hard for them to understand. The teachers kept reports of what happened week by week and even day by day, and the records here included show the infinitesimal steps that led to virtual miracles. One must conclude that there is nothing truly important except little things — but, of course, it was just such a process that Darwin used in gradually developing his theory of evolution.

Out of the process here described the teachers learned as much or more than the children, but of a different order. The authors include rich summaries of these learnings, which are easily translatable into one's own practice. And after watching almost day by day how the Indian child, the Spanish-speaking child, and the child of migrant workers are gradually turned into successful, confident learners, one begins to see how one might improve his own efforts at overcoming deprivation.

Esther M. Lloyd-Jones

La Jolla, California
February, 1970

Why This Book Was Written

Problem children—those who are disadvantaged or for one reason or another "different" from other children—have always been of special concern to their teachers. Until recently, however, teachers have been given little basic encouragement in their efforts to help such children.

Not long ago, behavioral scientists envisioned a child as an individual with latent traits that would gradually be developed as the child matured. In other words, a child had a high or low "potential"; tests measured what was there and indicated to a teacher what to expect. Intelligence was relatively unchanging and potential essentially fixed. Therefore, a child's inability to learn was interpreted as a deficiency in physiological, intellectual, emotional, or social readiness. Educators seldom envisaged themselves or what *they* did for a child as influencing his development in a strategic sense.

During the last decade, though, influential behavioral scientists and educators have modified these concepts and reorganized these views. They know now that a child cannot be appraised as an entity apart from his cultural experience. The particular areas in which the child is functioning well or poorly when he enters school reflects what he has or has not learned in his preschool environment. They furnish clues to his intelligence level, but do not define its limits. A child's behavior, used to measure his adequacy in life situations, cannot be understood apart from the context in which it occurs. Therefore, simply giving a child an intelligence test will not necessarily tell you how bright he is. It will only tell you how he is functioning today.

The challenge now directed at the school is to enhance the child's intelligence, not simply wait for him to mature until we can say this child is "ready" for school. Today's effective teacher will directly and deliberately supply the kinds of experiences and environment in school that hopefully will, in time, not only make up for gaps in the child's early learning, but also arm him with the tools to continue learning to the limits of his potential. Such a teacher, as Maslow points out, sees "adequacy as a function of the development of inner nature and sees growth emerging through expression and need gratification. He views man as moving toward self-actualization—unless growth is thwarted by need frustration. . . . This is, indeed, a refreshing and hopeful view of man."[1]

This shift in point of view has taken place largely because during the last few years social scientists, behavioral scientists, and educators have devoted increasing attention to educational problems of culturally disadvantaged children. Until then, public schools had often neglected this major source of manpower and of creative talent in our school population. For these children, it was "Up the Up Staircase" all the way; even being admitted into school presented difficult problems, and then they were confronted with the dilemma of keeping up with the others in order to stay in school.

The usual teachers did not "reach" these children; they were not able to understand them, their backgrounds, their culture, or their parents. The usual school tests did not identify these pupils' assets and abilities; the usual curricula did not challenge them or meet their needs.

Now research has helped to determine specific steps that *can* be taken to reorganize our educational system so that the intellectual—or academic—handicaps of these children can be overcome, their functioning intelligence "improved," and their potential realized. Pilot studies across the country have demonstrated means to these ends: smaller classes; flexible, nongraded grouping, especially in the elementary school so that failure will be minimized and enrichment maximized; counseling for parents and children; individualized help for those who need to learn English as a second language; employment of experiential methods of learning to help make words more meaningful; textbooks and visual aids based on experiences disadvantaged children can understand; certified, specially prepared teachers who will be sensitive to their problems; assistance with their health and nutritional problems; an extended school day and week that will include trips to civic, cultural, and recreational centers of interest in their communities and provide them not only with places for study and recreation, but also with available adults who will coach them, individually or in small groups, in their academic skills, particularly in reading.

Most studies, however, have generally been made in large cities and have been based on teaching a *class* of disadvantaged boys and girls.

---

[1] Arthur Coombs, Chairman, *Perceiving, Behaving, Becoming.* Yearbook of the Association for Supervision and Curriculum Development, National Education Association, (Washington, D.C., 1962), p. 85.

Too little attention has been paid to the fact that there are disadvantaged children in almost every classroom in our country. The Southwest, for example, contains not only the country's largest concentration of our Indian population, but also 5 million Mexican-Americans who constitute the second largest disadvantaged minority in the United States. Most teachers will not be teaching a class of disadvantaged children; but almost every teacher, each year, will find perhaps five to fifteen disadvantaged boys and girls in his or her classroom. Throughout our fifty states, disadvantaged children in ever-increasing numbers enter our public schools: they come from economically poor homes, from migrant workers' camps or construction crews, from Indian reservations, from refugee groups, or as immigrants—Indians, Negroes, Eskimos, Puerto Ricans, Cubans, Orientals, and "poor whites."

Every study made has emphasized the urgent need for "better" teachers for these boys and girls. The term "better" is usually defined to mean someone who understands disadvantaged children, who has a set of assumptions about them different from the negative conceptions studies have shown many teachers of middle-class background to have. Descriptions have been given of the "effective" teacher's characteristics and behavior patterns; his ability to do "creative" teaching has consistently been stressed. But little of this research has helped the thousands of regular classroom teachers who want to know more, specifically, how to be more effective in *their* classes.

Teaching disadvantaged boys and girls effectively does not involve learning only a set of gimmicks or techniques! Underlying the methods of teaching is a teacher's ability to understand how a disadvantaged child—regardless of age—feels when he enters school: he finds himself in a new world, often an alien environment where expectations and values are different from those he has known, where habits he has never learned are necessary to success. Perhaps his parents have had little education; they may not speak English. They may even be hostile toward the idea of schooling, either because they see no economic value in it, because they have, in the past, been humiliated by school failure, or because they see education as a threat to their culture and traditions. Their child will not be motivated to work in school; it will be difficult to initiate his interest and to guide him successfully into learning. Unless the teacher understands all this, he cannot "get through" to the child, no matter how clever are his techniques. Every perceptive teacher knows that his basic attitudes toward children and the quality of his relationship with boys and girls determines their response to whatever he does.

Many teachers have the potential to be effective teachers of these boys and girls. But the potential needs to be nurtured. Teachers need assistance in learning how to understand these children; they need, in addition, to know how to teach them—specifically how, day by day, they can work successfully in their own classrooms with these pupils.

Suppose a well-meaning teacher is confronted with a child so verbally inadequate that the teacher despairs of his ability to communicate with the child, or the teacher faces a hostile child who "does not want to learn," although the teacher is eager to help him. How does a teacher work toward achieving rapport with these children?

The teacher interested in disadvantaged boys and girls wants to believe that it is possible to have positive learning experiences with these children; he wants to be shown *how* to do so. In this book, he is shown; he observes teachers working successfully with disadvantaged children who have a variety of learning difficulties. Many specific techniques are demonstrated and discussed. Many different approaches are used by teachers in this book; they believe that there is no one *right* approach. Teachers who tell their stories in this book are working with white and Negro, Indian and Mexican children—including children of migrant workers. You, the teacher reading their stories, may be teaching Puerto Ricans, Eskimos, Orientals, or Cubans new to our country. These teachers are working with elementary school children. Although you may be teaching on the junior high or high school level, it will become clear to you that, in spite of age differences, similarities in disadvantaged boys' and girls' basic needs and responses are evident beyond doubt.

The perceptive teacher-observer will learn ways of coping with the basic—the *real* problems—involved in helping disadvantaged children to learn. Perhaps you choose not to emulate the pattern you see? You'll evolve your own style? Good! The important end result of your observation of these teachers is that you, a potentially effective teacher, discover the manifold sources of your own strength.

The aim of this book is to provide potentially effective teachers of disadvantaged boys and girls with the insight, knowledge, understanding, and second-hand, day-by-day practice that will build into them the confidence that they *know how* to teach such boys and girls. You cannot *tell* people to be confident, but you can provide a situation that builds confidence! The authors believe that one of the best confidence-builders any teacher can have is the sharing of daily experiences with a teacher who is so working with children that the children are beginning to feel their own power, to see the value of their own ideas, and to realize what they can do with knowledge. Such children are being won to learning!

The authors invite classroom teachers throughout the country to share such an experience with teachers of boys and girls who began the school year as culturally disadvantaged children, strangers to the school environment, and who ended it wanting to come to school and wanting to learn.

The authors gratefully acknowledge the advice, encouragement, and assistance of many people in this writing project. The numerous graduate students at Northern Arizona University who, working as teachers among Indian, Mexican, and Negro children, or who, as representatives of these groups themselves, read and criticized parts of the manuscript pertinent to their experience; those teachers who contributed material used in the actual compilation of the manuscript—Patricia Berman, Alice Huff, Mary Margaret Wedgworth, Famous McElwee, Jr., Herbert Marshall, and especially Elizabeth James of the Tempe Public Schools in Tempe, Arizona, for her story of Anthony in Chapter 6, Louis Carillo, a high school teacher in El Centro, California, for Victor's story in Chapter 5, and Tony Gabaldon, principal of the Sechrist Elementary School in Flagstaff, Arizona, for background information on Chapter 5.

Without the enthusiasm and assistance of all these people—and their conviction that this material must be made available to teachers—the manuscript may never have gone beyond the stage of "concern about the problem."

Ruth Fedder
Jacqueline Gabaldon

Flagstaff, Arizona
February, 1970

CHAPTER 1

A Reading Problem – or Something Else?

Every September, teachers everywhere wonder about their new classes: What kind of children will I have? How many will be eager to learn? How many will find school difficult – and *be* difficult? How many will merely sit out the year? Primary teachers wonder: will they learn to read? Teachers of older children question: why didn't they learn to read? If they can't read, how will I be able to reach them? Or will there be some who just don't respond to my efforts?

Before school has been in session more than a few days, some answers are obvious to a teacher. The class is an average group: a few boys and girls whose behavior leaves much to be desired, some who are shy, some who are bright, some who are lazy, some who have problems, and some who are good workers. They are average, too, in nationality background – some Indians, mostly Navajos and Hopis, some Spanish-speaking children, a couple of Negroes – maybe half are primarily English-speaking children. Yes, that's a pretty average class in our school. Maybe in yours, there are Puerto Ricans, Cubans, Eskimos, children of Chinese and Japanese background in addition to the "white" children.

Already the fast learners stand out from the rest; they read well. Some read fairly well, although they need lots of help. Then, just as the teacher feared – there is a group to whom books seem almost unknown. Every year, too many children are at the "bottom" of the scale in reading!

Let's suppose that you are a second grade teacher, concerned about this situation. (Or, perhaps, you teach fourth or sixth grade, junior

1

high or even high school.) You wonder why? What is the matter with these children? Are they retarded mentally? Surely not all of them! Maybe they don't like school. They might be just plain lazy. Then you ask yourself, maybe it's my fault? This is only my second year of teaching and, when I did my practice teaching in training school, we didn't have children like this. Maybe I don't know how to teach them. On the other hand, maybe their last teacher didn't know what *she* was doing: it doesn't seem that she taught them anything. They don't even pay attention. I go over and over the same thing, but they still don't know it. Sometimes, I wish they'd go somewhere else, so I wouldn't have to teach them. I'm afraid it's a waste of time to try. Look at the ones who are bad readers and non-readers. They're usually those Indians, Mexicans, and Negroes. Everyone says they don't want to learn. Maybe I should give most of my time to the rest of the class.

How often do teachers think this way? More often than they themselves realize. We all become discouraged sometimes — and as a result, pessimistic. Some teachers, of course, do admit, to themselves at least, that they really would rather not have to teach "this type of child." Other teachers perhaps will not put forth the necessary effort to reach these children?

Many teachers do *want* to help children like this — if only they knew what to do! They feel frustrated; it seems as though they cannot teach them anything! Since they don't know why these children cannot learn, they may assume that the fault lies with the child. "He doesn't want to learn. He's lazy or stupid." How accurate is such an analysis of these children's learning problems which, usually, take the form of reading problems?

It would be a grave mistake to pretend that there is one easy, simple solution for reading and learning problems. There are as many problems as there are children, and as many responses to problems as there are children to respond.

Suppose you begin by making a diagnosis of each child in your class who has a reading problem. Why can't this Indian — or this Mexican — or white or Negro child in my class read?

"Now suppose, just for a moment, that part of the reading problems are not reading problems at all," Mrs. Brown, a teacher experienced in working with these children, suggests.

"How ridiculous!" is often the instant retort of an inexperienced second-grade teacher like Mrs. King, a new teacher in our school. "What do you mean, 'reading problems are not reading problems'? That's double talk."

"But just suppose that this statement was true."

"Well, even if it was true, what would it prove? Nothing."

"Not yet, no, but it is necessary as a first assumption. Next, if the problems are not reading problems, why can't the children read? What kind of problems are these?" Mrs. Brown goes on,

"First, look at the non-readers. Is there any *one* thing that most of the children have in common? Not all of them, but most?"

"Well, I don't see it. They're all different! Some are Navajos, some are Hopis, some are Mexicans plus a few Negro and Anglo. How does that help? Wait a minute—do you mean they are all different? They just aren't like us?"

"What makes them different besides their nationality background and the color of their skins?"

"Well, maybe they don't live like we do."

"That's the idea. Their culture is not the same as ours."

"You mean that they don't *have* any culture, don't you?"

"No, that's not the idea at all. Each group has its own culture, and each is different from our culture. Sometimes we call them 'culturally disadvantaged' children, but we mean this only in the sense that they have little knowledge of the predominant, middle-class culture which those children have who 'fit' into our school. It doesn't mean they have none of their own."

"Well, all right, they have a culture, but they aren't used to ours. Is that it? I still don't see how that can affect their reading."

"I think it might. This cue gives us a place to start. Can we begin to see something they have in common with each other?"

"I don't understand. First, you say they are all different, and now they have something in common. The only thing I can see is that they're all bad readers."

"True. But why should this be so? Perhaps you will find some answers if I tell you a story."

MRS. BROWN DISCOVERS DISADVANTAGED CHILDREN

Mrs. Brown began, "A struggling school teacher whose main problem was trying to teach her low group to read was discouraged at the immensity of her task, but convinced there must be *something* she could do. She tried everything the books said, and everything she knew how to do, and everything other teachers told her. The children—mostly—tried to cooperate with her and please her. She taught them sounds and letters and words. She used all kinds of word cards; she taught them the alphabet—how to say their letters and recognize and write them. The children seemed to understand about letters and sounds; they could say the words sometimes, but they seldom remembered them. So, they just weren't improving in reading.

"Then one day, the teacher thought about a discussion held in a college class the previous summer about learning being a two-way proposition; how teachers could learn from children, as children learned from them. She decided to watch the children, to listen to them and to see what she could learn from them about themselves. She began to keep a record of some of the things the children said and did — in the halls and on the playground — when they did not know she was really watching and listening. Maybe, she reasoned, if she could find out what they said and did on their own, she could find cues about how they would learn. She began carrying 3x5 cards around with her and making notes on each non-reader whenever she could do so unobtrusively. Most important, she began really to listen to the children and to *look* at their behavior more closely.

"She remembered that behavior is language. She asked herself, 'What is each child trying to say?' After a week of listening and watching and making notes on each child who was having reading difficulties, the teacher began to find patterns in the children's behavior. For example, one little Navajo girl never seemed to talk to anyone in class if she could possibly avoid it, yet on the playground she chattered in Navajo to an older Navajo girl. Why? One little Mexican girl wouldn't talk to anyone in the class. She would only answer the teacher's questions by whispering in her ear, speaking disjointedly and hesitantly. Why? One larger, older white girl from the Tennessee mountains talked so strangely — to the children's ears — that they had laughed at her, so now she talked only to the teacher and then only in monosyllables in response to questions. An Indian boy didn't seem to understand anything his classmates said in their attempts to be friendly with him. No wonder, then, that he did not respond to the teacher's questions!

"The teacher tried to put herself in their places. How does it feel to a boy or girl to be confronted with words he can hear, but cannot comprehend; with expressions that stand for ideas in a culture he knows little about and in which he feels uncomfortable; with sounds which have a tonal quality, pitch, and inflection that his tongue cannot manage?

"After another week of observations, the teacher sat down again to read over the daily notations she had made on each child in her lowest reading group, and one fact emerged clearly: each of these children was having difficulty in communicating with his classmates and with her. Was it possible, she thought, that *she* wasn't communicating with these children? How ridiculous! She always spoke clearly and slowly. Of course they understood her! When she talked to the other children in her classroom, *they* knew what she meant. Her directions were always given clearly; what she wanted done should be perfectly obvious to everyone—that is (a new idea occurred to her) to everyone brought up as she had been—understanding the vocabulary, the customs, and manners she took for granted!

"Maybe these children who didn't understand her or their classmates didn't have the same frame of reference? If their experiences were different, the words she used might as well be Greek as English for all they understood. Maybe, all this time, she had been talking *her* words and ideas and *assuming* that, because they had meaning to her, all the children would understand her and would learn. Maybe her first problem *was* to communicate with these children? How could they read if they couldn't talk to her? And, if they didn't even understand what she said, how could they be expected to understand words in print?

"The teacher pursued this idea. Could she communicate with them? Would they understand what she said? Could she and they carry on a conversation? The next time she sat down with her non-reader group, she took some of the time she thought she couldn't spare from the mechanics of reading and talked *with* them instead of *to* them. At first, they wouldn't talk—except for a monosyllable now and then, or a few words whispered in her ear alone. But, gradually, as they learned that she really was interested in things they did and liked—in their pets, their families, their friends, their food, or their amusements—very gradually they began to talk during their reading lesson. The teacher listened carefully to the children. She discovered, to her amazement, that many words common to her had absolutely no meaning to these children. So, the teacher watched the children; whenever there seemed to be the slightest doubt as to anyone's understanding a word or phrase she or someone else used, the group would all talk it over, draw pictures of it, act it out—and then try to find the word or a picture representing it in their reading book.

"At first, the teacher found that she and they could be looking at the same picture, yet not observing it in the same way. For example, one day she discovered that these children didn't know the difference between lettuce and cabbage even when they talked about them and were looking at pictures of them. Obviously, the children had never eaten these and had, apparently, not had them pointed out either in the town market or as they grew in truck gardens near town. So how could they know the meaning of the words? The next day, the teacher brought some lettuce and cabbage from home. The children felt and smelled some of the leaves of each, talked about them, compared them, and discussed what they tasted like. Then, the teacher and the children were all talking about the same things, each listening to the other and understanding — as well as hearing — what the other said.

"Or were they? In one workbook question, the children were to choose whether a person could eat a chair or a cherry. The children were quite sure you could not eat a chair, but what was a cherry? After school that day, the teacher went to the store. Next day, she brought to class cherries and strawberries for the children to see and feel and taste and compare. Another day, she brought her knitting and knitting needles to illustrate a phrase in the reading book.

"So it went. The teacher discovered, for example, that shapes mentioned in the book had to be demonstrated. She taught the children to look around the room to find squares and circles and triangles; they drew these shapes, colored them, cut them out, pasted and made designs with them. To learn words like *across, around,* or *under,* they acted them out; a girl walked around the table, a boy crawled across, another crouched under it. To reinforce and broaden the meanings of these words, everyone looked around the room and across it; they went under it to the gym.

"At first, less actual sight or oral reading was done during each reading lesson than before the teacher used this method; but, when the children read now, their faces beamed. Their behavior revealed that they were beginning to understand what they were reading. Their satisfaction in their accomplishment was creating not only confidence that they could learn to read, but also interest in learning to read as well as possible and as much as possible.

"As the teacher continued to devote time each day to listening to them talk and to helping them to express themselves, words began to have more meaning for the children; they wanted to use them more often. Then, when words they knew were pointed out to them on the printed page, the words were friends; the children began to recognize and remember them. Their reading began to improve — slowly at first, but dramatically. The children blossomed in their enthusiasm to be first to identify some word they now could understand because they had talked about it and learned its meaning. They began to want to read as they began to believe they *could* do so.

"The teacher made available to them many easy books; she encouraged them to read, just for fun, to their parents, younger brothers and sisters, and friends. She came early and stayed after school so that they could read to her. She encouraged them by sending them to read a story to the school nurse, principal, other teachers—anyone who knew what she was doing and who would be sympathetic and interested in the children. She sent them to these people to deliver messages or to do errands so that they could practice this language still new to them. She encouraged them to talk in class, although this was difficult for these children. She kept inventing ways that they could speak inconspicuously if they were not yet ready to stand up in front of the class. She helped them to become class members in every sense of the word."

"It sounds like a fairy story, Mrs. Brown. Do you mean that if I could get Henry Yazzie to talk, he would automatically learn to read?" Mrs. King asked.

"No. *We're* having the same difficulty that the children have—the same words do not always mean the same thing to each of us. Each of us hears the same word; but we each interpret it in terms of what we have learned to understand by it.

"Reading is a word that conveys a multiplicity of meanings. Some people think that to learn to read is to voice aloud one word after another from a printed page; others think it is imbibing ideas from a printed page and interpreting these—and so on. I am saying that, when children have difficulty with this process of reading—however you define it—there are reasons for their problems.

"One reason definitely is, I am sure, that no child can learn to read, comprehend, or remember words that have no meaning to him. And this reading problem is not only confined to elementary school! A New York high school teacher wrote about the disadvantaged students in his classes: 'Their trouble is basic. They have not been taught the meaning of words. They cannot read with any facility. Consequently, they cannot grasp what is being taught . . . and have slipped further and further behind.'[1] No one—child or adolescent or college student—can even respond to words unless they understand them!—"

The young teacher interrupted Mrs. Brown. "Maybe that's what's the matter with Henry Yazzie. He just sits in his seat and stares at me. He doesn't respond when I ask him a question or tell him to do something. Sometimes I think he doesn't hear me. Oh, I don't mean he *can't* hear me; he just doesn't listen to me. And he never says anything."

"Do you know why Henry acts like that?"

"I haven't the faintest notion," she replied, adding apologetically, "I've never worked before with children of as mixed nationality as

---

[1] John Tebbel, "Teacher of the Unteachables," *Saturday Review,* May 15, 1965, p. 72.

those in this school. I've seldom even *seen* an Indian in my life. I wish I had time to learn something about them. Do you know some good books that would teach me what I need to know—fast?"

"I have a better idea," Mrs. Brown said eagerly. "Let me explore it—and I'll tell you more tomorrow."

CULTURALLY DISADVANTAGED—THEIR FRAME OF REFERENCE

All the way home, Mrs. King kept thinking about Mrs. Brown's story. Was she really trying to tell you that these children are special? She used the phrase "culturally disadvantaged."

Let us examine the all-purpose phrase "culturally disadvantaged" more closely. It refers to many social, economic, educational, ethnic, or racial factors and social pressures which impede an individual's full freedom of choice and hinder or destroy his right to maximum opportunity in our society. Culturally disadvantaged families retain the lowest social status, lowest income, highest unemployment rate, poorest health and housing standards, and poorest education in our society. In the past, the Irish, Germans, Scandinavians, and many people with Central and Eastern European or Mediterranean backgrounds who immigrated to this country and who existed in poor living conditions were referred to as culturally disadvantaged. Now, more writers are recognizing the plight of the Negroes, Indians, Mexicans, Puerto Ricans, Cubans, Eskimos, Orientals, and the indigent urban and rural whites as members of this culturally disadvantaged population. Today's culturally disadvantaged children generally come from families who have had no educational tradition and little formal schooling. Some parents are so busy, even harried, trying to obtain the necessities for sheer survival that they are unable to provide their children with intellectually stimulating experiences.

The Children

Many children from lower socio-economic backgrounds have had limited opportunity to learn the language patterns expected of them in school, and to explore areas outside of their immediate home environment. When and if they get to school, they find the going hard! Because of the dearth of intellectually stimulating experiences which they had prior to their school entrance, they are at a disadvantage in adjusting to most school environments. Before they can hope to make a satisfactory school adjustment, the unique needs created by their life situations must be met. In other words, their teachers must take into account the range of handicaps with which these children come to school: they may be handicapped by reactions of fear, apathy, anger, inferiority, and ambivalence toward the schools. They may not speak English—at least not the school's language. Many, in fact, will be deficient both in English and in their native language. Their daily speech, usually, is concerned with their immediate environment; it is sparse, colloquial, and concrete. If they speak at all! To some of them, silence is a way of life; the unstimulated and neglected are sad, passive, listless, and withdrawn. The unwanted and rejected express in their speech and action the fact that they are habitually angry, reckless, and aggressive. Few of them have been able to develop positive self-concepts. All this behavior is dramatically demonstrated by the children described in the following chapters.

Some of these children give the impression of being mentally retarded because they do not "respond" in the classroom when, actually, the problem may be their lack of experience with words, the language of the classroom. Or, they may be untrained in listening to and following directions, not inclined to abstract thought, and unaccustomed to regimentation and supervision by adults. They may lack training in independent problem-solving situations which engender motivation and stimulate achievement. They could be unfamiliar with the varied experiences necessary to the manipulation of school materials.

Confronted with learning problems in these children, the teacher's appropriate response is not to attribute the problems to nature, heredity, or even environment, but to analyze the causes and gradually to eliminate them. The diagnosis should be child-focused rather than test-focused; it should take into account the particular child's family background and developmental history.

Such analysis requires also a continuing study of the *nature of learning*. Numerous schools have been experimenting to find out as much as possible about the conditions under which such children learn best. Current developments allow us to be optimistic about our ability to vastly increase their level of education. We have found for example, that if we begin language enrichment programs in the preschool years, not only do we foster children's curiosity, initiative, and language facility, but also, we nullify—sometimes even prevent—negative feelings toward the school or negative experiences in later grades. Thus we win another child to learning.

Without a doubt, our human resources are our nation's most valuable asset. The school's greatest challenge, therefore, is not only to conserve, but to develop the talents of every boy or girl in our population by providing each with those educational experiences which will enhance the development of *his* or *her* potentiality.

Does every child have access to this kind of an education? True,

our children all can go to free public schools housed in the best buildings, offering the best equipment, and taught by the best teachers that
the people of their respective school districts are willing to support.
Accordingly, all children have equality of educational opportunity.
Or do they? The description in the preceding sentence, to the degree
that it is accurate, would indicate equality of educational *offerings*.
To create genuine equality of educational opportunity, experience in
recent years has taught us, educational offerings often have to be
decidedly unequal. Why?

The Home

Since our immediate concern is with culturally disadvantaged
children, the most pertinent answer is: because children learn at home
as well as in school. In middle-class homes, children learn from the
conversation, the respect for the child, the concern about his education and his future, the stimulation furnished by books, periodicals,
music, trips to the theatres, museums, concerts, zoos, ball games. For
the child whose home is characterized by poverty or a struggle for
survival, by disease, instability or conflict, the educative process is
complicated. Although the parents may want "something better" for
their child, such a home tends to produce a child who is tired, hungry,
ill, apathetic, or emotionally unstable. A boy or girl from such a home
where physical punishment is common—as it is in many disadvantaged
homes—may also have learned that violence is his best weapon and
often his only defense.

These last statements are not to be construed as having, altogether,
a negative implication. Riessman states that "one of the great difficulties with formulations like 'culturally deprived—disadvantaged—
handicapped—impoverished'—and the like is that they connote inadequacy in a culture rather than present a rounded picture of the
culture: the latter would include a culture's strengths as well as its
deficiencies."[2] Understanding the culture of the underprivileged,
then, "is not the same thing as recognizing the economic difficulties
and general life conditions of the educationally deprived."[3]

Some of the values these children have learned, although different
from those of dominant groups in our society, are not only utilitarian
but also worthy of emulation. Many of their patterns of behavior have
developed because they are compatible with, even necessary to a
group's way of life, be it crowded urban living or life on a Navajo

---

[2] Frank Riessman, *The Culturally Deprived Child* (New York: Harper and Row, 1962),
    p. 113.
[3] Ibid., p. 112.

reservation. As such, they deserve respect and understanding—even though they may need modification if they are to be effective in the dominant American culture. Examples and implications of these statements will be discussed in later chapters.

The disadvantaged child's parents may oppose—or tolerate—the idea of schooling for him. They may see little value in academic routines; they may be alienated from the school because of personal past experience with failure in school or fear of the negative effect of schooling on their indigenous culture and traditions; or they may consider schooling a waste of time which could be better spent earning money. On the other hand, some parents of children like these may be eager to help their children "to learn English—to get a good job—to have a better life than I did."

Whatever his home background, to the culturally disadvantaged child, the school will be a completely different world from his home. For example, in school, he is expected to function in a language which his parents may not speak and, therefore, could not teach him. Lest he be called "stupid," he is expected to respond to directions he does not understand, to use equipment and materials he never saw before, and perhaps to behave in ways contrary to values he was taught to cherish. In his response to these unrealistic expectations, the child may show withdrawal, indifference, or even outright hostility to the school; without doubt, he will have difficulty concentrating on learning.

The School

Children from bilingual homes, different cultural backgrounds, and economically poor families are being found, in varying numbers, in almost every school in our country—urban, town, rural, even suburban. What are schools doing to make up for the inequality of opportunity between their homes and those of their more fortunate classmates? Many schools during the last few years have manifested interest in discovering and developing the talents which undoubtedly exist among these millions of children from disadvantaged backgrounds.

Demonstration programs in outstanding schools have proven that educational opportunity can be equalized; these children are being helped with extra effort, extra time, extra equipment, and well-prepared personnel who understand the exigencies of education for these children, and who design and put into operation positive programs of education. These programs bring hope and purpose to the disadvantaged of all groups and help these children successfully to gain an education in spite of learning deficits in their early years. In other words, it has been proven that disadvantaged children *can* be motivated to stay in school, *can* learn to like school and enjoy learning, *can* be prepared to advance on the socioeconomic scale, *can* be imbued with behavioral and intellectual values different from those with which they entered school.

Instead of the school's reinforcing the sense of personal insignificance and inadequacy which life has imposed on some of these children as preschoolers, many schools are accepting more realistic approaches and responsibilities: *recognizing* the uniqueness of every child; *identifying* his interests, aptitudes, needs, and desires; *stimulating* him to want, more fully, to know both himself and the changing, challenging world in which he lives; *helping* him to define for himself goals which will be personally and socially satisfying and productive; and *providing* him with incentives to fulfill these goals. This process must begin, at the latest, when a child enters school, as the following chapters emphasize.

The Society

Naturally, such a program of education must take social factors into account: the hatreds, prejudices, and conflicts of the adult world are reflected in the child's world. Caused in part by factors of status, economic pressures, and the need for group identification, they also stem, in part, from the very multiplicity of groups in American life and the tendency to identify with one's own "in-group." In American society, the effect of mere membership in a disadvantaged group may produce such feelings of rejection by the majority group that psychological and real barriers are built between a child and his peers. Prejudice, we know, hinders—or warps—the development of an individual. In short, a child's inherited potentialities are either encouraged or inhibited by the social pattern into which he is born.

Truly to understand the disadvantaged child's possibilities and problems, the school must appraise the entire complex of factors in which the child must learn to interact: the structure and functioning of his family; his values and behavior patterns; the present state of his education; his future prospects for education and economic opportunity; and the attitude of his community—a society often indifferent and sometimes hostile to his plight. Each facet in this complex is inseparably connected; deficiency or improvement in one area affects all the others positively or adversely. Facing this fact realistically helps a school to define, not only its own possibilities and limitations in helping the individual child, but also its responsibility in so working in the community that community members will be led to examine *their* attitudes, values, and actions toward groups culturally different from the majority.

This teacher's thoughts about these boys and girls have been "long, long thoughts"! Who wouldn't be baffled by their numerous problems? Baffled, yes—but not frustrated any longer. "These children *can* be helped, I'm sure of that now. Mrs. Brown did it! Tomorrow, I'll ask her to tell me more about exactly what she did."

A SCHOOL ORGANIZES TO LEARN ABOUT CULTURALLY DISADVANTAGED CHILDREN

Mrs. Brown teaches in a school where there is intelligent concern about these children. The concern is manifested not only in teachers' positive attitudes toward these children and in their skill and understanding in teaching them, but also in the administrator's determination that teachers receive the support and assistance they need and that new teachers, like you, have the opportunity to share their colleagues' skill and to gain knowledge from anyone in the school or community who can contribute to their education.

What elements are essential in developing this type of school situation? First, of course, an effective teacher, one who tries to make a genuine contact with each child, tries to convey to the child his or her desire to understand his interests and needs. In the light of this teacher's knowledge about each particular child, classroom activities to which he can contribute are provided, ones in which he can continuously improve his performance and through which he can earn the respect of his classmates. Within such a framework, each boy and girl can experience a fair measure of success and failure. Repeated success encourages self-respect and challenges the child to try again, thus stimulating him to further progress and gradually developing a sense that his school experience is important to him.

Whether or not this educational process takes place in the classroom depends totally upon the teacher-child relationship. The most important quality in this relationship is the teacher's respect for the child, a respect which involves persistent confidence in the child's potential. Respect for a child is important in working with any child, anywhere. To children accustomed to drabness, conflict, and failure, the genuine interest and respect of an adult is all-important.

Intelligent respect for the disadvantaged child is, in fact, the secret of contact between the child and the school. Intelligent respect is based on a teacher's awareness of the circumstances affecting the child, an awareness which involves sensitivity but is not judgmental. The teacher is not repelled by deviations from his own standards. Instead of judging a child by his "shortcomings," the teacher is encouraged by the child's ability to do as well as he does, despite his handicaps. The teacher knows that, if a boy or girl's present behavior and attitudes are such as to hinder his development, they can be unlearned and replaced by more positive ones. The teacher encourages each effort the child makes in this direction—and the teacher's recognition becomes a powerful motivating force for the boy or girl, as incidents in the next chapters repeatedly demonstrate.

However, teaching disadvantaged children involves many problems which cannot be handled by the teacher alone. The effective school provides other essential professionals: remedial teachers, guidance counselors, psychologists, psychiatrists, nurses, and school social workers to observe and work with children and to provide specialized help for teachers. Examples of teacher-specialist cooperation are cited in the following chapters. The number and type of specialists varies with the size of the school and with the philosophy of its faculty or administration concerning the specific problems inherent in a given community.

In small communities, the principal may be the only "specialist." The principal's skill in human relationships and his respect for people of different cultures are essential; for he can encourage and foster the willingness of teachers and other specialists to consult one another. He can sustain the morale of both staff and children, encourage experimentation and continuous learning, give recognition to teachers for good performance and make of the school a vibrant, creative situation where there are ample opportunities—and challenges—to promote the best possible development of human beings.

All school personnel can profit from opportunities to learn from one another—and from representatives of cultural groups in their community—if the administration will set up the mechanics which make learning possible. Examples of such "mechanics" are cited throughout this book. In the next chapter, for example, the principal makes it possible for a faculty to become increasingly effective teachers of disadvantaged children by providing them access to insights of psychology, sociology, anthropology, and the science of human behavior as he plans for them to learn from culturally "different" people in their profession and their community, people whom they know and respect.

Through such experiences, teachers are sensitized, also, to their own attitudes toward culturally different children. They begin to understand the interaction between all facets of their "selves": the impact of their *own* background on their personality and behavior, their attitudes, values, and actions. These insights provide a realistic basis for awareness of the children's problems as well as for that genuine respect accorded each child which is the mark of an effective teacher of disadvantaged children.

CHAPTER 2

Learning About the Navajo

Mrs. Brown had an appointment with Mr. Jackson, the school principal: "Mr. Jackson, I've been talking to Mrs. King, one of our new teachers. She's having reading problems with her Indian children—" Mr. Jackson smiled, "Yes, I know. Several new teachers are worried because they've never worked with Indian, or Spanish-speaking, or Negro children before—they say they can't 'reach them.' You've lived here all your life and taught these children for several years now—successfully. I know! I've been wondering whether you and some of our other experienced teachers could meet with our new-comers and give them some help—and confidence!"

"I'd be glad to," Mrs. Brown responded eagerly. "But we have other resources—the experienced teachers in our school system who themselves are Indians, Mexicans, Negroes, or Puerto Ricans, and the faculty people at the college who have studied these children's cultural backgrounds. Then, too, some of our leading community citizens who are Indians or Mexicans or Negroes could help our teachers to understand what they *were*—and what their children *are*—up against when they come to school—"

"Sounds excellent," Mr. Jackson interrupted. "Any ideas as to how we begin?"

Mrs. Brown volunteered, "When I was talking to Mrs. King, she was very concerned about Henry Yazzie, a young Navajo boy in her class, so I immediately thought of Mary Lou Begay who teaches at Roosevelt School. She's Navajo, as are so many children in our schools. I've heard her talk—very effectively—in a college class

17

about the problems that the bilingual Navajo child has in our public
schools. I think she could be very helpful to all of us who work with
Indian children."

"Agreed," Mr. Jackson said. "I'll inquire among our teachers for
a convenient meeting date next week and invite Mary Lou. In addition,
I wonder whether sometime soon, you could organize the observations you did last year on Peggy Blackgoat and discuss with the new
teachers how you worked in your classroom with one difficult Navajo
child?"

"Of course," Mrs. Brown assured him.

MISS BEGAY INTRODUCES THE INDIANS

Miss Begay began, "I am very pleased that you asked me to come
and talk to you about Indian people. I am glad to help anyone become
better acquainted with us, especially people like yourselves who work
with our children. Every effective first grade, or fourth grade, or
ninth grade teacher wants to know as much as possible about every
child in his or her room. It is not easy to understand Indians. We have
some ways and customs which may, at first, seem strange to you.

"There are over 100 Indian reservations west of the Mississippi,
but the Navajo is the greatest in extent and the tribe the largest in
number.[1] Let us concentrate on Navajo children today, since the
Navajo are so numerous, and since, popularly, the Navajo is thought
of as the typical Indian — a shepherd and horseman, dressed in brilliant
colors dramatized by a velvet blouse and silver handwrought ornaments. His silverwork and the colorful handmade blankets woven by
women of the tribe are sold all over the country; his sandpaintings of
pollen and powdered rock fascinate art lovers everywhere.

"However, this pattern of life is inadequate for today's world which
the Navajo is being reluctantly pushed to enter. The Navajos — to an
extent, all Indians, and all minority groups — are *in* our American world,
but not yet part *of* it. Each group, for different reasons, is being forced
to move into our country's dominant culture.

"For Navajos, the major problem is that they are increasing rapidly
in numbers, yet their lands have been depleted by erosion — and adja-
cent areas can no longer absorb the population overflow. In order to

---

[1] Information in the next two sections is based primarily upon the following studies:
Clyde Kluckhohn and Dorothea Leighton, *The Navaho* (Rev. Ed., Garden City, N.Y.:
Anchor Books, The Natural History Library, 1962).
Ruth M. Underhill, *The Navajos* (Norman: University of Oklahoma Press, 1956).

make a living, their people are being drawn, imperceptibly, into the white economy whether they remain on the reservation or move to nearby cities for work or schooling. Every day the demands of different ways of life—alien ways often antagonistic to theirs—press upon them.

"What is distinct about the Navajo way of life—or that of any minority group? Knowing a people's history, its hopes and fears, its unspoken assumptions about the nature of human life is vital in communicating with *any* people of a different tradition, if facts stated are to be understood rather than distorted, if changes are to be reconciled with human habits and emotional needs, and cooperation to be evoked in making changes, rather than resistance encountered. Teachers, administrators—and anyone interested in human ways—must grasp the significance of this approach as they try to teach the Henry Yazzies and other children of minority groups lest they rouse only resentment to new learning because they are dealing with them patronizingly, as though they were strange folks with strange ways!

"Navajos have faced all the perennial problems with which mankind must deal—as have Mexicans, Negroes, Eskimos, and other minority groups. The unique solutions which each cultural group, through generations of trial and error learning, have worked out must have some meaning to those of us who have met the same issues in different contexts and have worked out other answers. What lessons can we draw from the special Navajo—or Mexican or Negro—situation and from their traditional solutions? And, as we work with their children, what relationships do we see between a given child's culture and the kind of individual produced by a given way of life?

"Culture, in the technical, anthropological sense, 'is any given people's way of life, as distinct from the life-ways of other peoples . . . Any culture consists of the set of habitual and traditional ways of thinking, feeling and reacting that are characteristic of the ways a particular society meets its problems at a particular point in time.'[2] To most recurrent and inevitable human problems, there is a variety of possible solutions. The solution chosen by any one group depends upon the way the people choosing see the facts involved. Clearly, facts have different meanings to different peoples, meanings derived from the premises, categories, and goals in terms of which that people, consciously or unconsciously, evaluate the facts.

"To work effectively with Navajo, or Mexican, or any minority children in school, you must understand, then, that their psychological

---

[2]Clyde Kluckhohn and Dorothea Leighton, *The Navaho*, p. 28.

processes and assumptions differ in some ways from yours. You must
consider their human needs as well as their physical needs and comprehend the problems in human relations which they face upon entering this white society—the school. Perhaps you are more concerned
about teaching them new—and what you consider better—ways of
life. To change a way of life, however, you must change a person. But
before you can change people, you must understand how they came to
be the way they are.

Who Are the Navajo?

"If a child is a Navajo, he comes from the largest group of Indians
in the United States, a tribe who proudly call themselves *diné,* the
People, a title suggestive of their ancient culture with its indigenous
customs and values, a constant reminder that the Navajo constitute a
society in which each individual has a strong sense of belonging. The
name Navajo is not even in their language. In their tales, or their bible,
they and their blood brothers, the Apache, are the Earth People who
climbed up to the earth's flat disk from her dark, underground womb.

"The farming Tewa Indians of New Mexico used the word *Apachu*
to mean strangers or enemies. They applied it to these strangers when
they first wandered into New Mexico. Later, when these strangers, in
turn, had settled into agriculture, they became known to the next new
arrivals, the Spaniards, as *Apaches du Nabahu* or 'Strangers of the
Cultivated Fields'—or Navajo. The Anglicised spelling—Navaho—is
standard anthropological usage, developed also because the *j* is apt to
be mispronounced by anyone unfamiliar with Spanish.

"The People speak a language different from any other Indians. It
has been identified as Athapascan, a northern tongue known in Canada's Northwest territory. Tales indicate that the Athapascans of
Canada came there via Alaska from Siberia. Groups of Athapascans
have been found among the Eskimos on the Bering Sea; other offshoots
are the Tlingit and Haida, famous canoe and totem-pole builders of
Alaska; others are in Oregon and California. Though primitive
hunters, the Athapascans were enterprising travelers and colonizers.
They remind one of the Norsemen who, having entered an area as
conquerors, learned the customs of the new country and took their
place among its foremost citizens. Even today, the Navajo are the
greatest learners and adapters among American Indians.

"These Athapascans of the north woods poured their vigor into
Indian culture up and down western North America. In small bands,
they wandered into the Southwest. They wore skin clothing and
moccasins. Their homes were conical frames made of tall poles leaned

together and covered, generally, with bark and leaves. Some Navajos today build such a 'forked-stick' home, but, in their dry country, they cover it with earth.

"It is believed that, like today's Navajo, Athapascans counted their descent through women. As now, the mother-right families may have been gathered into clans. The young husband went to live with his wife's family where he probably practiced mother-in-law avoidance as do many Navajo today. Some Navajo will not stay in the same room with his wife's mother, nor speak to her directly—a device to keep peace in the family but, to some, a taboo so strong that the price of disregarding it is considered to be insanity.

"Other customs of these ancients were the maiden's rite and the belief in the power of the dead. Ceremonies surrounding these events are, even today, more elaborate among Navajos and Apaches than among other Indians. The maiden's rite, meant to tame the supernatural power that is thought to take possession of a maiden at maturity, still takes place. The fear of magical contamination from the dead still causes some Navajo today to desert the home where someone died, never to approach it again. Some even burn their dwellings. This fear explains some Navajos' lack of interest in better housing. Another example of this fear is the fact that a cradle board is burned if a baby dies while he is of cradle age and using it. In truth, no cradleboard or clothing is prepared for a baby before it is actually born since all of a person's personal possessions are destroyed upon his death.

"When and by what route these ancients traveled from the North is not known. It is certain that they traveled in small bands, living off the land. The foraging and camping which constituted the journey of many small bands over many years in many kinds of country involved many contacts and resulted in intermixture with other groups. Navajo today are a number of distinguishable groups, each specializing in certain traditions, skills, even dialects.

"The mixing with other groups continued in the Southwest. Epochmaking change confronted the People here in the country of the corngrowers. They knew nothing of planting and farming—or permanent settlement made possible by a stationery food supply. Arriving in what is now New Mexico, they found the small city-states of the Pueblo Indians and a civilization made possible by the growth of corn which, by 1100 A.D., had freed Indians here—and in Mexico and Central America—from wandering. Villages of stone and clay—often great terraced apartments housing several hundred people—had been built. Men tended nearby fields where they grew corn in six colors, beans, squash, sunflowers, tobacco, and cotton. Women ground the corn and cooked it in many different ways; they made pottery, mats, and baskets. Both men and women wove cotton into garments and decorated them with paint and embroidery. In the plazas, a constant round of sacred pageants was staged by masked and kilted men representing rain-bringing spirits. Today, Navajo ceremonies and sand-paintings represent their gods in this kilted Pueblo costume.

"The date when the infiltration of the People began in the Southwest is thought to be around 1100 A.D. Pueblo farmers, about this time, began to concentrate their scattered settlements into larger towns and to guard their cliff dwellings with stone towers. Around 1254 A.D., the settlements began to be attacked by prowling strangers who stole corn and women. The strangers' most valuable equipment was a sinew-backed bow, a strong, short weapon of wood or horn in a double curve, reinforced with sinew glued to its back and sometimes wound around its length. Its powerful spring made it a much more formidable weapon than the Southwest Indian's simple stick of wood bent into shape by the bow spring. The Athapascans also had armor – a heavy shirt of elk or moose hide.

"The People undoubtedly married their women prisoners, thus procuring ready-made pottery-makers and teachers of agriculture. In fact, their myths are a metaphor of this merging of Navajo and Pueblo people – although Navajo will maintain that they were 'created' in *Dinetah,* old Navajoland in New Mexico, by the gods themselves. Never speak to a Navajo about 'coming' from the North! He can draw pictures of these ancestors who were created, dressed like Pueblo dancers in mask and cotton kilt! The creator gods also set up the boundaries of Navajoland by the four sacred mountains – north, east, south, and west. The four points of the compass in this order plus the zenith and nadir of the earth – these constitute Navajo conception of directions.

"This merging of peoples explains why the Navajo have many arts and ceremonies unknown to their wilder brothers, the Apaches. This varied ancestry is also indicated in the range of physical characteristics of the Navajos – some tall and rangy, some small and plump.

"A relationship of fighting – and trading – continued for several centuries between wandering bands of Navajos and the historic Pueblos. The Navajo had deer in their country and, since the Pueblo had long since used up game nearby, Navajo hunters probably traded buckskin or even dried venison with nearby Pueblos such as Jemez and Taos. They did not trust the villagers, nor the villagers them; raids and counterraids continued. But the Navajo remained, learned agriculture and, by the 1600's, were an established people spoken of

by the Tewa of the Rio Grande as 'Strangers of the Cultivated Fields'
or *Apaches du Nabahu.* The Spanish adopted this name and spelled it
Navajo — and launched it into history.

The Arrival of the Spaniards. "The Spaniards' coming changed all
Indian life in the Southwest. Spaniards rode into the Rio Grande
Valley on horses with silver bridle ornaments jingling, and with their
herds of sheep and goats. Prior to this time, Indians had not seen sheep
or horses. On the Indians' journeys, women or dogs had been the burden bearers. Only mountain sheep and bison existed in their country —
and no one had tamed them. But never ask a Navajo how his tribe
obtained horses or sheep! His myths soar into poetry at this point.
They were gifts of the gods! He is right; the Navajo we know in recent
history did not exist until the Spaniards arrived with the animals
which would make the tribe rich and powerful.

"Beginning in 1598, the Spaniards subdued — and christianized —
Indians. In their permanent villages Pueblo Indians became a subjected people. Navajos, in their remote canyons, at first remained un-
touched. Pueblos learned from the Spanish how to bake bread in round,
earthen ovens from wheat that the Spaniards had brought from Spain.
They learned to grow wheat and watermelon and to use chili brought
from Mexico. They were given sheep, shown how to care for them,
how to shear the wool, dye it with indigo from Mexico, and spin and
weave it like their own cotton. Soon Pueblo men were wearing woolen
breech clothes and women a wrap-around blanket dress.

"In 1680, the Pueblo revolted against the Spaniards, killed several
hundred, plundered ranches and desecrated churches. The Navajo
hovered near, caught the sheep, goats and horses and received the
Pueblo refugees, many of whom fled their homes. Some spent years
with the Navajo, teaching them the new skills gained from the Spanish. Some remained permanently, their women becoming founders of
the Jemez clan, still noted among Navajo for their skill in agriculture.
Today Navajos are more closely related physically and ethnically to
the Pueblos than to the Apaches.

"From 1700 to about 1775, old Navajoland contained Navajo and
Pueblo houses — and adaptations — intermingled. Settlements often had
watchtowers four stories high because, now, the Navajos needed protection. They had acquired fields and flocks, and the Utes and Comanches were bearing down from the North, while the Spaniards were
nearby. Yet they prospered. Within a century, they were the dominant
group in New Mexico.

"The Pueblo women taught them to weave, although their myths say that 'Spider Woman taught them—in the beginning.' (Their technique exactly duplicates that of the Pueblos.) Moreover, all specimens are wool; therefore, they were made after the Navajo had sheep, hence after the Pueblo revolt. Soon Navajo men were wearing wool leggings and shirts and women a black woolen blanket wrapped around the body, held at the waist by a sash, bare on the right shoulder and fastened on the left, like that of Pueblo women.

"Navajo women began to adapt to their usual gray pottery, the color and design of Pueblo pottery, and Navajo men learned the complicated Pueblo rituals for bringing spirits to their ceremonies by drawing their symbols. These rituals the Navajo developed into sand-painting, accompanied by chants presided over by a medicine man who *sings* over a sick patient to bring him back into harmony with nature and restore him to health. Everyone is invited to the ceremony, which may be nine days long, so that all can share in the blessings inherent in the chants in which Navajo religion and Pueblo myth have become intertwined. Incidentally, medicine men are not regarded as magic-makers; they are respected for their learning.

"During the 1770's, the Pueblo and Navajo separated and, with their flocks, the Navajo began to rove the land. The sheep usually belonged to the women, horses to the men. They had acquired their first horses when the Spanish ranches were plundered and the horses captured. Later, young hunters of the tribe had fought and raided among other tribes—even into Mexico. Their captives had been sold to the Spaniards who needed field workers and house servants—or most often, had been exchanged for horses. Or the hunters had acquired horses by rushing a horse corral at dawn and stampeding the herd. As a result, herds of wild, unbroken ponies roamed throughout the Southwest.

The Navajos as Conquerors. "Thus Spanish herds were depleted and Navajos prospered. By about 1776, they were a recognized people—recognized as conquerors. Now they again became rovers. Loading their goods on horses, with their flocks following behind, the main body of Navajo moved to the Southwest, to the 'land between the four mountains'—on into Arizona, Colorado, Utah. Here, they had no ties of friendship; therefore, they took what they wanted—they raided Zunis and Hopis for flocks, food, and captives. They looted ranches throughout New Mexico and Arizona. From 1824 to 1865, they were the most dreaded raiders in the Southwest. They constantly grew richer and more powerful.

"Their country, now so barren, was lush with grass and threaded by streams. Their pride was in their horses and their flocks of sheep. They moved two or three times a year to assure their flocks good pasturage. Their weaving skill progressed because, now, women had all the wool they could use. Spanish soldiers were gone—and the country was theirs. True, it was United States Territory, but perhaps the white man could be driven out too, as the Spanish had been!

"The Navajo plundered the white ranches, particularly in New Mexico—even South of the Border. They plundered Hopi and Zuni cornfields; they took the children as slaves—sold them or traded them for horses. Indians were bought and sold in New Mexico much as Negroes elsewhere. However, Navajos, too, were raided by Apaches and Utes and sold into slavery. Some were sold among the Spanish whose dress and weaving, to this day, influences Navajo costume.

"New Mexico whites began to take the law into their own hands— but the Navajo were not intimidated by them. The Utes and Apaches were more of a menace to the Navajo, for they had never taken up agriculture or sheep raising; their way of life was raiding for food, horses, and captives. When the Utes, Apaches, or Comanches had the Navajos at a disadvantage, Hopis and Zunis would risk a quick attack on them too. Yet the Navajos, in the white man's eyes, were responsible for all the fighting.

"American military men and Indian agents, who succeeded one another at the rate of about one a year, held parleys with the Navajo and made peace treaties. However, these officials did not understand the tribal organization among Navajos—no one man can dictate nor be responsible for any behavior other than that of his own and related families. Respected older men signed treaties; but ambitious younger men who did not yet have flocks continued raiding. When it became apparent that U.S. troops were not numerous enough to protect one warring group from another, all Indians returned to raiding.

"Now the whites furnished guns to the Zunis and employment to the Utes who guided the whites to Navajo hideouts. Just as the situation became desperate, the Civil War began and the whites were gone. The Navajo and Apache overran the country. As far away as Sante Fe, they entered towns, drove off stock and murdered citizens.

U.S. Military vs. the Navajo. "In 1882—retribution! The government decided that the Indians not only must be defeated, they must also be removed far away from the scene of their ravaging. By 1863, the Apaches were beaten and sent to Fort Sumner in northeast New Mexico. Then Colonel Kit Carson was dispatched after the Navajo.

Utes, Zunis, and Hopis joined the Americans. These guerrillas put despair into the hearts of the People. They fled into hiding. A few who could do so collected their animals and stole out of Navajoland.

"The campaign lasted six months. Only 50 Indians were killed, but thousands surrendered. Carson burned their homes and crops and killed their herds to starve them into submission. When the soldiers methodically went through Canyon de Chelly, the Indians finally believed that there was no hiding place for them. They began to surrender and, on March 6, 1864, the first caravan was started on the *Long Walk* to Fort Sumner. The Navajo had promised to go peacefully — and New Mexico held a day of Thanksgiving. With their rations, horses, sheep, and goats, the Navajo walked 300 miles at 15 miles a day. Finally, some 7,000 of them reached Fort Sumner and were dumped on 40 square miles of flat, grassy land beside a small adobe fort from which 400 soldiers guarded them. There was no provision for them save a corral into which they walked to be counted.

"Here they were confined until June 18, 1868. The government, having found that they could not support themselves here, yielded to their entreaties to return to their lands if they would promise, in a treaty, never again to fight whites, Mexicans, or Indians, but to irrigate the soil and to send their children to school. In return for their signing this treaty, the government would supply rations, animals, and clothing to help them to a new start in life. After a 35-day march, some 8,000 Navajo returned home.

Probably no folk has ever had a greater shock. Proud, they saw their properties destroyed and knew what it was to be dependent on the largess of strangers. Accustomed to move freely over great spaces, they knew the misery of confinement — lived in a flat and colorless region, eating alien foods and drinking bitter water which made them ill. . . . One can no more understand Navaho attitudes — particularly toward white people — without knowing of Fort Sumner than he can comprehend Southern attitudes without knowing of the Civil War.[3]

Destitution on the Navajo Reservation. "When the people reached home, there were more privations and hardships. The government had not yet surveyed the reservation; they camped at Fort Wingate five months awaiting permission to reenter the homeland to which they were now to be confined. Finally, the reservation was designated as a long, narrow rectangle of 3½ million acres straddling Arizona

---

[3]Clyde Kluckhohn and Dorothea Leighton, *The Navaho*, p. 41.

and New Mexico. No one considered how they would make a living in this restricted area.

"They redistributed themselves. Some raised crops in the few fertile canyons; some roamed widely with their sheep. Each family preempted such planting or grazing land as it found and no one interfered. This is the Navajo way. The next comers passed on uncomplainingly to less fertile places. Eventually the government issued seeds, tools, and some livestock; but there were many delays and, for long periods of time, many families existed on rations issued by the government—or starved. To add to this distress, there came several years of drought, flood, heavy frosts, and resultant crop failure. The old equilibrium of their society removed, unrest prevailed. Misfortunes were attributed to witchcraft—and lynchings of victims took place.

Struggling Toward Self-Supporting Conditions. "In spite of their misery, the Navajo gradually moved toward stable conditions. A sheep industry, later valued at millions of dollars, was established. Women used the wool for weaving; men traded in the blankets and rugs the women made—while they themselves and their families wore flour sacks and lived in caves and mud huts. The making of silver ornaments began. This skill was initially introduced to the People by a respected medicine man who learned it from a New Mexican friend who, in turn, had learned in Mexico. By 1878, the Navajo had grown from a band of paupers to a rigorous and prosperous people. Their numbers had increased, in ten years, from about 8,000 to 11,850 people who owned horses and flocks numbering about 70,000.

"The persistent theme in their history, though, has been the struggle for land. By 1884, 8 million acres had been added to the reservation. But the railroad had come in 1881 and had taken some of their best watering places and finest winter range land. Now the reservation includes about 15 million acres, reaching north into Utah and west to the Colorado river. But lands have been taken away and use rights thrown in doubt. Today, in spite of the 1946 Indian Claims Act, the most critical problem which confronts the People and the Indian Service is that of making self-support possible for a rapidly growing population in an already overpopulated region on a reservation made up of unproductive, deteriorated land, striking for its appalling lack of moisture.

"By 1900, the population was 20,500, more than twice their original number after Sumner. The tribe owned twice as much wealth as before Sumner. They had learned agriculture from the Pueblos, sheepherding from the Spaniards, weaving from the Pueblos and traders, and silverwork from the Mexicans. Their costumes were adapted from the Spaniards. Their arts and ceremonies developed a new character as unique characteristics were absorbed from each people with whom they had come into contact. Through it all, they kept their own customs such as their family and clan loyalty, the mother-in-law taboo, and the maiden's rite—at least, groups of them had.

"One could not, now, talk of *the* Navajo. One must know whether, by Navajo, one meant the 'civilized' people around Fort Defiance who lived in frame houses with windows and doors and who sent their children to school or the people who lived in permanent agricultural settlements, or the isolated flock herders living in hogans in Canyon de Chelly—both wealthy and poor families, or the half-savage ones of the barren, western lands who lived in ancient, conical huts and fled at the sight of strangers.

"For, by 1900, life for the Navajo was a combination of Middle Age living conditions, ancient Pueblo customs and American influence. The railroad had come in 1881. Traders arrived; homesteaders surrounded the reservation. New equipment which the railroad brought and the traders sold to the Navajo spelled the end of handmade equipment. By 1890, traders had even gotten Navajo women to weave with commercial yarns; they made the gaudy rugs the market demanded from designs dictated to them by the traders. In return, they bought from the traders calico which the men wore, and velveteen for the women's blouses which, together with the long full skirts, they wear today. They had been taught to sew by the slaves who returned about 1872 from Mexican settlements where they, in turn, had learned sewing from their Spanish mistresses. The building of the railroad brought work for some of the men; but the increase in white population accompanying it also brought economic exploitation, intoxicants, diseases, and other disrupting forces which added to the Indians' rancor toward whites.

'To Learn Paper.' "As did even the establishment of schools! At Fort Sumner, the Indians had pledged to compel their children to attend school and the United States had agreed that, for every 30 children, a schoolhouse and teacher would be provided. However, the government did not know that one cluster of two or three huts might be ten miles from the next, and that a family living in one place in autumn might desert that hogan by winter for a new pasturage. Navajo, in turn, did not know that schooling meant sitting in one room for three to ten years 'to learn paper.' Why? Their picture of the future was a new hogan, more fields, and flocks, and a peaceful life in the open with their children working with them learning their ways.

"The first school was opened in 1869 at Fort Defiance. Attendance was so irregular as to make learning impossible; in fact, by 1879, average attendance from the entire tribe was 11. In 1880, Congress passed a larger appropriation for education—which was used to build an adobe-style boarding school with bunks for 18 children and iron shutters to keep them in. Dragooned to enroll, children were terrified; they were shut up from the outdoors in dark buildings where they slept three in a bunk, and were forcefully bathed on Fridays, and their long hair was cut because they had lice. The latter experience panicked them—'you can't dance in ceremonies unless you have long hair.' They disliked the white man's food; they caught measles and other illnesses. Imagine the horror of a child who found himself among these impersonal strangers—a child taught, frequently, to regard strangers as sorcerers. His refuge was the Navajo expedient, to which many children today still resort in school: be silent, make no move.

"By 1887, when it had become evident that only arbitrary means could compel school attendance, Congress made education compulsory. Navajos, however, refused to send their children away to school. What good was English, especially written English, to them? In those years, girls usually married at ten to 12 years of age, until which time they herded sheep. Boys were usually heads of families by the time they were 18; until they married, they herded horses.

"Indian agents drove around the reservation in buckboards, collected children and sent them off to boarding schools. Parents, not notified, thought them dead. Children frequently escaped from the schools to return home; some died in the mountains enroute. By 1892, only 75 children from a tribe of more than 16,000 were in school.

"By 1903, 300 children from a tribe of 23,000 were in boarding schools. Many children came because their families were poor and the schools supplied free board, lodging, and clothing; but many other children hid out and refused to go to school. Children hated the regimented life where they were kept busy and sternly disciplined from dawn to bedtime marching to meals, to class, and to the 'detail work' in kitchen, field or shop where their labor was needed in the understaffed schools. Then, when they returned home, they were treated as strangers; a purification ceremony was held to take away the dangerous magic of strangers. Their 'paper learning' was impossible to put into practice; mates were hard to find for them.

"Yet jobs off the reservation were misery for them; they knew some English, but were not schooled in the ways of the white man. They met prejudice; they were laughed at, ignored or despised as stupid. So they 'went back to the blanket.'

Destitution Again! "In the 1920's, a cycle of bad weather and their population increase meant that some Navajos were starving again. Sheep was growing thin and yielding less wool because grass on the reservation was disappearing at an alarming rate. Overgrazing and destruction of the soil resulted in a disastrous drop in the level of prosperity until, in the barren western part of the reservation, income was $31 annually. Rations were rushed to the Navajos to keep them alive. Illness was prevalent, but hospitals were not used. In fact, Navajos hated the impersonality of hospitals. They were accustomed to the comfort and attention of an entire family when they were ill and to the personal ministrations of a medicine man centered on them at a *sing*. When they sent individuals to hospitals, it was usually only to die—so that they would not be contaminated by a corpse—let the white man bury him! They were shocked at the fact that people died in a building and neither the building nor the equipment was burned. Such an accumulation of evil frightened them!

Attempts to Rehabilitate the Navajo. "Then came 1934 and the New Deal. The Navajo were to be given work—which was to be of permanent benefit to the locality. They were to be paid a living wage—like other Americans. Soil conservation projects and waterworks were started. Men, some collected from remote areas in the reservation, learned to work on tractors and drag-lines building wells, reservoirs, dams, and roads. They worked regular hours and, in the evenings, attended classes where they learned a trade, were taught to use their new tools, and to make a start in learning English. The tribe permitted an oil company to drill test wells on the reservation. The government ruled that this underground wealth, when discovered, was to be the property of the tribe. They must organize to make leases and receive money.

"Although, even in 1940, the normal per capita income was only $81.89, some Navajo had more money. And money in hand began to undermine the Navajo feudal system. The solidarity of the family suffered. Money was wealth which could be concealed and kept or spent for oneself. One could avoid one's duty to the family. Wage-earners began buying pick-up trucks. Some young men were driving cars. Here and there, houses of modern frame were being built.

"However, for those who depended on flocks and herds, there was tragedy. Because of continued land deterioration, the government ruled that now they *must* cut down on the number of sheep and must get rid of their horses. They would be paid for doing so. But horses and sheep were a Navajo's life! They saw only a white man's plot in this edict. So the horses, sheep, and goats were collected, sold and slaughtered by the government—and the owners had only money. They refused to cooperate in any way with the government; they refused to send their children to school. The government was asking that the Navajo make the transition from the Middle Ages to modern civilization in one leap!

The Navajo and World War II. "Then came the Second World War! Soon their lives were so full that bitterness was forgotten. Thirty-six hundred Navajo men were in service; 12 Navajo women were WAC's. Army life was enjoyable to them; coarse food, irregular hours, and no privacy were not a hardship to Navajos. White men now were no longer mysterious enemies; Indians were no longer inferior. Both were 'buddies.' In the armed forces, Navajos performed a unique service. Their language was used as a code in the signal corps. A platoon of 29 Navajos was trained together. Then, in groups of two, carrying portable telephones and a two-way radio set, they conveyed messages across enemy lines. The platoon did service in the Pacific, in Sicily, and in Italy. The code was never broken by the enemy.

"When these service people returned to their earth-floored hogans, they understood what the white man worked for; they and their families wanted what could be had—money, possessions, and education. Now they wanted schooling. But the schools were not ready for them. Of 21,000 children of school age, less than 6,000 were enrolled in available schools. Congress appropriated money for repairing old schools and building new ones; special courses were developed for veterans who wanted to go to college—and concentrated programs for all children under 12.

"Life outside the reservation had changed other attitudes. Soldiers, to get their allotments, had to observe the white man's marriage laws and support only one wife and one family of children—not the entire clan or all their relatives. They had to register births, deaths, and divorces. They had to take a 'paper name,' one which they would keep all their lives. The white man considered their real name or Indian name less important because it might be changed according to crucial events in their lives.

Change of Reservation Traditions. "Some families were moving off

the reservation to work; some were breaking up and individuals going
off on their own to earn money. The output of weaving and silverwork
diminished; more money was to be made in other ways. The money
which came into the reservation bought silver ornaments, clothes,
stoves, dishes, glasses, radios—and, of course, cars and pick-up
trucks.

"The latter still are especially prized because, with them, a Navajo
can come into town where he can buy food at the chain store, sometimes cheaper and often in greater variety than from the Trading Post.
Then, there are the shopping plazas for kerosene or wood stoves, kerosene refrigerators and washing machines which the Navajo today buys
even if he lives in a dirt-floored hogan. Above all, he wants a battery
radio! These have become so common that the Tribe now broadcasts
radio programs in the Navajo language—and entire families and clans
gather to listen—their only concern with time! The time of day is
usually meaningless to a Navajo. Even now, however, their money is
not spent on housing as frequently as on other possessions because
some Navajo still cling to the idea that a home must be burned after
a death.

"However, many ceremonies, even those indicative of their attitude
toward death, are changing. After much debate, the Tribe had publicly
buried their war heroes and accepted a cemetery in their honor.
Certain old ceremonies are still performed. Even today, one may wit-
ness the performance of a *Yei-be-chai* dance or be present at a *sing*
and watch the making of a sand painting. Other ceremonies are less
frequently performed or are performed with a difference: the young no
longer consider purification necessary in order to be received back
into the family; the Squaw dance, formerly danced with couples facing
one another without touching is now sometimes danced arm in arm.
Religious significance of ceremonies has lessened for some young
people—and Christianity has not filled the void. Navajos, after all,
have never aimed for eternal bliss! They only want to be happy and
loved in the present life.

"Gradually, some Navajo learned to work eight hours daily, like
white men. When ordnance plants came to the reservation, many
worked regular shifts and went home to shower baths, wooden floors
and beds provided by their employers. One of the villages built for
them was given to the tribe when the war was over so that those
Navajo who wished could work and live as white men. Not all could
or would so so. In spite of their years in the army, many Navajo were
not prepared to work in the white man's world; some were not clock-
trained, others remained innocent of the techniques of getting ahead.

Consequently, many had no work and no money when their soldier pay of $20 monthly was used up. Then alcohol, procured from the white man, would take its toll.

"By 1947, some Navajos were still starving; many were still living in earth-floored huts and existing on a diet of fried bread and coffee. Their tuberculosis rate was one person in ten. Trachoma was on the increase as was the number of aged, crippled, and blind. Sheep were bigger and better—but fewer, and income from them was going to fewer people. There was not enough land and water on the reservation which, though increased to 15 million acres, the largest in the country, was insufficient now for the 1947 population of over 55,000 Navajos, a population continuing to increase by over 1,000 annually.

"A 1947 government survey emphasized that the depleted, now often barren land, could support only 35,000 of the People. Numbers of them must live off the reservation, be educated in trades, learn to work in small businesses—a frightening prospect to many Navajo! Their lives were to be severed from the fabric of their family and relatives and lived amongst whites who usually were not friendly! Indians have had the experience of being excluded from restaurants, hotels, and theatres, relegated to live in slums, and to having their children shunned in white schools. Nevertheless, some left the reservation, usually those provided by the government with a work contract. But many did not fulfill the contract; they returned to the reservation.

"Their Tribal Council tried to help them—for the Navajos have a representative body which, by 1954, owned 15 million dollars, five in the U.S. Treasury, subject to supervision, and ten in the bank to be drawn at the Council's decision. Millions more will be available because both oil and uranium have been discovered on the reservation. In 1950, a long-range program for the Navajo was enacted into law, basically a program of land improvement, modern land management, and continued search for mineral resources—supplemented with a program of service to people—hospitals, schools, roads, telephones, and aid in finding employment.

"The Council has encouraged individuals to borrow money to set themselves up in business; it has financed groups who have left the reservation together to set up a new life; it has given scholarships to bright young Navajos who seek higher education. Opposition to schools has disappeared—officially. Hospitals, gradually, are becoming more accepted. Yet, in 1958, there were, still, more than 5,000 cases of tuberculosis on the reservation; the death rate was 14 times higher than that of the rest of the nation—while three out of ten babies died at birth.

"Clearly, the old and the new ways have not yet meshed. Parents to whom children are economic assets still refuse to send them to school because they see no need for 'learning paper.' Living habits, for many Navajo have changed only slightly over the years; one can still see primitive homes, sweat baths, sheep corrals—and the ancient customs of the People. Just as one can admire the painstaking effort required in weaving the handmade rugs and producing the handmade silver ornaments, so one can wonder at the situation of the Navajo who 'succeeds,' then must deal with his family and relatives.

"Most Navajo are still expected to share what they have. Therefore, if a Navajo builds a house, 20 relatives may come to live with him. If he is elected to office, relatives expect jobs and benefits. If he is a foreman, he cannot discharge any relative, no matter how lazy or inefficient he may be. Indeed, he may not reprove him, lest he shame him.

"Moving away to work and live is one solution. But, the white man's world is too strange to many Navajo whose way of life has not included promptness and exactitude and has not been conducted in the extroverted manner of the white man. For some Navajo these qualities have been deprecated as 'white'; strangers have been regarded as intruders to be shunned, if not enemies to be fought. To these Navajo, the white man's world is too strange, and his answer to the white man's expectations is absenteeism from the job procured for him—then, perhaps, drunkenness, and next, return to the refuge of his family.

"This behavior is not peculiar to the Navajo. Many individual Navajo may fail because they encounter too many difficulties at one time. But the Navajo tribe, as a whole, is making determined efforts to remove the dangers to individual life in the broad society of our time just as it is learning to govern itself in this complicated modern world.

Life of the Navajo Child. "Therefore, as you look at one Navajo child, you must ask yourself what his way of life has been. Is his family one of the many—'well-off' and poor—who live in a dirt-floored hogan in one of the isolated areas of the 'Land of Time Enough and Room Enough'? (The Navajo affectionately use this term to describe their homeland.) Has he hidden out from school until this year, herding sheep, moving with his family from place to place for pasturage? Did his family encourage his remaining home—or do they want schooling for him? Does his family own a horse, a wagon, a pick-up truck? If the latter, he has probably come with them to town, to the chain store for food—and probably to the shopping plaza.

"However, many Navajo children have never been to town—or to school. Although the Tribal Council now officially urges education, the democratic practices of the tribe favor parents being persuaded rather than forced to send their children to school. Some parents resist. Navajos like to have many children, and they like to have their children around them; they are loath to send them away to school.

"To many families, a child's going to school involves his being separated from his family for nearly nine months a year from the time he attains school age. The children who live in isolated areas are the ones who must leave home for their schooling. If their families are poor, a child's leaving for school entails economic loss for the family as well as painful separation from the family. Moreover, many children refuse to go away to school and, in many Navajo families, decisions about what they will do are left up to the children themselves. Therefore, such parents will not force unwilling children to go to school. Nor are the parents inclined to send a child away if he has become an economic asset to the family. A boy may be in sole charge of a herd of sheep from an early age on, or a girl may take care of younger siblings while the mother is farming or herding sheep. Because of the great distances and sparsity of population on the reservation, no one may know of these children save their families who, as stated, may be uninterested in schooling, too poor to afford to give up their children or so uninformed that they do not know of the education available to their children.

"Some families may send their children to school reluctantly, not because they are interested in education, but because the child will be fed, will receive free clothing, toys, and presents. The family is poor—and sending a child to school gets him off the budget for most of the year. Again, a family may send a child to school to secure vocational training so that he will get a job. To many families, unemployment is very real; out of 30,000 people eligible for employment on the reservation, 19,000 are jobless. To them, poverty has been a way of life. They see schooling, especially learning English, as the key to a different future.

"Sometimes slowly, nevertheless increasingly, numbers of Navajo parents are coming to understand the value of children's learning English—even if only 'so they will not be dependent on interpreters all their lives' as most adult Navajo are today. About 44,000 or 62 per cent of the adults do not speak English. In *their* youth, the tribe saw little value in, even resisted, 'the white man's education.' In the last few years, according to reports from Tribal Council Headquarters in Window Rock, Arizona, increasing numbers of children are receiv-

ing an education: in a day school if they live in a town near enough to
walk to school; or in areas close by where they can be transported daily
by school bus; or in a boarding school on the reservation; or in public
schools in towns near the reservation where they live together in
dormitories. In the 1964–5 school year, 40,256 children were reported
to be in school. However, the Council reported 45,969 of school age.
This means approximately 6,000 were still not attending school. The
latter is an approximate number, for, it is believed, not all births are
being reported to the Tribal Council Headquarters. It is estimated,
however, that more than half the members of the tribe are between the
ages of one and 18, that the tribe, on and off the reservation, numbers
well over 100,000 and that it is increasing at the rate of 2.25 per cent,
faster than any other tribe.

What Are Henry Yazzie's Problems?

"Try, then, as the teacher of Henry Yazzie, to put yourself in his
place. Until now, he may have lived in an isolated area on the reservation or, if he were a Hopi, in a village apart from the mainstream of life
in our country. If so, his experiences and his values will inevitably be
different from those of children raised in a town or city. This will be
true, to an extent, of any Indian child you have.

"In fact, there will be dramatic differences in the backgrounds of
your *individual* Indian children. This is the reason that you need to
know: has a given child come to you straight from the reservation
without any previous schooling? Or has he had the experience of
attending a day or boarding school on the reservation before he came
here? Is he living in the Indian children's dormitory in town, having
his first experience away from home? Or are his family 'town' Indians
who return to the reservation only to visit relatives? Such information
is of inestimable assistance in understanding each child's behavior.

"Let us suppose that Henry is living in a dormitory for Indian children in a border town and is attending public school – your school –
the white man's school to Henry. He may or may not have had previous school experience on the reservation. This may or may not be
his first separation from his family. Henry may be anywhere from six
to 11 years old when he first attends school; he may not know English.

"His parents' mixed feelings about schooling are reflected in the
child. Henry may or may not know why he is going to school; he may
realize only that he had to leave home. Though his parents may have
made the decision to send him, they may not have been able to make it
plain to him why he was going to school. Left without guideposts, a
child may or may not be motivated to learn when he arrives at school.

"Is Henry culturally disadvantaged? Not in terms of *his* environment. In the desert land where he has lived and herded sheep, he knows his environment well. He can identify every trail, every footprint and stray goat that crosses the trail. In fact, he identifies most of his acquaintances by their footprints. He knows the tracks of his own horses and many of his neighbors'. He knows the springs of water nearby, the desert plants, animals, and reptiles. He is familiar with the Trading Post and Chapter House. He possesses an intellect which has enabled him to master one of the most difficult languages in the world and to display ingenuity in adapting himself to a harsh environment.

"Is he lacking in a positive self-concept? Navajo proudly claim their ancient culture; the People pass on their ceremonials and chants, their customs, and values to their children as prized possessions. Outward forms of ceremonies change, yet the impact remains. For example, the tribal observance of a given individual's coming of age is important to numbers of its young people.

"Only when a Navajo child is confronted with a middle-class white culture and with the attitude, 'our way is right and you Indians are hopelessly backward' is his self-concept threatened and his culture at a disadvantage. Confronted with the many 'things' that comprise so much of middle-class culture and in the context of a middle-class schoolroom, Henry *is* at a disadvantage; he may even function as pseudo-retarded. His values, his culture, his experience, his language background — all are liabilities here rather than assets.

"It is difficult for you to imagine Henry's plight. At the door of the classroom, he is expected to shed his language, his experience and his culture — to recite his ABC's and to respond positively in the classroom atmosphere. Though his ears are physically receptive to sound, he cannot associate English sounds with anything meaningful in his own language background. Since he cannot hear what is said in school and cannot speak the school's code, he remains unable to comprehend the messages the code carries. Nor is Henry faced only with learning a new language; he must also learn a new culture — the classroom way of doing things! This is a tremendous load of learning for a young child.

"Most threatening of all, the teacher not only asks his name, but uses it freely. Obviously, you, the teacher, must call the child something; it is necessary for you to use his name often in the classroom. It would not occur to you that you could offend a child by using his name. However, many Navajo people still consider a name semi-sacred, a very private possession. If you want to know what a Navajo's name is, ask one of his friends or acquaintances.

"Although many Navajos, especially since the Second World War, have learned that the white world demands a name, there are still many other Navajos who feel that strange people have no right to ask their real name, much less to speak it. Nevertheless, since the war, increasing numbers of Navajos—adults and the many children who have been in contact with whites in school—have learned that they must have a name to give on demand—but that the name demanded is not their real one, since whites usually do not even know its existence, much less its significance. Therefore, Indians have learned to handle this situation by using—or accepting from the whites—a 'paper name,' thus reserving their Indian name and never speaking it save in their families.

"Clearly, increasing numbers of Indian children today learn that, in school, it is accepted procedure to speak a person's name. But a particular young child may not know this. Give him time to become accustomed to hearing his name used publicly! This usage may be hard for him 'to take' at first; he may feel uncomfortable when he sees his new name displayed on the blackboard or bulletin board or on his desk or chair. However, gradually, he will begin to understand that, in this new culture, it is not offensive to speak a person's name; rather, it is an indication of concern about and interest in the person. After a while, he will accept, in this spirit, another person's use of his name.

"School problems comprise only part of Henry's total load. In the dormitory, he is constantly confronted with new experiences, details of which we shall discuss later. It is a long step for Henry to take from the hogan with its tightly-knit family group to a boarding school full of strangers and far away from the reservation where a new language, new motivations, and new values are expected of him. Some children do adapt with comparative ease. Some are full of fear; some become apathetic and lag far behind their classmates; some insulate or isolate themselves from their surroundings; some run away—back to their parents.

"No matter when a child goes to school, leaving his home is an emotional shock. Moving from the reservation, an area of approximately 25,000 square miles, much of it desolate plain and mountain—and being shut in a town dormitory is a frightening change to a child. So is leaving his large, extended family where he was loved and cherished. Now the child finds himself in a new world, mostly in the company of strange children, all of them vying for the attention of the comparatively few adults—strangers to him—who live in the dormitory with them.

"This impersonality is terrifying to a Navajo accustomed to living, from birth to death, in a warm circle of family and clan mates where strangers may be shunned as intruders, but where his place in his group is assured. Even if he sins against his group, perhaps by displaying a bad temper, his punishment is only admonition, "do you wish to shame your family?" a reminder that, no matter what he does, he belongs to them.

"To Henry, the biggest surprise is the dormitory and the school cafeteria. Perhaps he is met with the demand that he wash his hands or his socks, or even that he take a bath. For the first time in his life, he has all the water he can drink—and he is even to bathe in it. He is told to shed his clothing and get into a bathtub. At home, the family heated bricks in a sweathouse and had to wait until the steam came up before they could 'bathe'! He is given a 'white man's haircut'! Learning personal grooming is difficult; understanding that his clothes must be washed and kept clean is confusing. He is expected to sleep in a bed. He is told to put on pajamas—a wholly foreign experience to him! The idea of changing into special clothes just to sleep! A bell rings and it is *time* to eat. What does this mean? He knows only Indian time. In the cafeteria he has to stand in line (with the opposite sex)! Then, he must choose something to eat from bewildering foods whose names he may not even know, then eat these foods—at a table, with knives, forks, and spoons—and learn to drink milk through a straw! Can you imagine how frighteningly strange, to a child, is this new, antiseptic world of soap, baths, 'wash your hands,' 'launder your clothes,' 'eat with your knife and fork,' 'drink your milk,' 'eat your vegetables'?

"On the playground, he is expected to play with the other boys— and even girls. Some Indian children do not play with the opposite sex. In fact, many Indian children are inexperienced in any group play; they live in isolated family groups where 'others' are outsiders. The idea of mingling with everyone is new and strange. The idea of toys to play with—balls and wagons and swings and slides—is fantastic to some children! What—no horses to ride or sheep to herd?

Navajo Eating Habits. "Let us examine Henry's eating habits. To the Navajo, all food is good; they like to eat. They understand that food is necessary to life; therefore, to waste it is to do wrong. However, its relation to health is not always understood. And the diet of many Navajos is inadequate; eating may, indeed, be an alternation between much and little. On some days, there may be only coffee and fried bread. In fact, fried bread and mutton stew are staple foods for some families; for others, Anglo, Spanish, and Pueblo Indian foods have been added to the diet. Tortillas made from fried bread dough, but cooked on a griddle, or in a skillet, or on a wire mesh grill over coals are the everyday bread of many Navajos.

"Some families grow patches of squash, beans, pumpkins, and melons where there is suitable soil. Surplus commodity foods—flour, cornmeal, rice, and dry milk—were first distributed in 1958 and Navajos have learned to use these. In addition to these staples, they will buy at the trading post: lard, salt, sugar, coffee, and baking powder; then, if the family has sufficient credit, meats, pinto beans, squash, pumpkins, melons, tomatoes, peaches, canned milk, 'pop,' and candy. Many still do not usually eat eggs or fish. The selection of foods they buy depends on their likes and dislikes, not on food values.

"Some Navajos may also use native plants for food: the bee plant or wild spinach, sourberries or red sumac, cactus fruit or prickly pear, wild onion, wild rhubarb, pinon nuts and yucca fruit. Several native plants are used to make hot tea. Tea, coffee, and pop, especially strawberry pop, are their usual beverages. Even the poorest families will have coffee with sugar in it to drink along with their bread or tortillas.

"What a family eats is determined partly by their personal preferences, but also by the amount, location, and potability of water for cooking, for in some areas, water has to be carried ten miles; by the amount and location of firewood which is very scarce in some areas; by the income of the family; by the availability of the food, and by the transportation available to them. If the family owns a pick-up truck, food is easily available at the trading post or even at a supermarket in a nearby town. But what if they own only a wagon?

"Space for storage of food in a hogan is limited and refrigeration is available only to those comparatively wealthy families who can buy kerosene refrigerators. Some families have a root cellar for storage of such items as squash and pumpkins. Water storage facilities in a hogan vary also, from an open bucket to safe running water. Obviously, all these are determining factors in the amount of food purchased or the variety available to a family.

"Usually, no electricity is available for cooking. An open fire or small wood—sometimes kerosene—stove is used. Occasionally, a family may have an oven in a stove, or a beehive oven, or a Dutch oven. Because firewood is often scarce, cooking must often be done as quickly as possible and women must be skillful in handling a fire. Therefore, most foods are prepared by frying, boiling, or cooking over or in hot coals. Basic cooking utensils are a stewpot, skillet, and coffee pot. Other pots and pans are improvised. Newer homes will have more modern equipment.

"In many families, eating utensils are shared. Some foods are eaten from a common bowl, with the fingers—by both adults and children. Enamel or aluminum plates and cups are used by many families. Knives and forks may be used by town Indians. Spoons are generally available to hold pieces of meat or to dig up gravy, but bread is usually used for this purpose. In earlier days, the mother sometimes fed the children, especially the youngest, from her plate. Now most children have their own plates. Many families now eat off a table, covered perhaps with oilcloth. Some families have chairs; others use boxes or orange crates for chairs. Some eat off the ground.

"On the reservation, Henry may have eaten two meals a day, or he may have eaten when he was hungry—or when food was available. Navajo eating patterns vary. For example, a child herding sheep leaves early in the morning and takes fried bread to eat during the day. He comes back to join his family for the evening meal; or, if he is late, food is saved for him. The amount of food eaten in a family fluctuates. When a family has food, all eat well. When food is scarce, all go without. It is a fact that, when some children return to school after a summer at home, they have lost ten to 20 pounds.

"Henry may be one of the many Navajo children who are undersized. After their first year, these Navajo children fail to maintain the same growth curve as other American preschool children. Cases of malnutrition and undernutrition are not unusual. Enteric diseases—dysentery and diarrhea, in addition to pneumonia and influenza—are leading causes of death among Navajo children where the infant mortality rate still is about 40.3 per 1,000 as against 25.3 per 1,000 in our country as a whole. Some Navajo children seem to lack resistance to illness; they become seriously ill in a shorter period of time than most children—and they recover more slowly. They seem to be subject to repeated infections; anemia and nutritional deficiencies may be the basis of this situation.

"Not only will Henry find many fruits, vegetables, and other foods strange to him, almost nothing will be familiar in this new environment at the dormitory. If he has come to school directly from the reservation, he may seldom have handled a book, magazine, or newspaper save at the trading post. He may never have been to a movie, seen a TV program, or heard a nursery rhyme. He has probably not slept in a bed of his own, washed his hands in running water, taken

a bath, or used a flush toilet; these children have had the entire outdoors for toileting! Henry may not have seen or used electrical appliances such as irons, toasters, or washers.

Navajo Homes. "On the contrary, Henry may have lived, along with
his maternal grand-parents, his parents, his maternal uncles, and
cousins in a small, one-room six- or eight-sided house called a hogan.
The traditional, conical-shaped one is constructed of logs and mud,
with no windows, a packed dirt floor, a blanket-covered doorway
facing east, and an open fire in the center of the floor with the smoke
going out a hole in the roof. The more commonly-used modern hogan
is six-sided and built of larger timber to support the heavier roof.
An oil drum or wood stove — sometimes a kerosene one — may now be
used instead of an open fire. A wooden door may replace the blanket
at its entrance. Since the coming of the Rural Electrification Association in 1964, some hogans have electricity; a few have running water.

"Usually, the family who lives in a hogan sleeps and eats together.
Sheepskins and blankets are used as bedding on the floor where everyone sleeps with his feet to the fire and head to the wall like spokes of
a wheel. They sleep with their clothes on. Because of lack of water,
clothes are not usually laundered. Some modern Navajos live in
frame houses in town, sleep in beds and take their clothes in to wash
them at laundromats; but many Navajos simply discard clothes when
they are too filthy for use. Their bodies, however, are washed in the
sweat bath and rubbed in sand periodically; and their hair is washed
weekly with yucca root.

"Or perhaps, the Henry Yazzie you know lives with his family in
town? Even then, his life is more like that of other Indians than it is
like yours and mine. Probably his parents speak only Navajo at home.
They probably eat the food they were taught to eat, dress the way they
were taught to dress, live the way in which they were taught to live,
and rear their children as they were taught to do on the reservation.

"If Henry has lived in town for one or two years before he comes
to school, he will have seen some of the foods, utensils, and appliances
mentioned, but he may not have used them. He may not even know the
English names for them. Even in town, he will not, in his home, necessarily have been exposed to experiences and ideas — or even to foods
and clothing — which most of your children take for granted. His
mother probably provides the foods she has learned to cook; she may
even dress her girls in clothes like those she wears and has worn all
her life: the long, full, satin or cotton skirt with bright-colored velvet
top and turquoise ornaments which, for most of a century, Navajo

women have worn for all occasions from sheep-herding to dancing.

"Moreover, even though the Indian family has moved to town, the Indian—Hopi, Navajo, or whatever he may be—is intensively devoted to his homeland. Despite the harshness of village and reservation lands, the cold winters, hot and dry summers, floods and violent dust storms of spring, the Indian's homeland and his family are the focal points of his culture. These values he teaches his children: an intense attachment to native soil, a reverent disposition toward ancestral ways, a restraint on individual self-seeking in favor of family and community, a relaxed attitude toward life and an appreciation of the beautiful.

Navajo Values. "Most of these values are different from the values Henry encounters in school. Both the child and the teacher are confused—sometimes hurt and frustrated—when these differences in culture are not understood. Let us examine several areas of possible conflict. I shall use Navajos as examples; but all Indian children have school problems caused by cultural differences.

"First, the difference between your concept of time and the Navajo's is worlds apart. The pace of Navajo life out in the reservation is leisurely and relaxed. Time means little; therefore, adjustment to a schedule of any kind is extremely difficult for the Indian child. Henry finds classroom routine very strange. There are no clocks or watches on most of the reservations. There are no hours of the day—there is only sunrise and sunset. There is no time when you must get a specific amount of work done. The fact that Indian people see no need for time as such poses a severe problem when the Indian child must adjust to the school's way of doing things. Is it surprising that Henry has not yet learned that, when the bell rings, the teacher expects him to line up *now,* not *pretty soon* or that the bus comes *at a certain time* to take him home from school and that he must be waiting for it *in a certain place,* and not expect the teacher to come and find him wherever he is playing?

"A second difficulty for Henry is that his culture is a cooperative one, while in school he must learn to be competitive. Henry has been taught that polite phrases, non-aggressiveness and self-control are highly valued. Cooperation with one's fellows and generosity in judgment of others have been expected of him. Navajos never praise anyone for doing good nor do they censure evil as such; they weigh and judge each word or deed in terms of its effect on other people. A Navajo does not fight for personal rights nor try to be better than someone else. Personal competitiveness is especially deplored. Such conduct brings shame and ridicule—powerful weapons in Indian culture! Specifically, Navajos consider it undesirable for an individual to call attention to his own achievements or to excel the group.

"This does not mean that Henry has no personal pride or will not work to accomplish something. Henry may, for example, labor for hours memorizing long chants in order to take part in *sings*. He wants to know the chants perfectly—but not in order to garner personal praise. His motive for perfect memorization is that, if he made one mistake in the chant, the entire ceremony would be nullified and he and his family would be publicly shamed because he had not done his part right.

"In school, however, teachers who do not understand these attitudes of Indian people may publicly praise a child extravagantly for something he has done well, believing that, in this way, they are rewarding him for his efforts. Actually, singling out a child, in front of his friends or in class, and praising the child verbally, embarrasses him seriously. Indian children enjoy praise, but, to feel comfortable with it, it needs to be group praise. The best way for the teacher to handle this situation is to praise three or four—or a group of children—or to display together the best work done among all in the group. A child's friends will ostracize him if he is singled out for special attention. This will be especially true of children who have come directly from the reservation.

"After Indian children have been in our schools for several years, they usually learn to adapt gradually—or at least to understand the attitude toward praise held by their non-Indian classmates. Meanwhile, a teacher's knowledge of this Indian attitude toward praise will help the teacher to understand why a given child turns against him or even refuses to cooperate after a teacher has publicly praised him. The reason is that the child's Indian friends would reject him if he seemed to seek—or if he responded favorably to—individual recognition.

"A third classroom problem is that of Henry's *obeying* his teacher. What is involved here? We might describe as permissive the discipline which the Indian child has known; he receives gentle encouragement to do what is expected of him—but he learns what the expectations are! An Indian child is cherished and respected as an individual but not pampered. In fact, many Indian children are given great responsibility at an early age. A young child may have sole responsibility for an entire flock of sheep or for a still younger sibling. He or she, therefore, has had to learn to make decisions on his own. In school, then, he continues making decisions. Such a child may unconsciously alienate his teacher by assuming that he is to continue to make decisions for himself—decisions which, in school, are the province of the teacher. Consequently, when a teacher says, 'We'll now put away our drawings and get out our arithmetic books,' Henry Yazzie may decide that it would be better for him to finish his drawing than to participate in arithmetic today. He has heard you, so you wonder why he doesn't obey you. How can you tolerate such a situation? In Henry's eyes, he is not being disobedient. He is doing what seems to him the best thing to do. Early in his life, Henry was forced by circumstances to make his own decisions. Moreover, Henry's family may have been one of the many Navajo families in which it is customary for children themselves to make important decisions relating to their own welfare. We noted earlier that children in some families decided whether or not they would attend school. They may even make decisions as important as whether or not they will go to the hospital for necessary treatment.

"If a Navajo parent, however, feels that a child has deliberately disobeyed or done something wrong, he handles the situation, not by physical punishment as do parents of comparable economic status in some other cultures, but rather by shaming the child into acceptable behavior. The Indian parent takes for granted that the child does not know any better. Thus, he disapproves of his behavior, lets him know by precept and example what behavior is expected of him, and invokes the force of public opinion to secure compliance. The child obeys because he does not wish to disgrace his parents or himself. No one wants people to 'talk about him!'

"Obviously, Henry's relationship with his parents is a cordial one. Navajos like children. A small family is a disappointment. Navajos are proud of their children, are careful in training them, and enjoy having them about. If you have an opportunity to visit their homes, you feel the cordiality, although there might be little conversation. Upon your arrival, you would shake hands with everyone, even with the smallest toddler, but not the hard, quick hand-pumping to which you are accustomed, though, for Navajos measure you by the duration and 'sincerity' of your handshake. Lest you lose their respect, remember that Navajos clasp one another's hands gently, but long and fervently, especially if there has been an interval since their last meeting. In public, Navajo are not demonstrative; this prolonged handclasp and a low murmur is their form of greeting.

"Suppose that you are being brought by a Navajo child to visit his home on the reservation. As you approach the home, the family may go inside. If they want a visitor to come inside their home, the entire family goes inside when they see the visitor arriving. The visitor is expected to enter without knocking. If a family prefers not to have a visitor come into the house, they will be outside to greet him and will remain there. In any event, they will seat the visitor comfortably — and quietly allow him time to become accustomed to them. It is considered rude to plunge at once into talk about the reason for the visit. Should you, during the visit, talk favorably about their children to the parents, you will find that they are very pleased. They are not accustomed to expressing the appreciation in words — but you can see it in their shining eyes.

"That one be esteemed by his fellows is of utmost importance to Henry and to his parents. All of their conduct shows this concern. For example, if a Navajo has wronged someone, an apology or even punishment of the offender is insufficient; compensation must be made to the person wronged. One never says, 'Excuse me' or 'I'm sorry' because words are inadequate! Nor is appreciation shown by a 'thank-you'; one must *do* something to prove one's appreciation.

"This attitude also explains the Indian emphasis on generosity: one must share all one has with one's entire extended family — in fact, with anyone who asks. For example, when an Indian is traveling anywhere on the reservation, he may stop at any home and be assured of food. If a family has food, it is Navajo custom to share it. A visitor is expected to join a family meal if he arrives when the family is eating. If he comes at another time, a woman promptly places food within reach and the guest is expected to help himself. This expression of hospitality shows that the woman is a good wife — a credit to her parents and husband. On the other hand, for a guest to refuse proffered food can be considered an insult.

"Food, particularly abundance of food, is a status symbol. In the past, a fat person was considered to be one who had done well; he could afford to become fat. Times are changing, though! Today's teenagers prefer slimness or, at least, a well-proportioned figure. The extended family, however, will still gather together mountains of food, should someone be ill and some individual family need to give a *sing*. This involves inviting and paying the fee of the Medicine Man who chants and prays for the patient's recovery and, as mentioned earlier, it includes inviting everyone in the community. All, therefore, must be fed for the duration of the *sing* which may extend for a week or longer.

"Moreover, if an individual in any one group in the extended family is regularly employed — or if an individual family has a vegetable patch or a fruit orchard — each is expected to share what they have with everyone in the extended family. In times of extreme drought, this generosity includes everyone in the tribe. Each family will share the water hole with all who need water; in fact, Navajo are so considerate that they never camp too near water lest they frighten away the wild life who also need it to live.

"With Navajos, then, everyone has a claim on what anyone possesses. An unfortunate corollary of this concept, according to general American standards, is that, sometimes, no one feels personal responsibility for the care of possessions. Obviously, if property is perceived by Navajos as common property, private property is not understood in the non-Navajo sense of the word. Generous sharing of all one possesses with every one in one's family and clan is expected of every Navajo. Whether each person contributes his share or not, a Navajo does not say that a relative is lazy or selfish or ineffective. He is expected to be friendly and helpful to all. One must keep in mind, though, that with the introduction of money into the daily lives of more and more of the People, this practice of generosity, too, is changing. Also, this discussion does not imply that an individual Navajo may not own anything. They do; children, for example, may be given sheep at an early age.

"In school, behavior stemming from this Navajo attitude toward personal property is sometimes interpreted as stealing. Think how confusing to an Indian child is your distribution of pencils, papers, and supplies and your telling him on one day to 'take one' — then accusing him the next day of 'stealing' someone's pencil! Indian children do not understand what you mean by stealing. With many Navajo, you are expected to take, without asking, what you need for yourself. Therefore, when a child is caught 'taking something' in school, he is not ashamed of this behavior — but he does learn, from your shocked reaction, to be more careful next time!

"Thus, to the teacher who is not knowledgeable about Indians, the Indian child may seem careless about time, uninterested in achievement, disobedient, perhaps a thief! On the other hand, he may seem unresponsive.

"Navajo children are taught self-control. Verbally and by imitation, a child learns behavior — as he is taught skills — by watching adults in his family. They show him, over and over, what is expected of him. The boy or girl watches. He does not question or discuss what is being taught him. Such passivity, carried over into school, may be interpreted by his teacher as unresponsiveness.

"Navajo children have many learning experiences with adults because, as previously stated, many of them live in an extended family.

Their concept of family relationships, therefore, are different from yours. The household they know is usually that of the maternal grandparents. Here maternal uncles may have as much influence on a child as his father, and maternal cousins are often considered brothers and sisters. Is it surprising, then, that these children have difficulty understanding what their school readers mean by 'brothers,' 'sisters,' 'fathers,' and 'mothers'? To the Navajo child, his mother is the person of greatest importance both in his family and to him. The child is part of his mother's clan, even if he is illegitimate; illegitimacy is not something to be ashamed of! The Indian child honors his mother, in fact, he is constantly admonished to 'be nice to your mother.' An adult's neglect of his mother is harshly censured by the community.

"Navajo women have always been esteemed. Although their marriages may have been arranged, women are the center of the family's social life. They do the cooking, make the clothes and blankets, own the home which the husband is expected to build. They own the children, the sheep, and the goats, while the fathers own the horses and cattle. The women usually share the farm work with the men and do the trading for provisions and domestic supplies. They are industrious and self-sufficient. This concept of a mother is very different from that of the middle class American mother or of the mother of Dick and Jane in your readers.

Teaching the Navajo Children

The Navajo Language. "In 1961, 62 per cent of the adult Navajos did not speak English. So, it is probable that English isn't spoken in Henry's home. English words will not only be unfamiliar to Henry, but, also, he will find that new words have meanings confusing to him. For example, teachers talk of four directions; Henry knows six—north, east, south, west, zenith and nadir. Or teachers may feel that Navajo children are 'slow' to learn color. This is true. Henry *is* confused because in Navajo, a single word denotes blue and green; another single word denotes grey or brown, while there are two words for black, the black of darkness and the black of 'things' such as coal or tar. Finally, Henry's language has no *p, q, r, f, v, u,* or *w.** These letters and their sounds will be especially difficult for him. Clearly, Henry will need special help with language. One of your faculty meetings, I am glad to learn, will be devoted to specific ways to give language help.

"Henry's language problem reminds me of my visit to Expo 67

---

* See page 82 for more information concerning the Navajo language.

where the Canadian Indian pavilion was used wisely and well by Canadian Indians to get across, in moving and touching signs, some messages one cannot soon forget:

An Indian child begins school by learning a foreign language. The White Man's school is an alien land for an Indian child.

When the White Man came, we welcomed him with love. We sheltered him, fed him, and led him through the wilderness. He could not have lived without us.

The early missionaries thought we were pagans. They imposed on us their stories of God. But we spoke with God — the Great Spirit — in our own way.

The Navajo's Learning Experience. "Not only will English be — on the whole — a foreign language to Henry, but most of what he sees around him in school will be strange to him. He may not recognize by name nor know how to use drinking fountains, paper towels, flush toilets, clocks, desks, blackboards, chalk, pencils, and crayons. The nurse's bathroom scales, the playground equipment, your record player, fairy tales, and nursery rhymes may either fascinate or frighten him. Henry will try not to look at his teacher, or to show how he feels — because he has been taught this way — but, in spite of himself, he may crouch under the table if he becomes overwhelmed with too many new experiences. As previously mentioned, no matter how interested he is in something, he will not interrupt his teacher or ask questions; such behavior is considered rude.

"A Navajo child learns a skill by watching an adult practice it. The adult shows the child, over and over again, how to do something. No verbal directions are given; there is usually no conversation during the learning experience — no discussion — and no asking of questions. Finally, the child tries on his own. Navajos are unaccustomed to learning by means of words. Consequently, a Navajo child has had no experience in asking or answering questions. In fact, many an adult Navajo does not like to be asked a direct question. Fearing, perhaps, that his answer will be considered wrong, he may reply 'maybe' in a non-committal tone. Nor is it likely that he will offer information, advice, or help unless it is specifically requested. This practice is considered rude. Therefore, do not be surprised if an Indian pupil does not tell you that he has a pass to leave your classroom and go to the nurse — or does not tell the bus driver where he lives.

"In the classroom, Henry may seldom look directly at his teacher, but rather at what the teacher is doing. He expects to memorize what

he is to do. Discussing the lesson being taught him might involve con-
tradiction of his elders which is 'never done.' In the light of this background, Indian children will find it most difficult to listen to verbal
directions and to follow them. No wonder that teachers say that Indian
children are bad listeners! Listening is a new experience to them!

"What can teachers do in this situation? Some teachers think that,
by raising the tone or volume of their voices, by pressuring the children, or by threatening them with poor grades if they don't listen,
teachers will ensure good listening. To the contrary, such responses
will only frustrate the teacher! Indian children simply 'go into a shell'
when pressured. Since they are not personally competitive, pressuring
them to make good grades is more a threat than a stimulus to them. And
should a teacher say to an Indian child that, if he cannot understand and read and speak well, he will not be promoted, this does not
concern such a child. He does not know the urgent need to 'get ahead'
which drives the white man.

"One positive way for a teacher to handle this situation is to give
the Indian child only one direction at a time. A list of directions will
confuse him. If you say to Henry, 'First color this picture, then do
your arithmetic, then read the story in your reader,' what will Henry
do? Color his picture, that's what. And he will probably still be color-
ing when everyone else is reading because he is unaccustomed to
thinking about time and planning ahead. Only very gradually will he
learn to follow a list of directions. At first, give him one at a time,
a simple one which contains only two or three words telling him definitely what is expected! In addition, show him as well as tell him what
you want him to do.

"And if Henry appears not to be listening—or seems deliberately un-
communicative? Some teachers may think he is being sullen. In reality,
he is observing the rules of politeness as he knows them. Navajos are
taught never to look directly into the eyes of a speaker, although they
may watch the lips. Moreover, a Navajo child is taught to observe the
rule of silence when he enters another's home; remember, it is courtesy
to allow time for the various individuals to 'get used to each other.'
The Indian child considers the schoolroom the teacher's domain.
Therefore, he sits silent. He was taught that polite people are quiet,
slow of approach, never aggressive.

"Henry's teacher, however, in need of information about him or in
an effort to be friendly, may ask him question after question. The
teacher may even have pointed at him. Perhaps the teacher receives
only confused looks from the child. Henry is puzzled by this strange
new person who so aggressively demands answers to personal, prying

questions, since Henry has been taught that asking questions, especially personal ones, is the height of rudeness! And pointing with the finger is highly improper. To direct attention to someone, one uses facial expressions or lip gestures.

Combining the Two Cultures. "Henry Yazzie and his friends *want* to learn all that you can teach them; but they also want to remain Indians. They want to hold on, whenever feasible, to their culture and to their way of life. They want an education which will help them to find a way to combine the best from two cultures! I think that this is commendable; they should do exactly that! A number of nationality groups in our country have kept their values and traditions—their celebrations, their dishes, their religion, their ways of life; yet they think of themselves as basically Americans. Indians, too, may want to see themselves accepted as American citizens—with a special cultural heritage. Teachers and schools have helped other groups to become Americans in this sense. You can help the Henry Yazzies to develop their special potentialities as they, concurrently, learn to become good American citizens. Teachers will do this most effectively as they learn who the Henry Yazzies are, what they are striving for, and what they can contribute, from their particular heritage, to the composite of the culture that is America.

"The wisest teachers, as they work with the Henry Yazzies, will conscientiously ponder such questions as: what alien ways must these children learn in order to live in today's society? how can they absorb technical knowledge necessary for their survival without disrupting the whole fabric of their lives? how much of the old pattern of life can they safely preserve? how can the human values by which they live be conserved in the heritage of all humanity?"

Mr. Jackson thanked Miss Begay, emphasizing, "You've told us things today that, I am sure, some of us never knew before." Miss Begay responded graciously, "Others of you, however, know a great deal about Indian children and do a superb job of teaching them. I am so happy to learn that these experienced teachers are planning to share their experiences with the new teachers all of whom, I am sure, are looking forward to hearing Mrs. Brown, at your next meeting, talk about her problems and successes in teaching Peggy Blackgoat, a Navajo child who was in her second grade last year."

CHAPTER 3

My Year with Peggy

Mrs. Brown began the next teachers' meeting with, "Last week we discussed Indian children as one group of culturally disadvantaged children whom we would like to understand better. Peggy Blackgoat is a seven-year-old Navajo child. Were Peggy in your class, you might consider her either a problem or a challenge. She had problems, but she was not a problem child. She never seemed upset or unduly concerned about anything. She sounds like an ideal pupil? Yes, but Peggy had a learning problem. Peggy couldn't read."

"'Oh,' you say. 'What's special about that? We all have nonreaders. Do we have to hear about another child who can't read?'

"I didn't say Peggy *can't* read. Last year when she entered second grade, she *couldn't* read. She acted stupid at first, yet she seemed bright too. Was she a nonreader? She's reading now. What happened?

"What kind of miracle method did I use? If I had one, I'd be a millionaire. No, I shall not talk of miracles. I began by asking myself — of what is my class composed? Individuals.

"Do I hear groans? — 'Oh, you're going to give us the old story about how a good teacher individualizes instruction. You know there isn't enough time in the day for that!'

"You're jumping to conclusions. Individual instruction is necessary and valuable. Moreover, up to a point, it can be and is given by every good teacher. But — I do know — it isn't possible all the time or in every subject. However, you have learned, children with 'different' cultural backgrounds have specific learning deficiencies. There are equally specific reasons for every child's *particular* deficiencies.

"Although this story is primarily about Peggy, she isn't my only reading problem. In her group are two Mexican children, two Negroes, one white child from the Tennessee mountains and one from the slums of a middle-western city. These children, whose backgrounds are not similar to Peggy's, are also lacking in cultural experiences. They need, as much as she does, to have explanations of words — simple words we take for granted — before reading can be meaningful to them.

"If a teacher can identify each individual's particular problems, consider them carefully, then develop specific remedial methods, techniques, and understandings to fill in the gaps or deficiencies in the child's experiences, that individual will gradually improve in his response to school — in his learning and his reading. At least, so I reasoned about Peggy.

"I was not satisfied that I was teaching Navajo children effectively. When I became aware of Peggy's reading problems, I decided to learn as much as I could about her. I vowed I would keep a detailed record on her in order to try to find out what her specific difficulties were and what their source might be. Using this information, I resolved to try to develop specific ways to help her, then to evaluate what I did in terms of what was useful to her and what was not. I hoped that this record could become the story of Peggy's *progress* in school. Let me share it with you."

PEGGY'S PROGRESS RECORD

First Week of School. "During the first days, I had the children 'trial reading' in preprimers. Although she needed repeated reminders about words she had encountered last year and 'forgotten,' Peggy 'read' fairly well at the preprimer level. However, upon questioning her, I found out what the experts mean when they say that the learning of English necessitates not only saying the new words, but also forming new concepts and developing the vocabulary to express these in spoken English.

"Peggy had learned to recognize a limited number of English words by configuration, association, or by rote. She could recognize and reproduce, after a fashion, a few vowel and consonant sounds; she could even divide some words into syllables and, sometimes, indicate the accent correctly. In other words, Peggy could pronounce these words. But they did not constitute a meaningful vocabulary because Peggy did not know what the words meant. To her, they were merely strange sounds in a strange language.

"In class, Peggy was shy, almost withdrawn. It was difficult to establish rapport with her because of her silence, her down-cast eyes and lack of response to directions. Now I realized that, even though Peggy had attended school — spasmodically — last year, she still did not understand enough spoken English to know what I was saying *most* of the time. To her, I was a strange person using a strange language, making requests of her which she did not understand. My directions only confused and bewildered her. No wonder she would not venture to speak even a single word!

"I made inquiries about Peggy. Her family has lived in town for several years, yet they still speak Navajo at home. In fact, her parents know very little English. Her home and her ways are more Indian than American.

"Peggy's parents haven't much use for school. Peggy is fifth in a family of eight children. Her older brothers and sisters have each been retained in the lower grades; all were nonreaders. All had poor attendance records.

"The home is poor and Peggy's appearance reflects lack of care. She has a round face and attractive brown eyes, but also stringy black hair which usually needs both washing and combing. Her clothes are like those of other children from economically poor homes; cotton dresses or skirts and blouses. The clothes are frequently dirty, with buttons and belts missing.

"As is the case with many disadvantaged children, linguistic and cultural differences are greater barriers to Peggy's school learning than are racial differences. Peggy's rate of learning in school, therefore, will depend upon the rate at which she can and does accept new ways and a new language. Can I find a way to bridge the gap between the language I speak and that which she understands — can I break the sound barrier? Can I get across to her that she is accepted, that she 'belongs' in our class? If she feels secure with us, especially with me, she will be *willing to learn* our ways and our language. Then, like most children, she will, I am sure, respond when she knows how to respond.

"My first step was to learn a few key words and phrases in Navajo. The teacher can gain the confidence of a child who comes to school speaking a language different from English if he shows the child that he respects the child's language enough to have learned something about it. Simultaneously, as the teacher struggles with the child's language, he develops rapport with the child because he actually shares the child's transitional struggle. Moreover, even limited knowledge of the child's language will help the teacher to anticipate particular difficulties which that language presents to a child in learning English. I have prepared some material for you in Navajo and have indicated specific difficulties which the Navajo-speaking child will encounter in learning English.[1] You can prepare similar materials in Spanish, for example. Now — to return to Peggy!

"In order for Peggy to understand English, she must have experiences which will make each new word meaningful — so that, when she pronounces a word, she will 'know what she is talking about.' This knowledge will give her confidence to try the word on her own — to speak. If you think this process is simple, ask Peggy to say a few words in her language; then you try to repeat *them*. You may not even be able to reproduce the sounds, much less understand the words. Your attempts will probably draw a polite smile. I remember two Hopi girls who giggled for 15 minutes at my attempt to reproduce one four-syllable word of their language. I finally gave up; no matter how I said it, it seemed to sound funnier and funnier to them.

"By means of well-planned classroom experiences, Peggy can learn new words everyday. Her language can develop functionally; speaking and learning a new word can accompany purposeful activity. For example, when we use pencils, chalk, crayons, paste, scissors, chairs, tables, we talk about these items. We take things out of the cupboard, borrow them, lend them, put them away. We use the drinking fountain, the washroom, the cafeteria. We need to be shown how to use them, where we put our paper towels after we've washed our hands, how to use straws to drink with, and silverware for eating.

"Vocabulary grows out of experiences like these. The new words must be repeated day after day before Peggy can be certain enough of their meaning and of their pronunciation to venture to use them herself. She will listen and watch and try to learn them because she understands that there is a purpose in learning these words. Thus, day by day, her functional vocabulary will be built. Playground activities demand another set of new words to understand, to pronounce, and to learn how to use. Of course, the most natural way for Peggy — or any child — to learn to speak what the school considers acceptable English is by talking with people who speak in this fashion: namely, with her teacher and her classmates, by playing with children who have learned some language skill, by participating in classroom activities which, daily, develop language skill."

Third Week of School. Peggy never speaks except in response to a direct question. Then she responds in a low monosyllable, without ever looking at me. She has great difficulty in communicating with me, and I certainly am not "getting across" to her. Is she shy? Doesn't she understand me — or is she in-

---

[1] See end of chapter: p. 84.

capable of learning? I wonder. She is *trying* to read *Fun with Dick and Jane* with a group of four other children. Several of them are having serious difficulties, especially Peggy. Her specific learning problems are that she
(1) Cannot remember words;
(2) Cannot figure out words—apparently phonics previously "taught" her did not "reach her";
(3) Gets no help from context clues.

Since Peggy is not learning to read by methods I am using now, I will have to do something else. But what? How can I teach her? Or maybe I can't; maybe she is mentally retarded.

I have arranged to have Peggy given an individual intelligence test. This may give me a clue as to whether she is retarded. Maybe she is.

"Her brothers and sisters have been regarded by other teachers as slow learners—or nonlearners. Peggy's sister Nancy, a year older, was tested last year, and earned an overall IQ score of 65. Of course, the validity of most intelligence tests for bilingual children should be questioned. The children may be insecure in the testing situation—with a strange person giving directions they may not really understand. Moreover, these children may have little incentive to learn; the home may provide them little or no motivation. Therefore, they may not work hard or try to do their best on a test."

I shall not take Peggy's actual test score too seriously. However, a test may give clues about her strengths and weaknesses. Though I sometimes doubt my ability to teach Peggy, I don't really doubt her. I think Peggy can learn. We'll see what the test shows—and go on from there.

Tuesday: I told Peggy about the test; what I said was that Mr. Jackson wanted someone to try some new games with him this afternoon; he wanted to see if second graders liked them. Would she like to try them? She said "O.K."; but this afternoon she didn't come back to school.

Wednesday: Mr. Jackson came in at 2:00 P.M. and asked Peggy if she would like to go with him to play games. Impassively she said, "O.K.," and went along.

Mr. Jackson had suggested that I come in at 2:30, after my class was dismissed, to see how Peggy was doing. She seemed rather pleased at the attention she was getting; she was trying to cooperate, but she obviously could not tell what he wanted, especially when directions were given verbally. At such times, she would look at both of us blankly, barely perceptibly shrug her shoulders—then do something—usually based on visual clues she had gotten from the directions.

Thursday: Peggy's test results are in! Here they are:

RE: Peggy Blackgoat, Age 7   Date of Test   2-11-67
    Birthdate   6-28-59

Peggy was given the Wechsler Intelligence Scale for Children on which she scored an IQ of 76 on the Verbal Scale and 94 on the Performance Scale. Full Scale IQ was 83. The sub-test breakdown is as follows:

VERBAL TESTS		PERFORMANCE TESTS	
Information	6	Picture Completion	9
Comprehension	5	Picture Arrangement	7
Arithmetic	7	Block Design	10
Similarities	6	Object Assembly	6
Vocabulary	5	Coding	14
Digit Span	8		

Using the Full Scale IQ as reference, Peggy is shown to have an M.A. of 6.3 years. This is determined by the standard formula $MA/CA \times 100 = IQ$. However, if her Performance IQ is used, which, in the examiner's opinion, is probably closer to her actual ability due to her language deficiency, she is shown to have an M.A. of approximately 7.1 years. This is not too different from her C.A. of 7.7 years and means that she probably has average ability for school work.

Peggy cooperated well and did not seem frightened. This was a good test situation.

Just as I suspected—Peggy can learn! I certainly agree with Mr. Jackson that her performance IQ is more nearly correct than the verbal one because of her language deficiency. She may have even more ability than this test indicates. At any rate, she should be retested when she has gained facility in English.

Now, what to do about Peggy? First, I'd better try to analyze the problem. What can I learn from her behavior that might give me clues about her learning problems?

"I decided to watch her for a week and to record my impressions. The following is what I had written down after a week":

Observing: Peggy seems to be oblivious to most things going on around her. She doesn't talk to, listen to, or even watch the other children most of the time. Drawing—mostly pictures of hogans "out home"—or playing quietly with clay or a puzzle—occupy most of her free time in class (and some of the time when she should be doing something else).

Listening: She doesn't listen to directions at all—doesn't even seem to know that I am giving directions! She doesn't listen to stories that I read aloud to the class—something most children enjoy!

Speaking: Peggy has still not said a word voluntarily. When I ask her a direct question, sometimes she just stares—or answers with a monosyllable "yes" or "no"—or an occasional "don't know." She never says anything in front of the other children.

Reading: Peggy still cannot remember or figure out words or use context clues. However, she does seem to get help from pictorial clues—just as she did when Mr. Jackson tested her! What should I learn from this observation?

Relationship to Other Adults: She will not speak to other teachers or adults with the exception of her last year's first grade teacher.

Social Activity: Nancy, her third grade sister, is her only playmate. She has no friends in our room.

I have just re-read my notes. How do I expect Peggy to read if she can't listen, and won't talk? She probably isn't talking because many words that we use are meaningless to her—but I don't know which ones. And if I can't get her to talk, how will I ever find out?

Peggy's Reading Group Learns New Words. "I had been thinking about Peggy and the others in her group. I had not been really aware of them. I realized that not one of them spoke more than the necessary monosyllables. I asked myself, 'Why won't they talk?' Maybe it's because I haven't shown them that I really want to listen to what they have to say. I'm always so busy trying to stuff information into them! Why don't I stop and see if they have any for me? If I could quit worrying about how much actual reading we can get done each day, if I would relax and talk *with* them instead of *to* them, and show them I really like to hear what they have to say, in these ways I could help them to learn the meanings of new words and teach them how to *use* the words. So, my first job was to teach them to talk!"

Today, Monday, I conducted my *reading group* this way: "Our story today is about pets. Does anyone know what a pet is?" No answer. "Could anyone think of something that could be a pet?"

Debbie barely whispered, "A dog?"

"That's right. Fine, Debbie." I beamed at her and repeated "dog" so that everyone could hear. Then I went on. "Lots of people have dogs for pets. A pet is an animal that usually lives in your house or yard. It might have a name." I paused. No response. I went on, "What do we do with a pet?"

John said, slowly, "We can play with it."

"Yes, we like to play with pets. Does anyone know another pet?"

"A cat?" asked Peggy in a low voice.

"Good, Peggy. Cats make nice pets." I paused again. No more volunteers —
so again I went on, "Who knows the name of any of the pets in our book?
Lyle?" (He looked as though, with encouragement, he might say something.)
"Puff."
"Yes, Puff is a pet. What kind of pet is she, John?"
"A cat."
"Do you know what we call a baby cat? Debbie?" She looked as though she
was gathering courage to raise her hand.
"A kitten."
"That's right. I'm pleased that you are all such good thinkers. Is there
another pet we know from the book?"
Peggy said, a bit louder this time, "Spot."
"Good, Peggy. What kind of animal is Spot?"
"He's a dog."
"Do any of you have a dog?" Four hands went up.
Lyle said, "I don't got any."
"Susan, do you have one?" No answer — but she nodded her head slowly.
"John, what does yours look like?"
"He gots spots."
"What color spots? Is he like the one in our book?"
"No, he gots brown spots."
"Peggy, do you have a dog?"
"Ony on da reservation."
"What does he look like, or is it a girl dog?"
"He's a girl."
"Does she have puppies?"
"Long time 'go."
"What color is she?"
"Black."
"Does she have a name?"
"No."
Debbie interrupted, "Mine's name is Bingo."
"Susan, what do you call yours?" No answer.
John broke in, "Mine is Spot, too." No more volunteers, so I said, "I'm glad
you told me about your pets. I like to have you tell me things. And when you
do, we all find out things we didn't know about one another. Do you know
something now that you didn't know before?" No answer. "Well, I do. I
know what color Peggy's dog is. Do you?" This elicited a chorus of "Black."
"That's right, and I know that John's dog has brown spots. How many know
that?" All hands went up. "Does anybody know the names of John's and
Debbie's dogs?" Hands shot up again. "See, you know lots of things you
didn't know before. I think you even know whether Peggy's dog is a boy or a
girl, don't you?" Heads nodded. "How did we find out all these things?"
Debbie said softly, "Somebody told us."
"That's right, and do you know what we did whenever somebody talked?

We listened to what they said. I can tell we're all good listeners because we learned so many things today. Do you know how else we could learn something, besides by listening?" No answer. "Well, I'll tell you — by looking. Let's play a game called 'Looking.' Tomorrow on the way to school, look around, and see if you can find something in your yard or by the road that you could bring for us to look at. It can be anything you want, but be sure it doesn't belong to somebody else. Will you do that?"

"O.K."

It was almost like pulling teeth, but four out of five of them *did* talk when they were sure they knew what I wanted! *Not a word out of Susan — but Peggy talked more than she ever has! I think I'm on the right track; listening to them and encouraging them to talk is a prelude to teaching reading!*

"Perhaps, in their overcrowded homes, nobody talks *to* them except to give orders or to scold them. Nobody wants to hear their ideas on anything. It probably hasn't occurred to their parents that children could have an opinion or idea that adults might want to listen to."

Well, they're going to know that I want to listen! Then we'll see if they'll talk.

Tuesday reading group: "Did anybody bring anything to show us today?" (I had something ready in case no one had.) Debbie held up a rock. "How nice! Debbie remembered to bring something."

Lyle said, "It's just a rock. That's all." Debbie looked crestfallen. I immediately interposed, "That's fine, Debbie. It's a beautiful rock. We can all find out something about it. Debbie, what did you like best about this rock?"

"It's red."

"Yes, it has a pretty color. Can we tell anything else from it?" No answer. "Well, is it hard or soft?"

"Hard,"

"How do you know it is hard? Can you hear it is hard?"

"No."

"Can you see it is hard?"

"Yes."

"You can see it is a rock, and rocks are usually hard. But what could you do to be sure?"

Peggy — "We could touch it."

"That's very good thinking. We can all touch it, and be sure whether it's hard or not." The stone was passed around the group. We all agreed it was hard. "How about if we smell it, would that tell us anything about it?"

Some of the children laughed. "Rocks don't smell!"

"No, they usually don't. Well then, could we taste it?"

Debbie — "Ugh! It's dirty!"

"That's right, we don't want to taste it because it's dirty. What did we do to it so far to tell us something about it?"

John said, "We feeled it."

"Yes, we felt it. What else?" No answer. "Did we see it?"

"Yes."

"What else could we do to learn about it? Do you think we could hear it?"

"No."

"Let's close our eyes and listen. Do you hear anything?"

"No."

"Keep your eyes closed and listen again — now do you hear anything?" I dropped it on the table.

"Yes, yes, I hear it."

"Tomorrow, let's see if we could bring something we could smell. All right?"

Wednesday: Before school, Peggy came up with a flower in her hand. "Here."

"Oh, is that for us to smell?"

"Yes."

"Good. I'm so glad you remembered to bring it. You're getting to be a good helper for me and a very good listener, too." She smiled and went to her seat. Debbie handed me another flower. "Thank you, Debbie. I'm glad you remembered, too. I'm very pleased with you."

Reading group: We passed around Peggy's dandelion and Debbie's aster. None of them had known the flowers' names — so we learned those. The children talked about the smells, the colors, and how the flowers felt. They agreed we didn't want to taste them.

I still have to carry most of the conversation and to ask many questions, but the children are talking a bit more each day. (I'm sure it's very novel to some of them not to have a grown-up always telling them to shut up.) Tomorrow, they agreed, we will bring something to taste.

Thursday: Lyle brought a flour tortilla. They all knew what it was, but everyone tasted a little bit anyway. We talked about how it looks, feels, and smells. I had brought small chocolate candies for a surprise. We had fun watching a candy melt a little. Of course, we talked about melting. We also smelled the candies with our eyes closed; then we tasted them.

"When I brought surprises like candy, the other children in class had some too — during their reading groups. I explained to them that there are many ways to learn to read and that some of us are learning about words and about things we see in our books before we read in our books. The rest of the class accepted this explanation. Children are amazingly perceptive and tolerant. They may think it's a funny way to read; in fact, one day when we were munching on lettuce and cabbage, one boy stood near us watching for a few moments, muttered, 'Silliest way to learn to read!' and walked off. Yet neither he nor any of the others have ever teased these children about their reading. Presumably, the class has accepted the fact that people need to learn in different ways—just so *they* don't miss out on any treats!"

Two Weeks Later. I've been too busy to keep notes every day on Peggy. In her reading group, at every opportunity, we've been tasting, smelling, feeling, listening, and looking—and the process seems to have resulted in some learning. I had my first "result" today—after more than two months of school!

I have an established policy of giving the entire class directions for independent seatwork only once each morning. I've been checking Peggy's group for listening habits, and commending them as they improve. After I gave directions today, I asked if there were any questions. One child asked, "What page is our arithmetic?" The page number was written on the board; moreover, I had just mentioned it. I said, "Who has been a good listener and can tell Joe what page we are going to do?" Peggy's hand was up with most of the others. I was delighted and asked, "Peggy, what number is it?" When everyone looked at her, she shrank down into her seat. But she did answer in a very small voice, "21." I immediately repeated it. "Yes, 21. That's fine, Peggy. I'm glad you are such a good listener. And I see others who know how to listen, too."

In Peggy's group, we aren't reading orally very much yet; but we do read some each day. We're reading slowly and we spend much time in group discussion of new words we meet. I let them tell me what *they* think the words mean, then we amplify and clarify definitions. Sometimes we act out difficult words, particularly abstract words like *in front, behind, beside, here, before, there.* We're working on letter recognition and sounds, too. We play word games and sound games—sound games like "What sound does this word begin with, or end with?" We use flash cards to help find rhyming words; "what sounds like this word?" They love these games—and look forward to the treats everyone gets when they've been particularly good players.

"It's a slow process—perhaps *you* wouldn't see much progress in their reading. But they were beginning to feel that they *could* use words. Most of them, Peggy especially, in their own small group would talk—and they knew that we would always listen. I'm convinced that this observing, listening, and talking is necessary before any boy or girl of any age can read with any comprehension—or before they want to read! Motivating them to read, as you know, is more than half the battle.

"Most of them *wanted* to participate in group activities too. I'm sure they sensed my interest in what they contributed; and they were so pleased when I praised them—as I did for every attempt to participate. I remembered to include every child in my commendation. You can always find something good to say about a child, even if it's no more than how well he keeps his place as we read. Being praised — even being noticed — is such a unique experience for some of them that they are eager to please in order to share the group's satisfaction and feeling of accomplishment."

Peggy will generally answer me now whenever I speak directly to her. She seems to feel enough confidence in her reading group so that she readily speaks there. Perhaps, she realizes that they all have trouble expressing themselves. In group discussions in class, however, she will seldom respond. She isn't ready yet to venture to speak in a large group. I never force her; but I try to encourage her. I keep thinking of ways to coax her, like asking questions she can answer with a monosyllable.

Wednesday: Yesterday, as we were using *Weekly Readers,* the entire class was discussing pumpkins, pumpkin pies, and seeds. This morning Debbie brought me some pumpkin seeds.

Reading group: I began with, "Do you remember when we were talking about pumpkins yesterday? Well, Debbie brought some pumpkin seeds. Where did you get them, Debbie?"
"My mother cut open a pumpkin and took them out."
"We're very glad to have them. Be sure to tell your mother thank you for us. Now what could we do with them?"
"Let's plant 'em."
"I think that's a fine idea, John. Do you think we could raise pumpkins in our room?" They were doubtful. "I don't know either. I don't think they will grow to be pumpkins, but let's plant them and see if the pumpkin vines will come up (we discussed vines yesterday) and maybe they will have flowers. Now, what will we need?" They discussed what we should have to plant them in and how we should do it. Tomorrow we will plant them. (I seize every opportunity to initiate a new meaningful activity.)

Friday: Peggy came up to my desk. She still speaks slowly; "Teacher — may — I — go — to — da — bafroom? I — want — to — trow — up." I quickly gave my consent; I was afraid she wouldn't make it, but she did. Upon her return, I expressed my concern — but she did not seem upset by the incident. Teachers need to know that these children seem to have periodic stomach upsets, perhaps related to dietary habits. I have discovered though that, unless they are really ill, they seem to feel that the less said about it, the better.

Four Weeks Later. In Peggy's reading group, we've been working on listening, observing, and speaking every day. It's remarkable how well the children respond. I never dreamed Peggy would come along so quickly. We're reading now, too—as much as we can possibly squeeze in every day. Now they *want* to read because the words mean something to them.

Monday: For the first time this year, Peggy came in bursting to talk. "Guess what! Tonight they gonna trow me in da water—at church—and I'm gonna wear a white dress!" I told her that would be very nice. She scarcely heard as she went on, "They gonna trow my whole family in da water—even my fadder too!" Just to see what she would say, I smiled and asked, "Is he going to wear a white dress, too?" With a straight face, she answered, "No, he gots a white pants and shirt."

One thing I never, never do is attempt to correct Peggy's speech—not yet! What I want now is for her to speak. No matter how she says words! I cannot risk cutting off, by any criticism, the trickle of speech I'm beginning to get. Later, when she is secure enough and confident enough of my concern about her, I shall have plenty of opportunity to improve her speech habits.

"I have learned that these bilingual children, once they feel secure enough to express themselves in English, will imitate the English they hear. They haven't learned any poor speech patterns at home, which they would have to unlearn."

I shall see to it that they hear me speaking only correct English. Since they are good imitators, they will gradually learn to speak correctly—once they have the courage to speak at all! To encourage them, I let them know that I am interested in what they have to say and that I will listen to anything they want to say, whether in reading group, before or after class, or at recess.

Friday: Yesterday, as we were reading a story, I found that children in this group did not know the difference between cabbage and lettuce. I brought some of each to school. I asked them to guess which was which. Peggy didn't know. We all ate a little lettuce and then a little cabbage. I asked how the cabbage tasted. Peggy said, "It's hot—tastes funny."

We had a vocabulary test. Peggy noticed the word *scat* and told me, "Just take the *s* off and it says *cat*." This is real progress!

Recess: Peggy didn't play, just walked around. She still seems to have no friends. Although she talks in our reading group, she does not talk to individuals in it at any other time.

Afternoon: She didn't come back to school. I don't know why.

Progress Week by Week:
Monday: I asked Peggy why she hadn't come to school on Friday after-

noon. She said she had to baby-sit with her little sister. Family responsibilities take precedence over school attendance in many families like Peggy's.

Recess: She played with a Navajo girl in the other second grade. They played catch. This is the first time that she has played with anyone other than her sister.

Noon: When she came in, Peggy spontaneously told me about the kindergarten parade — "Dose kindergartens, dey got hats and flags and dey go all around."

After school: She wanted to stay and do something; she sharpened pencils for me, silently except for one remark, "Oh, I 'most sharp dis end wif da 'raser on it." When she finished the pencils, I sent her to her last year's teacher to ask for some of her *Weekly Readers* in exchange for some of ours. Peggy brought back some first grade ones and said, "She gots lots of dese." To reward her, I gave Peggy a puzzle test, one of identifying letters in one of the first grade *Weekly Readers*. She got every one right, and when I said, "Maybe that's too easy," she said, "Yes, it's too easy." But she continued working for several moments, when suddenly she said, "My fadder always wants to move, but my mudder says, 'Dem kids has got to go to school.'" This is encouraging. We, in school, thought that both parents were uninterested in the children's school attendance. Peggy offered no further information on the subject.

Now that she knows I will listen to anything she says, Peggy is beginning to talk — somewhat disjointedly, as though she weren't accustomed to talking. She doesn't talk about one subject — she hops from one thing to another. She tells me whatever she thinks might interest me or whatever interests her. I don't interrupt or question what she says. I'm just glad she talks at all; besides, I'm learning more about her all the time.

She's able to talk to other people, too. Today, after she finished the puzzle, she wanted something more to do. I sent her to a third grade teacher to borrow third grade readers. I am trying to give Peggy every possible opportunity to do errands which involve speaking to people. The other teachers understand my purpose and encourage her to speak when she comes to them. She is responding — perhaps because the sense of importance she feels in being chosen to deliver my messages helps to overcome her fear of saying something that might be wrong or might make poeple laugh at her!

Tuesday: After school, I asked Peggy to stay and help me put away our library books. As she brought me some books, I suggested she pick out ones she liked best. She chose five: *Hop on Pop, Dr. Seuss ABC, If I Ran the Zoo, Green Eggs and Ham* and *Chicken Little — Count to Ten.* I asked her which one she thought was the easiest to read. She picked *Hop on Pop,* which is much easier than the others. When I suggested next that she read some of it for me, she sat right down and began. After she had read two or three pages, she began to sneeze. I said, "Oops!" Promptly she read *oops* instead of *he*. Then she stopped and looked at me, and said, "Is dat *oops?*" She didn't really think it was, but she had wondered whether I was telling her a word. When I explained, we both laughed.

Wednesday: In our reading group, we had a story about a lamb and a rabbit. (There are seven children in our group now. We have many transients—children whose migrant families move into town and away again in a few weeks or months.) Peggy volunteered, "Out home—on da reservation—we got seven rabbits, six babies and dere mudder." We discussed the difference between pet rabbits and jack rabbits. Peggy said, "Oh, dose kind—dey live up dere in da rocks. One morning I catch one." I asked how and she said, "When he just come outta da hole, he didn't see me—I was behin' da tree and I catch him." I asked what she did with him. "I just put him inna house (hogan) onda floor and he just run out 'gain and everybody surprise."

Recess: Peggy was standing near some of her classmates who were jumping rope. I encouraged her and another girl to join in. They did and they both seemed pleased that they were having fun with the others.

Friday: In reading group, we talked about "Aunt Mary" and her pony. Peggy said, "I got a little sister name Mary—she almost big—'bout four years old." Later, I asked if any of them had ever ridden a pony. Peggy said, "I ride a big horse on da reservation." "Is it your horse?" "No, it belong to my brudder. He have tree horses."

After school: I sent Peggy with a note to another second grade teacher to ask her if she had time to listen to Peggy read. In a few minutes, Peggy came back and said fearfully, "Dere's lots of kids still dere." I told her they were waiting for the bus, that she should go back and deliver the note. She went back, but merely stood outside the teacher's door until the janitor told the teacher there was a little girl to see her. Then the teacher brought her in the room and asked her to read. She read remarkably well—she only confused *in* and *on* and she missed *what* once. The book she read was one that she had previously read to me.

Monday: In our reading group, I asked if anyone remembered what a *brook* was. We had talked about it the day before. Peggy said, "I know. It's a little water." Peggy is learning many new words, and she enjoys reading. In fact, today we had to stop reading a little early because of a school schedule change. Peggy thought we were stopping to let the next group read. She grumbled, "Dey waste our time lots. Let's go on and read." Not only does she *want* to read now, but she will tackle whatever I give her. I must be careful not to expect too much of her or to give her books that will discourage her. She is trying so hard to read!

Tuesday: In our reading group, one of our new words was *bee*. We were talking about how bees sound and how they sting. Peggy said to all of us in the group (we have five now), "You know — long time 'go, we go someplace — my family and me — way out somewhere to eat and were lots bees dere and one crawl on my leg — right here — and I was so scare and I didn't move, and it go away. But on da way home it bite me, and it reely, reely hurt."

We discussed beehives and honey and honeycomb and how they tasted. Peggy said, "Don't know. I never eat any honeys." None of the others had tasted it either.

Wednesday: I brought five little plastic containers of honey for the children in Peggy's group. They each tasted a little and took the rest home. I told them they could eat it on bread or just plain. Peggy didn't want to taste it. "Looks like glue," she said distastefully. I said it did look like glue, but it tasted good. So she tried it. "Is good," she smiled.

Thursday: Peggy was eager to tell me this morning, "I ate my honeys last night." I said, "On bread or with a spoon?" "On a bread. It was good."

Friday: Peggy greeted me today with, "My mudder make a cake for my sister's birthday. This mudder, Lena, is not my reely mudder. My reely mudder live on da reservation wif my grandfadder." "What is her name?" "Rose. My udder sister, Ruthie, she's 'most big like me — she live wif my mudder at reservation. My udder sister, she's name is Ruthie too — she live wif me. Lena is my big sister."

"Family relationships are very intricate on the reservation. Sometimes a child is raised by a grandmother, or by an aunt whom she calls mother; or a child may be sent to live with an older, married sister in order to go to school in town. We haven't been able to find out whether Lena is or is not Peggy's true mother. She seems to be. Peggy has lived with her long enough for her to be — but Peggy says she isn't."

I noticed Peggy had a large sore by her mouth and asked her about it. "Las' night a girl chased me, my mudder burn me when she make bread." I was unable to clarify the situation, but sent Peggy to the nurse to have the burn cared for. While she was in the health room, the nurse gave Peggy some almost-new shoes, which she needed badly. In her excitement over these, the burn was forgotten.

Peggy also told me, in a pleased tone, "Da nurse and Mrs. Drexell (our attendance officer) want me to read after school." She went after school to read to them, taking a story we had read about two weeks ago. They told me that Peggy missed only a few words and seemed to like reading to them.

Monday: Peggy could hardly wait to tell me, "Yesterday at reservation, two sheeps got babies — new little babies. My grandfadder he count sheeps and was only nine sheeps, not eleven. He go look and he find one wif a new little baby." We talked about the sheep. Then I said, "You're early this morning." Peggy smiled. "My mudder chased me up early dis morning cause she go to work."

Wednesday: We were talking about yarn in our reading group. They didn't seem to understand. Tomorrow I will bring knitting needles and yarn to show them.

Peggy was reading. She called the new word *seesaw* a *teety-totter*. However, she knew what it was supposed to be; she was just using the word she was accustomed to instead of the new word. When I told her to stop and look at the new word carefully, she read it correctly, then explained her error most perceptively, "Is one of da words jus' like it, but not like it." I complimented her; I was delighted that she had understood the idea of synonyms.

That afternoon Peggy did not return to school. I suspect she went to town with her sister. When I asked her, next day, why she hadn't come to school, she replied, "Don't know." Never pry — you'll be told only what you are supposed to know anyhow!

Peggy had other concerns today. "It hurts all here," pointing under her ear. I suspected she had mumps, sent her to the nurse, and she was taken home.

Two Weeks Later. "I'm glad to see you back, Peggy. I met your mother at the store. She said you had mumps. Did she tell you she saw me?" — "Yes, she tell me. She not my reely mudder. It's just my big sister Lena."

Peggy had her hair braided across the back of her head. Usually it isn't even combed. She doesn't like it braided, so she refused to remove her scarf all day. Twice before she has worn her scarf all day — once when she had had lice. The nurse checked heads in our room today. Peggy didn't have any lice.

Tuesday: Only two children were present in Peggy's reading group today. Peggy was delighted to have extra turns reading. "It's my turn on dis word and den Susan and den me and den Susan and den me 'cause nobody is here 'cept us."

Peggy came to school after lunch and said to me, "You know what we ate for lunch? Some corn and some 'tato chips and some hot beans chili." We had been talking in class about foods and food values.

Wednesday: In writing class, Peggy is doing very well. I showed her paper to the class as an example of neatness and good writing. She seemed very pleased. I wouldn't have dared to single her out in this way earlier in the year.

In the morning during her free time, I noticed her reading a copy of *Fun with*

Dick and Jane which we are not using in her reading group. I asked Peggy if she would like to read it to me today after school. She said, "Yes."

At noon, Peggy again reported, "Guess what I eat today, for lunch. Corn wif butter and bread and hot beans chili 'gain." If Peggy hasn't learned anything else about our class discussion of diets, she does know that I am concerned about what they eat!

As Peggy prepared to read to me after school, she picked a story near the end of the book, one about zoo animals. She had difficulty on kangaroo and on hippopotamus — not in reading, but in identifying their pictures! She also confused lion and tiger. She finished one story and went right on to the next and the next until it was time for me to load the busses. I told her that, since she was reading so much better now than when her first grade teacher had heard her before, I would ask Mrs. Branson to listen to her read tomorrow. She took her book home to practice. Nearly every night now, she wants to take home a book she likes.

Thursday: I scolded her for not wearing her boots in the deep snow and told her to be sure to wear them in the afternoon. She came back from lunch, beaming as she showed me she was wearing them. "See, like you tell me." Apparently, my relationship with her is now one in which she trusts me and listens to me.

Friday: Every morning now, Peggy has something to tell me. This morning, she greeted me with, "Last night when my baby sister eat ice cream, she get it all over she's face." "What kind of ice cream?" "Brown." "Chocolate?" "Yes." I commented to Peggy on how nice her hair looked; it was combed back into a pony tail. "My mudder fix it for me," she said, proudly.

Recess: A little Mexican girl who had just come back to our class after two months at another school came up to me and said she wanted to play ball. I asked Peggy to play with her; Peggy did so willingly. Soon two other girls in our room joined them — one a Mexican child and one Anglo. They played until the bell rang. Peggy likes to play with anybody; but she does not like to ask someone if she may play, nor will she just join a group.

During the class spelling lesson this afternoon, Peggy volunteered to spell "she" orally. Since I knew she could, I called on her. She is beginning to muster courage to speak in front of the whole class occasionally — when she is sure of her ground!

Monday: I brought some sweet peas for Peggy's reading group. We all smelled them, but nobody knew a name for them except *flowers*. After we had named them and talked about them, we worked on rhyming words. Peggy is finally beginning to get the idea of rhyming. She matched *rain* and *train, bee* and *tree,* and *met* with *pet.*

Tuesday: This morning, Peggy said to me, "Let our group read first. O.K.? Yesterday, we didn't get to be first."

In the reading group: Susan couldn't find the place. Peggy said, "Let me help her, O.K.?" She showed Susan the place. Later, we were talking about mice when Peggy said, "Sometimes dey get under da covers and dey go 'grounj,' 'grounj,' eating something wif dere teef and dey wake you up." What discoveries one can make about these children's lives when they feel free to talk!

This afternoon, several children stayed after school to make up tests. I was giving a vocabulary test to a girl in our top reading group. Peggy stood near me. She followed the words over my shoulder and said them after me. When I had finished, she told me that she had picked out a story to read to me. It was in a first grade primer and was about a girl named Peggy and some balloons. She read it very well. When she finished reading, she asked to straighten out our library books. She likes to do any job around the room; she will stay as long as I will let her. Apparently, if she goes home, only the younger children are there — with one bigger sister to look after them. Peggy often tells me that her mother wanted her to stay home that day to baby-sit. However, Peggy seems to want to come to school — and manages to get here regularly.

After school: Peggy wanted to read to me. But I had to tell her that I would be busy with a parent who was coming to visit me. I assured her that tomorrow she could stay.

"When you really gain the confidence of a child, you find that the child frequently wants to be with you, do things for you, read to you or visit with you. Peggy isn't the only one. Every year, there are several in my classes who want and need extra attention and encouragement. They get it, too, so far as I'm able to give it. However, on some days, I am faced with situations when it just isn't convenient — or possible — for me to stay after school with a child.

"When these occasions arise with you, be honest with the child. Tell the child matter-of-factly that a parent is coming or that you must go to the office or to a meeting, or that you just don't have time today because you have too much work to do. Tell them, at the same time, when you *will* see them. Thus, Peggy and others like her learn that you are not pushing them off; on the contrary, they understand exactly why you cannot stay with them when you cannot. They also have your assurance that you *will* give them whatever time you can."

Wednesday reading group: When we finished reading our story, I went to the blackboard to introduce vocabulary for the next story. Peggy started to read the next story by herself instead of watching me. She laughed when I told her to stop. "Now I like to read stories." I have noticed that, at class story time, Peggy now listens eagerly to stories instead of playing listlessly. She still does not understand all of them—or perhaps not all interest her. But early this year she didn't listen to any!

After school, when I remarked that I had forgotten to give a girl a paper to take home, Peggy grinned. "You're just like my *mother*. She's always forget to do something. When she cook potatoes, she forget to make bread."

Now that Peggy and her group have come to feel secure in their relationship with me, we have begun to work on improving their speech patterns. Because Navajos do not have a *th* sound in their language, most Navajo children have to work hard to overcome a tendency to say, *mudder, fadder, dis,* etc. I have been helping Peggy to say the *th* sound correctly.

"I have said before that Indian children and Mexican children who speak very little English pick up or imitate your correct speech habits—like, 'my brother and I,' instead of 'me and my brother'—much faster than an English-speaking child from a deprived background who has used the wrong forms all his life. The latter may even tell you, 'My daddy says it that way.' Indian and Mexican children have not had opportunities to acquire bad speech habits in English; therefore, it is not too difficult to help them to learn correct ones—once they are willing to try talking English!"

Thursday: We were to have individual class pictures taken this afternoon. This morning Peggy came with her hair uncombed and her dress dirty.

Afternoon: "My father tell me to stay home dis afternoon, but I just go out and come to school." "Why did he want you to stay home?" "Don't know." Had she mentioned the class pictures? Were the two situations connected? She was to have brought a note stating whether her parents wanted to buy any pictures. She did not do so. Had she understood directions? Had her parents understood her? How little I really know about her language capability, even yet!

It began to rain when school was over, so some of the children stayed inside to wait for the bus. While waiting, Peggy picked another story to read to me—about a trip on a train. Peggy once had a short train trip. She had learned new words in the story; all by herself, she had figured out—*today, bags, Buster, Daddy*. A girl waiting for the bus looked over Peggy's shoulder while she read. Peggy didn't seem to mind. This *is* progress! Then, three children insisted on reading to me. Peggy stayed to listen. She was very pleased to be able to tell one of these good readers a word (basket).

Friday: We came to a story which involved going *around* and *across* a pond. *Peggy walked around* our table and Susan crawled *across* it. We looked all *around* the room to see what we could see; then we looked straight *across* it. We put our hands *on* the table and *under* it, *behind* our books and on *top* of them. We have discovered we can't put our hands *in* the table, but we can put them *in* our books. Any word that confuses us we try to act out. I have tried also to give them group experiences with numerous words that are names of objects that can be felt, smelled, tasted, seen, or heard. Among others that we have tasted are lettuce, cabbage, honey, fresh strawberries, and popcorn (which we made ourselves). We have felt the differences between silk and sandpaper and cotton and cactus. We have smelled sweet peas, garlic, cologne, and a fresh rainy day.

Monday: After school, I tried to arrange for Peggy to be alone with me, but our new Hopi boy and middle-western girl stayed to visit. Undeterred by their presence, Peggy began to talk. She probably talked more in that half-hour than she had in the last four months. A piece of rock on my desk reminded her of a man — "way, way far away from here who died and me and Elsie (her sister) saw where dey put him, and were lots of rocks like this all around and lots flowers, too. Oh, I mean Elsie and I." She had corrected herself, for which I complimented her warmly. She was also beginning to say *th!*

Then she began talking about sandwiches. She said she could make egg sandwiches and cheese and bologna. Only she had difficulty saying *bologna* and had to repeat it three times after me. For half an hour, conversation flowed with Peggy doing most of the talking. Occasionally, I would ask a question. She talked about a little boy on the reservation who ran away from his grandmother and got lost. "We look and look for him long time and we didn't find him." He was part of her family but she doesn't know what relation; not a brother, nor a cousin. He was found the next day.

She was not at all self-conscious as she chatted with me and the other two children. In fact, she was still talking when I had to go, a half an hour later. This is what I've been working for! She's really talking now.

Tuesday: We read a story about a monkey and an organ grinder in our reading group this morning. I had made arrangements with another teacher who is showing the film, "The Monkey and the Organ Grinder" to her class to have Peggy's group join them. I told the children and, of course, they were delighted at the prospect. Then I put the word *money* on the board and suggested that they look in their books to see what letter could be put in the word *money* to make it *monkey*. Peggy found it first, and came to the board and put the *k* in the right place.

Wednesday: I asked Peggy if her father had returned from California. "No." "Does he have a job yet?" "Yes, they gotta job (her father and older brother). He wrote a letter to my mother." "Are you going to move to live with him?" "No, but this summer I go to Oak Creek and the reservation and everywhere. My grampa lives all by herself (then she corrected herself), I mean by *heself,* and we have to go. My mother's sister was take care of him, but all her teef fall out and she had to go to hospital, so he's all by heself now, and we're going to stay dere. I might not come to school here anymore. I might go to school on da reservation." I told her that I would miss her.

Monday: Peggy's hair was curled. I asked who did it for her. "My mother." With careful deliberation, she pronounced the *th*. "Why didn't you come to school on Friday?" "I fall down and bump my head and it hurt." She showed me a large scab on her face next to her eye. "That little girl in the first grade push me down. She's a Navajo girl but her hair is short like yours. I got my hair cut too. They make it curly—look like a 'Beatle.' I don't like it." It was curled all over, but I didn't think it looked at all like a "Beatle."

The movie about the monkey and organ grinder was scheduled for this afternoon and Peggy's group was eager to see it. All of them watched the clock for the big hand to get to two and Peggy reminded me one minute before time to go.

Later, Peggy told me about the film. "The man with the organ go to sleep and the monkey climb out the window and he run, and he want to go to the park and some children see him and they know him and they try catch him and he go in the park but they catch him and take him back to the man, and he's still asleep but the monkey climb up the stairs and on the porch and the man come out and make music with the organ box and the monkey dance and the children give the monkey some money and first he put it in he's pocket and den he give it to the man."

"Did you like it?" "Yeah! It was reely, reely good."

It all came out in one long sentence—just like this. Mixed up syntax, yes, but her speech was much better than at the first of the year when she was saying only one or two monosyllables! Peggy has learned to observe, to listen, and to speak. How it shows in her reading! She knows what she is reading about—and she wants to read now!

Tuesday: Peggy didn't come to school today. The attendance officer found that her family and a neighbor family had gone to an Indian Hospital in a neighboring town. Children in both families have some kind of chest infection. Indian children in our school seem, frequently, to have respiratory infections. Recently, Peggy's infant sister was in the hospital several weeks with pneumonia.

Thursday: When Peggy returned to school, she told me, "Elsie, my sister, she quit school 'cause my fadder is not here and Elsie has to baby-sit 'cause my mother is working." As she came in after lunch, she said, "Today I eat crackers wif hot chili 'gain." Sometimes she manages *th* and sometimes not!

During our class oral language period, the children were supposed to make up a story about three pictures in their book; a boy and girl on a donkey cart, the children in the cart going down the road, and the donkey sitting down and refusing to move. To my amazement, Peggy volunteered, got up in front of the class, and said, "A boy and girl went to the movie. They pay to get in. When they in there, the donkey go home by heself, and the boy and girl have to walk home." She actually stood before the entire class to tell this story! Although she didn't speak very loudly, most of the children could hear all she said. A few months ago, she wouldn't say a word in front of one other person!

After school, Peggy went to read to Mrs. Branson again. Mrs. Branson praised her warmly, and later told me that she could see great improvement in Peggy — she not only read well at her level, but talked easily with Mrs. Branson.

Friday: Our principal came to listen to Peggy's group read. When he had promised to come today, Peggy had taken her book home to practice. She read three pages beautifully, missing only the endings on two words — *moving* and *going*.

Peggy's older sister dropped out of school today. Her mother said that Peggy's sister had to take care of the babies while her mother went to work. Mr. Jackson made the mother promise, however, to send Peggy and Nancy to school every day before she left for work. According to a remark of Peggy's quoted earlier, her mother *does* want the children in school.

The entire class talks about health frequently. Today, Peggy, for the first time, took part in the discussion. I knew, from her frequent reports to me about what she ate, that she understood something about the relationship between food and health. As we talked about foods we eat to stay healthy, she raised her hand and said, "milk." When we discussed good health habits, she volunteered again, "wash your hands."

Monday: At recess, Peggy saved a seesaw for her sister, Nancy. With another Navajo girl and a little Chinese girl on the adjoining seesaw, they played a game of touching hands. This is the first game Peggy has initiated.

In reading group today, we were talking about neckties. Although the others said their fathers had one, Peggy unhesitatingly said her father didn't. Apparently, she is secure enough in the group to be herself and not to mind being different sometimes.

Tuesday: During class discussion, we were making suggestions for our bulletin board of things we can see, hear, feel, and smell in the spring. Peggy raised her hand several times. Some of her suggestions were good; others did not apply to the spring season. Under things we can see, she said, "Flowers and animals and snow" (the latter does apply to our spring). Under things we can feel, she said, "A kitten, a pillow, rain, and wind." Under things we can smell, she volunteered, "Perfume and water." (Our water had just begun to smell bad because of algae in the lake. Every spring it smells terrible, so we put that one down!)

Wednesday: In Peggy's reading group, we were talking about food. Peggy told about a TV show she had seen at a friend's house. The mother and father in the show were jailed because they were drunks (something she sees frequently among her neighbors, although I don't know about her own parents). She seemed most impressed by the fact that the children in the show had no food. The way she told it, it ended with everyone out of jail, the father had a job again and the children had food again. This was the first time that Peggy talked so long in the group.

Later in the day, during class discussion, the children—row by row—were to choose any picture in their language book which they wanted to talk about. Peggy raised her hand and I chose her row first. She was the second one in her row. She took her turn. She chose a page with pictures of food, flowers, animals, and miscellaneous objects. Before the class, she rose and, in a louder voice than she had ever used, she said, "This is a car, drum, (she couldn't identify typewriter), jumprope, owl, (couldn't identify raccoon), turkey, kangaroo (she had asked me what it was just before we began the discussion) and a baby in its pocket, orange, cake, bread, apple, and flowers." (She couldn't identify individual flowers such as lily, rose, tulip, and dandelion.) After her row had finished, she came to me and, much to my surprise, asked if her row could have another turn later.

Thursday: Today was the next to last day of school, so I let Peggy's reading group choose any story they wanted to read in their books. Remember that they began this year with preprimers; they finished the first grade primer and first grade reader. Now, at the end of the year, they have read the first few units in our regular second grade reader. However, they have made a full year's progress, and I'm proud of them, especially of Peggy.

Today they chose to read *Lazy Jack,* a story they hadn't read in class. It was near the back of their books. Some words were too hard for them, so I helped them. Peggy started reading as fast as she could. I could tell she had practiced at home. She said she knew the story and that it was her favorite story.

She missed some words; she said *her* for *his* and she had trouble with abstract words such as *that* and *then.* But she read better than anyone in her group—and she knew what she was reading! When I suggested that the boy in the story looked quite a bit like someone in our room and I wondered if they had noticed the resemblance, Peggy said, "I know. He looks like Brent." She was right. Both boys had shaggy blonde hair, blue eyes, and an impish expression.

Friday: Peggy had never been in the cafeteria. She always went home to lunch. I bought a ticket and asked her if she would like to go. She said, "Yes." I knew her mother wouldn't be home at noon; but she told Nancy to tell her older sister she would eat lunch at school. We had hamburgers, potato chips, milk, pickles, olives, lettuce, tomato, and ice cream. Although much of the food was something she had never before eaten—in fact, some had to be identified—Peggy ate everything except the tomato and olives. I asked her if she liked the lunch and she said, "Yes."

WHAT I LEARNED FROM PEGGY

"When school was out for the summer, I sat down to collect my thoughts about Peggy. I reread my notes and tried to jot down specific things that I did to help Peggy and others in her group to learn to read. With this year's experience as a guide, perhaps next year I can think of more ways to help these culturally disadvantaged children to become interested in learning—to understand words, to express ideas, to want to read and finally, to enjoy reading because it means something to them. Also because it is fun—an experience that symbolizes success and achievement!

"The specific techniques I tried this year I want to share with you. Perhaps you can add to these. I wish that I could share also the deep sense of satisfaction I feel in having learned something about these children. Try getting to know them; their eager response to your interest in them will more than repay your efforts—even though you'll make mistakes and, sometimes, you'll wonder what progress really is! The following ideas will get *you* started":

1. We talked about nearly every word we came to in our reading in order to be certain that everyone knew what it meant. We acted out words like *there, here, across, around, behind, under, far, near, before, beside,* and *over.*

2. We practiced listening. Many times daily, I had Peggy and the others repeat directions or explain what someone had just said. Frequently, I would ask the boys and girls to tell me parts of a story we had read.

3. I brought things the children hadn't seen or didn't recognize words for, such as *strawberries, lettuce, honey,* and *cabbage.* We had demonstrations of such things as knitting to help explain the words *yarn* and *knitting.* We talked about how things feel, look, sound, taste, and smell—in order to sharpen their observation and to develop their understanding. Our class activities also included growing things, trying out musical instruments, and a variety of media in art.

4. Whenever we discussed anything in the class as a whole which I thought some of these boys and girls might not understand, I drew pictures. The word in question may have been *vine, plant, tree,* or *bush.* Drawing it, talking about it, or bringing in actual examples afforded opportunities to develop meanings which would encompass and explain associated words. Obviously, this idea can be expanded as far as your time and ingenuity permit.

5. I used all sorts of audio-visual aids—such as stories, both hand and string puppets, records, pictures, filmstrips, movies, giant plaster teeth, a large tooth-

brush, telephones from the phone company which actually work—anything which could possibly help to explain anything or to persuade the children to talk!

6. We made several field trips including one to the library (where I signed for Peggy and the others so that they became eligible for library cards), and to the fire station where Peggy squirted the fire hose (with the help of a fireman), where the children sat in the cab of a fire truck, watched raptly as a fireman slid down the pole, and listened attentively to another fireman's explanation of their duties. We also visited a house under construction; we visited an orchard to see apples and peaches growing; and we invited a policeman to come and speak to our class.

7. Above all, Peggy and the others were given time and encouragement to talk in their reading group. Peggy began saying a few words fairly early in the year after she had become convinced that I really wanted to listen to what the children had to say. The fact that the group was small and that the others were not proficient in English either probably encouraged her.

Next, Peggy began to talk to me—only a few words at first! But, as she sensed my interest in her and in what she had to say, she initiated more and more conversation with me, revealing constantly more intimate insights into her personal life and family relationships.

Only much later, after about seven months of encouragement, did Peggy want to or venture to say anything in front of the entire class. But when she did begin to talk in class, she joined class activities eagerly.

8. From the beginning, Peggy responded to my praise of her reading. She tried harder and harder to read better. She was delighted—though somewhat frightened—when I asked her to read to her last year's teacher, to other teachers, to the school attendance officer, to the nurse, and the principal. They were all interested in her and took time to listen to her. They all praised her for her good reading. In fact, they were all especially interested because her two older brothers and two older sisters (who have all gone to our school) are considered virtually non-readers. Peggy is the first in her family to like school and to come instead of staying out frequently, as her brothers and sisters have done.

9. Whenever possible, Peggy was sent to other school personnel to deliver a message, to do an errand, or to read to someone. The more she used language, the more her confidence in its use increased.

10. She frequently stayed after school and we talked about anything and everything imaginable. Other children often stayed too. Gradually, Peggy not only lost her shyness with them and learned how to converse with other children, but also began to see others as friendly and interested in her.

A COMPARISON: PEGGY'S FIRST AND LAST WEEKS OF SCHOOL

Observation — First Week: Peggy seemed oblivious to everything and everyone around her. She didn't watch or even notice other children most of the time. She just sat quietly by herself in class; she played alone on the playground.

Observation — Last Week: What a change! In the last few weeks, Peggy noticed and commented about many things in and outside the classroom. She even joined repeatedly in class discussions.

Listening — First Week: Peggy didn't listen to directions or to stories read aloud to the class. Nothing I said seemed to reach her; the children ignored her.

Listening — Last Week: At the end of the school year, Peggy listened carefully to directions every day, tried her best to follow them, and usually did so accurately. She began to enjoy many of the stories I read aloud to the class. However, if she wasn't interested in the subject, or if the words were too hard for her, she would still "turn me off." In general, though, her listening showed marked improvement.

Speaking — First Week: Peggy would never volunteer a word. She would only answer "yes," "no," or "don't know" to a question from me — if she answered at all. She never said anything in front of the other children.

Speaking — Last Week: Not only did Peggy, on several occasions, take part in class discussions, but also, in conversation with me, or in her reading group where she felt "at home," Peggy would volunteer conversation every day — about herself, her family, what she saw or did — anything that interested her, or that she thought might interest me, or the children in the reading group.

In total class discussion, she began by volunteering to tell the answer to a number problem or to spell a word she was sure she knew. Then she volunteered answers to word games; she grew to like being chosen to participate in these games. Her answers weren't always right, of course; but I always praised her for good thinking. I made a point of calling on her anytime she volunteered. In the last weeks of school, she actually volunteered to get up in front of the class to tell a story.

Relations to Other Adults — First Week: Peggy would not speak to any other teachers — or to any adults — with the exception of her first grade teacher.

Relations to Other Adults — Last Week: She loved to deliver either written or short oral messages to any teacher; she enjoyed going to read for three other teachers and for our nurse and attendance officer. She even read for our principal. On the playground, she would sometimes go up to one or two of the teachers and initiate a conversation.

Social Activity — First Week: Her sister in the third grade was her only playmate. She made no friends in our room.

Social Activity—Last Week: She began to play with one or two Mexican girls in our room; she frequently teased one of the Hopi boys. She developed an unexplained feud with a third Mexican girl during the last weeks of school; neither one would tell me what had happened. She played occasionally with a Chinese girl in the first grade. She continued to play sometimes with her sister in the third grade, with another third grade Navajo girl, a Navajo girl in another second grade, and with a first grade Navajo girl.

"Just because Peggy is an Indian girl does not mean that these methods are applicable only with Indians. As I stated earlier, these principles and techniques were used with the reading group of which Peggy was a member, a group which included Spanish-speaking children, Negro children and the children of Anglo migrant workers.

"The most important thing I have learned is the vital necessity of taking time which *can* and *must* be spared from the mechanics of conducting groups in silent and oral reading—in order first to help these boys and girls learn to communicate. If they don't know the words I use, they can't talk and they can't listen. In which case, they certainly can't understand what I say or what the book says! Some boys and girls may have difficulty using words even when they understand them; in other words, for some, speaking may be harder than listening—and vice versa. Whatever the problem, I am convinced that two-way communication must be achieved between me and a child and between a child and a book before a child *can* read or will *want* to read.

"A difficult concept for teachers to accept is that disadvantaged boys and girls actually do not know the meaning of many words so common that, you are certain, they must be universally understood. When some of these boys and girls, especially the older ones, are able to repeat or even read words, you think they know what they are saying. They may or may not know. They probably will not tell you that they do not know. Perhaps you had better assume they do not, or at least ask questions about common words and abstractions. You may find that your pupils have not attached meanings to some words, or that they have developed some very peculiar meanings.

"Some disadvantaged boys and girls have simply not been exposed to words their teachers take for granted. Malinowski had defined language as a 'system of sounds that accompanies experience.'[2] Without experiential background, no boy or girl can comprehend language. The same truth applies to their speech. 'Any discussion of oral English

---

[2] Marie Hughes and George Sanchez, *Learning a New Language,* Association for Childhood Education International Bulletin 101 (Washington, D.C., 1958), p. 7.

must begin and end with their experiential background. . . . what a child learns is a function of the opportunity for learning as well as the capacity for learning.'[3]

"Because of these differences in experiential background, there will be wide differences in the facility with which your non-English-speaking students learn a second language. To help them learn English, boys and girls must hear English words and sentences *at the same time* that they encounter the objects or concepts the words symbolize. In school, they must have experience with objects — such as toys, classroom supplies, and playground equipment; their concepts must develop from experiences on field trips, in science experiments, in dramatics, or other shared learning activities in the classroom.

"Classroom activities are especially important to these children. 'Activities are a way by which speech is stimulated. The English-speaking child, before he comes to school, has five or six years of practice using English in child-like activities. The non-English-speaking child has not had such opportunity. Activities must be provided him in school — if the alert educator is to expand language usage and comprehension.'[4]

"In other words, the disadvantaged child needs practice in using English before he can be expected to read it. Lest non-English-speaking children merely pronounce and parrot words for which they have no concepts, educators who understand their problems recommend that these children be given two years of speaking and language experience — in prefirst and first grade — before they are given readers and expected to 'do book work.' If such language experience were available to all children who need it, through such agencies as the Head Start Program, then the discouragement and pseudo-retardation frequently seen with these boys and girls from fourth grade on might be avoided.

"Clearly, this problem of not understanding words is as real with fourth graders, sixth graders, and high school 'non-readers' as it is with second graders. By fourth grade, approximately, the vocabulary load necessitated for keeping up in their reading and subject-matter has so far outrun their experiential background that these pupils are swamped in words they do not understand. In earlier grades, when most key words in their readers stood for concrete objects, some of these boys and girls were able to comprehend them — or, at least, to

[3] Beth L. Wellman, "Some Misconceptions about Intelligence," *Childhood Education,* XXI, Number 3 (Nov. 1944).

[4] Robert Roessel, Jr., *Handbook for Indian Education* (Los Angeles: Amerindian Publishing Co., 1964), p. 98.

guess their meaning through context. By fourth grade, however, many words denote concepts and abstractions these pupils have never learned. Moreover, by fourth grade, facility in expressing words and concepts both in speech and writing is expected of them. They cannot compete because they are still struggling to master the language! Thus, they acquire the label 'slow-learner' or 'non-reader.'

"Basic to all I learned from Peggy was my realization that facility in language — knowing word meanings, understanding what one is reading about, knowing what one is to say, and being willing to speak because one feels competent to do so — this power over language develops slowly through shared experiences and activities. Moreover, it develops within a personal relationship of mutual confidence; language is a function of the total life situation of the individual.

"If the life situation of an individual has not afforded him opportunities to use language and to comprehend words comparable to the opportunities his classmates have had for such learning, then this gap in his experience means that he is not as 'ready' as his classmates to learn what the school has to teach. It will take endless time, patience, ingenuity, and understanding to fill this gap. Time, patience, and understanding have been denied many disadvantaged boys and girls in their early years. Now you, their teachers, are the key people to fill the gap. Have you the requisite ingenuity and patience to make up for the lost time? Have you the quality of understanding to develop a relationship which will make learning possible?"

Thus, Mrs. Brown ended her talk, giving the new teachers much to think about!

The following section contains fundamental information concerning the phonetic differences in the English and Navajo language which teachers of Navajo children can use as a valuable reference source.

A FEW FUNDAMENTALS CONCERNING THE NAVAJO LANGUAGE

In order to understand the specific difficulties which the Navajo child will have in learning English, it is essential that teachers know some of the differences between the two languages. The English alphabet has 26 letters; the Navajo has 22. Though some English letters have equivalents in the Navajo alphabet, pronunciation is different:

    c — is more like *sh*
    d — is like an unasperated *t* — it sounds like *t* in *stop*
    b — is unvoiced — it sounds like *p* in *spot*

m — is an uncommon source

th — sounds like *d*. This sound is particularly difficult; Navajos are likely to say *mudder* and *fodder* for mother and father.

Moreover, the Navajo language has no *p, q, f, v, u, w, r*.
The following are clues to *vowel sounds:*

a — always soft as in father
aa — designates a long vowel
e — like the *e* in *met*
i — like the *i* in *it*
o — like the *o* in *so*
ai — like the *y* in *my*
oi — like our *u*

English requires lip movement to form sounds. Navajos talk with very little lip movement; for example, they seem to say *auge* for *orange, waer* for *water*. The Navajo child must be taught to use his lips if he is to pronounce English correctly.

Number is a difficult concept for the Navajo to grasp because, in their language, number is expressed as singular while English emphasizes singular and plural forms of nouns, pronouns, and verbs. The Navajos' problems with color were mentioned earlier.

Gender is especially puzzling to a Navajo. Navajo pronouns seem to have a fourth person. The Navajo child will say: my brother, she; sister, he; grandfather, she; mother, he; father, she. "This is my brother. She wears brown pants" is not an unusual mistake!

Use simple, direct, correct English while teaching Navajo children. Do not allow a child to say "John is stick" when he means "John has a stick." The child must understand what he is saying.

Drill on specific sounds, showing the children how to place the tongue against the front teeth and open the mouth to force the sound out. Use a mirror and let the children see you and themselves in the mirror as the sounds are correctly formed. Make a game of learning sounds; praise the child as he says a word correctly. But, do not embarrass him, especially in front of others, if he has problems!

If you ask Navajo children questions, ask direct questions which involve direct answers, not ones which involve negatives. Never ask a Navajo child questions such as: "Don't you have a pencil?" or "Didn't you ride the bus?" The child will answer "yes." Then who is confused, teacher or child?

A device I have found useful in working with especially shy Navajo

children new in school is to have a short functional list of commonly
used words and phrases printed in both Navajo and English. (I keep a
third column, available to me only, to assist me with the Navajo pronunciation.) Then the child and I can begin to communicate, partly in
both languages. This list may be of use to you:

ENGLISH	NAVAJO	TEACHER'S PRONUNCIATION KEY
come	ha'go	huck'o
go away	acko'	akco'
hello	Ya'teha	ya ta hey
good bye	ha'go-sheh	hucko-ena
look	sho'	show'
work	nonish'	nawn' ish'
play	nush'ne	nush'na
cold	deskew	des' - Ka u se
say it	dine'	dina
paper, book	naaltsoos	nalt sos'
baby	a w a	a-way
boy	'ask kii	ā jé ete
mother	'ama	ā ma
father	'ashe'e	bish-a
yes	'ouu	oh
no	nda	nda
don't do that	doo teet	dō lē st'
cry	chah	e chah
milk	abe'	a ba'
water	too'	toe'
car	chidi	chi' de
what is this	has' at li sha'	ha' dish hol ya
where	has adisha'	a dish a
sheep	dibe	de ba
sit down	tsinede	sin'de'e
hurry up	tsinklo	sin'hklo
what do you want?	Ha de shon	hā dé shon
school	'o' lta	o' ltaw'
school teacher	ba' olta' i	bah ol tahe
hat	chah	chah
coat	ee tsoh	aate so'
repeat the word	dine'	dinay

CHAPTER 4

Your Spanish-Speaking Pupils

"Now that you have become better acquainted with Henry Yazzie and Peggy Blackgoat," Mr. Jackson remarked as he opened the next teachers' meeting, "you undoubtedly understand Miss Begay's concern that teachers who would work effectively with children of a different culture consider what is distinctive about that child's culture or way of life in order to comprehend part of what the child faces in adjusting his set of habitual and traditional ways of thinking to the school's new ways. Miss Begay said that you can change people and teach them new ways of life if you understand how they came to be the way they are. In other words, within a relationship where a teacher's personal understanding and concern for a child reaches that child, the child responds by learning. If you are sensitive to a child's human need for support and encouragement as he attempts this transition to a new way of life and you are able to supply this basic human need, *you can teach* that culturally disadvantaged child.

"What is true of Henry and Peggy is also true of Juan, Victor, and Tony, three Mexican-American children in our schools. During the next few weeks, we shall come to know them well. Our speaker, Roberto Gonzales, principal of one of our local elementary schools, and an educator familiar with the backgrounds of Spanish-speaking children, will introduce us to them: who are these Mexican-Americans, Bob?"

"I am glad that Mr. Jackson, who has been my friend since we were in grade school together, invited me to talk to you about Victor and about some of the difficulties you encounter in teaching Spanish-speaking children. I am even happier to know that, in the next two weeks, you will be hearing from some of your colleagues about their classroom experiences with two other Mexican children, both of whom so needed a teacher's help and understanding.

WHO YOUR SPANISH-SPEAKING PUPILS ARE

"You have, in your classroom, a Mexican or Spanish-speaking child. Is this child culturally disadvantaged? This term has many meanings. One pertains to economic conditions. If your child's father is a doctor or college professor, this child may have more economic advantages than you and I. His parents will expect him to do well in school. If his father is a clerk or mechanic, the amount of money he earns will not be as important in the child's school adjustment as the parents interest in education and their understanding of their child's need to compete and to 'do his best' if he is to succeed in his American culture. Victor's story — to be told in a few moments — will dramatically demonstrate the effect of such parental support. On the other hand, if the child in your classroom comes, as do a majority of Mexican-American children today, from a home where economic conditions are poor, not only will he be a victim of poor housing, poor nutrition, and perhaps disease, but he will also have cultural handicaps — not the least of which will be a language deficit. A child with this kind of background may not speak any English and even his Spanish may be poor! Yet each of the other children may also have come from bilingual homes — a fact which implies both advantages and disadvantages. Moreover, all three children will have absorbed cultural values different from yours. Therefore, each will have his specific problems in school — if not in learning the school's language, then certainly in becoming accustomed to school expectations and 'ways of life' different from his — what Miss Begay called 'the classroom way of doing things.'

"Let me emphasize that the educational and cultural background from which the Spanish or Mexican child in your classroom comes may vary widely. He may never hear English spoken until he enters school; he may speak both Spanish and English in his home — either well or poorly — or he may speak English to his parents and siblings and Spanish to his grandparents. His home may be a modern apartment, a small or commodious house owned by his parents, a tenement in the city or town slums, or a shack in a migratory labor camp.

"He may accompany his mother to the supermarket in a new automobile or may sit in a shabby car while father buys frijoles at the corner grocery. He may eat frijoles for breakfast or he may have cereal and milk. His clothes may be new and clean or old, dirty and shabby, given to him by the church or school. His family may have lived in your town for years; they may be new arrivals looking for work—or a family who entered our country illegally to work in the lettuce fields.

"The child, no matter what his family's income is, may have had personal experiences through which he learned that he was unacceptable in certain 'restricted' parks, swimming pools, movies, or even schools; he may have heard his parents discuss the refusal of certain stores to serve them or the policies of some employers to restrict Mexican-Americans to the least desirable jobs. He may have learned that, to some people, the word *Mexican* seems always to be coupled with 'dirty, greasy, lazy' or 'sneaky.' In school, he may have been teased because he 'talks funny' or scolded *when* he talked because 'we don't talk in Spanish here.' Such practices have resulted in 'the culturally disadvantaged child' whose problems we are discussing today, the boy or girl who finds 'the going' hard in our culture, for whom, in many schools, it is "Up the Up Staircase" all the way!

"The child's feelings—bewilderment, antagonism, resentment—which result from discriminatory practices obviously affect his learning. Gardner Murphy says that, when a child discovers that his family is somehow rejected by the large group, the 'shock involves not simply the loss of cherished landmarks of rightness and wrongness; it challenges the central rightness of the self and leads either to self-disparagement or to embittered protest against society.'[1]

"A boy or girl cannot identify with a teacher and a new language if he recognizes in the school situation only unhappiness for himself and a threat to his self-image. How will the child react? There is great variability in the manner in which individual Mexican children come to terms with the cultural differences and conflicts they face. Their specific reactions, of course, are governed partly by the attitudes and expressions of their parents and other members of their families.

"In fact, every culturally different child's attitude toward learning the language and culture of the larger society is colored by the complex of experiences which he and his family have had with the larger society. This burden differentiates the non-English speaking child from his classmates; it transcends the mere fact that he does not speak English. Moreover, it determines whether he feels it necessary or worthwhile to learn to do so!

"The Mexican-American child—like any other child in your classroom—has not lived in a vacuum during his preschool life. For those

---

[1] Gardner Murphy, *Personality: a Biosocial Approach to Origins and Structure* (New York: Harper and Brothers, 1947), p. 847.

five years, he was bombarded with cultural influences, often with dual language. Consequently, upon entering school, your pupil may be 10 per cent Mexican and 90 per cent Anglo—or 90 per cent Mexican and 10 per cent Anglo. Each child will be different—but none will be 100 per cent English-speaking and Anglicized. Moreover, that part of the child which is bilingual and bicultural is the most deep-seated part of his total personality.

"We, in schools, must realize that our usual curricula, teaching methods, and evaluating techniques will be ineffective with the Mexican-American boy or girl unless we adapt them to *his* 'facts of life': The bicultural community in which he lives; the degree of isolation or lack of acceptability which his family feels in the American society; the socioeconomic status peculiar to this degree of acceptability; and the social lag inherent in these barriers which not only prohibits his and his family's normal participation in the total community, but which also negatively influences his maximum personality growth.

"Because of the prejudice which they have met, the Mexican-American community—including some economically favored families—has, sometimes, built a wall around itself. Anglos charge them with being clannish. True, in protecting their personal and family lives from discrimination, they have restricted their experiences and relationships. On the other hand, their children have absorbed indigenous cultural influences and values which are basic in their personality development. Some of these are different from those accepted in the dominant culture, but does that make them less valuable?

"Many Mexican-Americans are confused about the role which they will play or will be allowed to play in the American scene. This is evident in the variety of their reactions. Their efforts to identify themselves with the American culture assume various forms, depending sometimes on the social level of the person concerned and sometimes on the community in which he resides. These efforts, all too ofteii, result in his allowing his Mexican culture to disintegrate; social pressures have caused him to be so ashamed of it that he disowns it. Perhaps even to the extent that Jose Martinez one day declares to the world that he is now Joe Martin!

"Joe is a victim of confusion, frustration, and insecurity. This Mexican-American has been made to feel so much a foreigner and a stranger that he is willing to disown part of himself in the desperate hope that the remaining part will become all-American. Are we forcing children in school into crises of identity like this one? What happens in your school?

"Perhaps we might begin by asking, 'What is the connotation of the word *Mexican* in your school?' Because of the fact that, in some schools and communities, it is derogatory, many people of Mexican descent (that is, whose ancestors actually came from Mexico) have resorted to a euphemism; they prefer, in fact, insist upon being called 'Spanish.' Such people are pleased when their Anglo friends who wish to flatter them, say, 'Oh, you aren't *Mexican,* you're *Spanish.*'

The Spanish

"There are, of course, people of Spanish descent in the United States. In California, especially, are many descendants of the early Spanish Dons, who were once extremely wealthy and whose blood lines were pure Spanish. However, they have been practically assimilated by the white, "upper-class" society of predominantly English-speaking people. These Spanish people have no problems of poverty, education, or discrimination. They do not belong in any discussion of culturally disadvantaged individuals.

"According to the 1960 census, there were 3,464,996 persons of Spanish surname mostly in the following five states: California, Texas, Arizona, New Mexico, and Colorado. Now, there are about 5 million Mexican-Americans, the second largest disadvantaged minority in America. There are likenesses and differences among these people who are predominantly Mexican. The term Mexican, as I shall use it, means any person of Mexican descent living in the United States, that is, any person whose ancestors were a mixture of Spanish and Indian blood. They may be Indians from Mexico or people from the southwestern United States.

The Mexicans

"In northern New Mexico are people whose historical antecedents differ from those of Spanish-speaking people of other states. These people are descended chiefly from early Spanish colonials who married Indian women, then intermarried for decades in the small isolated pockets where they happened to settle. They especially dislike being called Mexicans; they are, in fact, more nearly Spanish than any other mixed-blood group in the Southwest. In southern New Mexico, although people prefer to be called Spanish, they have a high percentage of Indian blood. Originally, they were also descendants of Spanish explorers and Indian women, but instead of intermarrying within their own group, their descendants married among many Indian groups until original blood lines became obscured.

"Among the Mexicans are also the Mexican migrant workers who will be considered separately because their problems are special ones. I shall also discuss Puerto Ricans — meaning people of Puerto Rican descent who live in the United States — as well as our new Cuban immigrants. The term 'Spanish-speaking' has been used interchangeably by some people to refer to any of the above-mentioned groups. I shall hope, however, to point out distinctions, as well as similarities, between these groups. You will note that, within each group, there is great variation in their cultural, economic, educational, and social advantages.

"I was born in a New Mexico farming community, lived there for 12 years, moved to California, lived in Los Angeles for three years, and have since resided in Arizona. Therefore I know, from experience, some of the similarities and differences in our cultural groups from state to state. On the whole, there are more similarities than there are differences. The differences which do exist are, to a degree, the sort of differences which arise in any culture because of variety of living conditions.

"The Mexican population of the United States is concentrated mainly in four states — New Mexico, Texas, California, and Arizona, perhaps because the Spanish explorers didn't get much farther before they stopped and settled down with local Indian women or with the women they had brought from Mexico.

"In New Mexico, until World War II, the Mexican population outnumbered that of any other group; but, when the War began, many Mexican people moved to California to work in defense plants. Later, when jobs became plentiful in New Mexico — especially in Albuquerque because of the development of the Sandia Air Force Base, other nationality groups moved in to fill them. Today, although Mexican people no longer constitute the majority of the population of New Mexico, there are still, in proportion, more Mexicans living there than in any other state. In New Mexico, you will find Mexicans working at any number of jobs. Many still own and work the same small farms which have been in their families for generations. Some work as laborers; some own small businesses, such as barber shops and groceries; others are clerks, government workers, or sales people; still others are school teachers and different types of professionals. They have been more completely assimilated in this state than in any other — or perhaps I should say that the other people have been assimilated, since the Mexicans were there first and were in the majority for so many years. At any rate, there is little friction among the various ethnic groups. Mexican architecture, food, customs, and culture in general are predominant features of New Mexican life.

"Mexicans have won more recognition for themselves in government, education, business, and law enforcement in New Mexico than in any other state. They have always owned land; in the early days, land was available from Spanish land grants. Mexicans could and did acquire it, and gradually became a dominant force in their communities and in state politics. A Mexican, Dennis Chavez, was elected to the the United States Senate more than 20 years ago. Since his death, he has been succeeded by another Mexican, Senator Joseph R. Montoya. Other Mexicans have been elected as congressmen and others have been appointed to such positions as sheriff, chief of police, and judge of the Supreme Court. Obviously, Mexicans in New Mexico have not felt discriminated against or unwelcome as have so many in California, Arizona, and Texas.

"In the last-named states, Mexicans have had a more difficult life. In California, many Mexicans live in poverty, both in large cities and in small farming communities. They work as laborers, farm hands, janitors, kitchen help, or gardeners unless they have managed to obtain an education. Some own small businesses such as corner groceries, barber shops, or shoe shops. Many work in factories. The better educated frequently go into teaching, law, medicine, and politics. The latter are still few in number although California has had two Mexican congressmen, one of whom, Edward Roybal, is still in Congress.

"Mexicans in Arizona for many years worked in the saw mills and the copper mines (where they were definitely considered second-class citizens), as farm hands, or as common laborers. Most of the uneducated ones still hold jobs such as these. However, more and more of them are earning an education and hoping for a different vocational future. Few Mexican people have acquired farmland in Arizona as they did in New Mexico. After all, most of Arizona's land is owned by mining companies, railroads, and the government. There have been no congressmen nor senators of Arizona who are Mexicans, although now Mexicans do hold some local offices.

"As an illustration of changing times, I was not long ago approached — separately — by two local candidates for sheriff. One had formerly held the office and been defeated; the other was the incumbent. The previous officeholder appealed to me to use my influence with Mexican people on his behalf. I asked, 'In your sixteen years in office, did you ever hire a Mexican deputy?'

'No, but lots of Mexican kids were "Junior Deputies."'

'Which do you think is better for a Mexican boy — to play at being deputy, or to feel that he has a chance actually to be one when he grows up?'

"He had no answer. The support of the Mexican people in our town went to the incumbent who had hired a Mexican deputy as soon as he took office. Our people will no longer sit back and be told what to do.

"In Texas, Mexicans have faced various problems. Many work at menial jobs; they are common laborers, farm hands, or migratory workers. Seemingly, Mexicans have made less social and economic progress here than have Mexicans in other states. Perhaps a basis for the prejudice against them lies in the historical relationship between Texas and Mexico, in the wars in which the Texans and Mexicans fought one another, particularly in the bitter feelings aroused at the time of 'The Alamo.' Feelings on both sides continued bitter for many years. It should be added, however, that Texas did elect one Mexican congressman in 1962, Henry Gonzales.

The Migrants. "Let us next consider the special problems of *braceros* or Mexican migrant farm workers; and then look briefly at the many striking similarities between our culture and that of the Spanish-speaking Puerto Ricans and Cubans.

"As recently as 1956, as many as 460,000 foreign workers, most of them Mexican, were allowed into the United States during peak harvest seasons in California, Michigan, Texas, Florida, New Jersey, and other major vegetable-fruit producing states. They joined about 500,000 native-born migratory workers, all of whom used to be, and still are, in some places, regarded as a necessary evil—unavoidable if crops are to be harvested. Once, a migrant was barely tolerated; he was watched to see that he 'knew his place' and that he did not spread crime and disease among 'respectable people.' Many people considered him, not a human being, but more like a machine or tool—except that he was not given that much care! When crops were to be picked, he was there, sometimes for a few weeks, sometimes for a couple of months; then he disappeared until the next year. He was the responsibility of no one; that he needed decent food, shelter, health care, and education was 'no concern of ours.' When he was working, he often had to camp in fields, barns, or chicken sheds. Perhaps no provision was made for bathing or even toileting. Is it surprising that epidemics of dysentery and other diseases were sometimes rampant? Many camps did not even have a place to wash. The fact that they were perpetually unclean, in turn, barred the migrants' entrance into restaurants, barber shops, theatres, and some stores when they went from their camp into a town in the old busses, trucks, or pick-ups in which they traveled—and sometimes lived.

"The following incident illustrates their plight: during the 1964 Christmas season, Arizona newspapers reported that in Buckeye,

Arizona, Mexican and other migratory workers were in desperate straits when unseasonal rains put them out of work for several weeks. Since they had no money, and with no possibility of work to earn any, many families slept in broken-down cars, busses or trucks—even in the fields in the pouring rain without warmth, food, or shelter.

"Since the migratory family moves from one state to another as crops are ready to harvest, it is they who suffer when a crop is delayed by cold, destroyed by rain, or flood, or hail. Such a family lives from hand to mouth; they may be fed poorly and irregularly and worked long hours during which they are exposed to heat, cold, wind, dust, and often harmful chemicals and mechanical hazards. Their housing may contain no sewage, no bathing or laundry facilities; it may expose them to dirt and health hazards. State Labor agencies do visit farm labor camps to see that they comply with minimum legal standards; but there are not enough inspectors to catch all violations.

"Migratory workers, of course, are not all Mexicans. Of about one million migrants in this country, many were formerly the rural poor of the South—both white and Negro. Some are of Mexican or Puerto Rican descent. True, many native Mexicans did remain in this country; some became American citizens; others are here as alien residents. However, since 1965, no more Mexican migrants are entering this country legally. In 1965, yielding to union pressure, Congress refused to renew Public Law 85 which had allowed Mexican nationals to become migratory workers here.

"With the ban on *braceros* from Mexico, farmers, fearful of losing their crops, did improve conditions somewhat for workers already here. The average wage of the migratory worker—countrywide—was $1600 in 1966, hardly enough for food and shelter and transportation—to say nothing of health care. Nor does the migratory worker have routine legal protection. In fact, he is often excluded from benefits routine to the other workers such as unemployment insurance, social security, and workmen's compensation, sometimes even from welfare assistance and child labor protection.

"Where conditions are improving, several factors combine: shortage of labor and union activity most notably. In California, the United Farm Workers Organizing Committee led by Cesar Chavez and organized in 1966 has produced 12 contracts with growers affecting 6,000 to 8,000 workers, has increased wages by 60 per cent, gained modest health and welfare plans, and some safety measures for machinery and farm chemicals.[2] Due to lack of workers from Mexico, some farmers in the West and Southwest have been short of labor for

[2] Richard Tobin, "One Million Migrants," *Saturday Review,* August 17, 1968, p. 12.

the last two summers in spite of the increasing help available from mechanized harvesting implements. Machines are being developed, notably for picking cotton, snap beans, lettuce, some apples, and tomatoes, and for topping sugar beets. Other harvests, tobacco, for example, must still be picked by hand – and sorting, grading, and separating crops are still frequently hand work. Hence, migratory labor is and will continue to be necessary to harvesting crops.

"For the last two summers, however, some farmers in the West and Southwest were so short of laborers that they recruited high school students as laborers in order to save their crops from rotting in the fields. These young people refused to pick crops unless decent living conditions were provided; they demanded and received adequate housing, better working conditions, and higher wages. As a result, all migratory workers, both Mexican and others, have benefited.

"In some places, conditions have improved so much that, not only are workers provided sanitation and decent housing, but also recreational and religious facilities. The Farm Labor Office has helped to upgrade their living conditions. Traveling priests and lay Catholic volunteers have done a great deal of welfare work among these people. Some cities have been aroused to their urgent needs; women's groups, social and church groups have, in some places, organized not only day care facilities for the children, health and medical services for young and old, but have provided schooling for the children and are developing educational programs for adults.

"To children from these camps, going to school truly is a new, often frightening experience. Not only is the English language 'a great booming, buzzing confusion,' but many Spanish terms are unknown to them too. What they speak is a patois of broken English and broken Spanish called in the Southwest 'Tex-Mex.' This speech enables them to live in the migrant worker's world, but nowhere else. If – and when – they get to school, then they are unable to understand or to speak what you call English. So, how can you expect them to read it or write it?

"As a matter of fact, recent studies have shown that comparatively few children from these migratory families, even now, attend school regularly. Sometimes they cannot; economic necessity forces them to stay home, perhaps to work – illegally – in the fields or to care for younger siblings. Sometimes illness, their own or that of another family member whom they must attend, forces them to remain at home. Finally, few receive encouragement from their parents to go to school since most parents had no education themselves – here or in Mexico – and they have difficulty in understanding their children's need of it.

"Moreover, some local school authorities make little effort to encourage these children to attend school. If the child does enter, he may be placed in the same grade over and over. Teachers may make little effort to teach him—'he'll soon be moving on.' Or the child may feel unwanted in school. You will note, in the story of Tony, a migrant child of whom one of your colleagues will speak, that Tony talks of being picked on and nagged at by the children and by 'everyone.' In addition, the child may be embarrassed because his clothes are different, or because he is not as strong as the other children. Tony always skipped gym because he couldn't 'lift weights like the other kids and they make fun of me.' How can a child with so many 'strikes' against him be motivated to learn? The miracle is that any of them wish to learn and *do* learn!

"Alert educators are becoming concerned about their problems. A variety of suggestions—some feasible and some questionable—has been made for educating these children. A number of school boards in the Southwest has tried to justify separate buildings or classrooms for these Mexican children because of their language handicap. Could it be that certain of these boards have distorted opinions and mixed motives; that some consider these people congenitally inferior; or that others do not understand why 'cheap labor' should not be perpetuated?

"My own feeling is that housing migrant children in a separate building will merely add another obstacle—physical separation—to the language and cultural barriers which already separate them from other children. If they are to learn to read and write English, they must be able to communicate in English and if they are to communicate in English, they must have *contact* with those who speak the language —the sooner, the better, as Mrs. Brown emphasized when she was teaching English to a Navajo-speaking child.

"Oh, I know well the obstacles they will encounter! Look at the many reasons why these culturally disadvantaged migrant children may not make satisfactory school progress—language, dress, indifference of parents, nutritional deficiencies, illness. Should their problems be complicated by the misfortune of attending a substandard, crowded school where teachers and children actively dislike them, they will have no incentive even to stay in school, much less to learn anything. And there *are* communities where indifference, even antagonism, are realities in the school life of the Mexican-American, especially of the migrant child.

"Those unfortunate children, like Tony, who must attend school under circumstances where they feel unwanted will appear stupid and lazy; or will become aggressive and troublesome to their teachers. Yet these migrant children desperately need what the school can teach them, particularly about health and personal hygiene. Who reacts favorably to a dirty, smelly child? And if teachers won't teach and help this deprived child, who will? That such a child can be helped is evident in both Juan's and Tony's stories which you will soon hear.

"It is undeniable that conditions for migratory workers have improved in the United States; it is hoped that they will continue to improve. Presently, thousands of these workers are living their lives without benefit of education, and for lack of it, are being denied better jobs! Even now, many children cannot attend school regularly because of their parents' frequent migrations. Recent studies indicate that their school achievement is usually under the fourth grade. Children of migrant workers have the lowest educational attainment of any group in our nation. Then, because of *their* lack of education, they, in turn, will not be able to secure better jobs than their parents'. This vicious cycle must be broken—or what hope do these children have?

"That the government is concerned about this problem is evidenced by the recent appointment of a Coordinator of Mexican-American Affairs in a new division of the U.S. Office of Education. This individual is to develop programs which, hopefully, will lower some of the barriers that keep so many Mexican-Americans in proud poverty.

"Already, specific grants have been made to State Educational Agencies for the development of migrant education programs. Six State Departments of Education are coordinating their efforts to enlarge educational opportunities for migrant children, to meet their special needs—health, nutrition, and language development are the foremost targets. Another function of these agencies is to provide local school districts with the financial support for lack of which these children, heretofore, had been unacceptable burdens. Programs like these will, at least, ease the economic burden of the *braceros* and *pochos,* the latter being a self-descriptive term used by the native-born Mexican-Americans which the more assimilated consider pejorative.

The Puerto Ricans

"Now let us consider some of the problems of Puerto Rican children. There are many similarities and differences between them and Mexicans. The most obvious bond is language; they both speak Spanish. Like the Mexicans, there are second and even third-generation Puerto Ricans, many of them New York-born and reared. Then, there are the recent immigrants.

"The customs and values of the two groups differ. Those born in this country tend to take on some values of the predominant culture. For example, they may value their ability to speak English, often at the expense of speaking Spanish. They may not like to be identified with the recent immigrants and 'their antiquated ideas' — which may include superstitions, different clothing, language, or accent, and such expectations as that their relatives should and would support them as long as necessary.

"Recent immigrants feel that the others have become 'modern' even though, interestingly enough, many in this second-generation group still cling to certain traditions such as the belief that women must be obedient to, even subservient to their husbands. However, the feeling of obligation to the entire *extended* family is lessening. Second and third-generation groups will give limited help to all their relatives; but they may be reluctant to have recent immigrants' entire families move in on them and expect to be supported until they can support themselves. Native-born generations often simply do not wish to be responsible for relatives they do not know or may never even have seen.

"The constant influx of new immigrants makes for social and cultural instability in Puerto Rican society in this country. On the other hand, Puerto Rican and other Spanish-speaking groups, especially in large cities, tend to remain together and to take on a certain solidarity as a refuge — or as protection from 'outsiders.' The latter need is strong because they usually find themselves subjected to prejudice in the large cities where most of the Puerto Ricans have settled.

"In large cities many Puerto Ricans are hired to do similar types of jobs to those which Negroes do. These groups may, then, become economic rivals, although Negroes have the advantages of speaking English and of having been there first! There is one exception: in New York especially, Puerto Rican women are in demand for garment work.

"In Eastern states, particularly in New Jersey, Puerto Ricans are 'field workers' like the Mexican *bracero* in the Southwest. Many Puerto Rican immigrants are recruited and hired through the Puerto Rican government for contract work in truck gardens and other agricultural specialties.

"However, Puerto Ricans rarely remain permanently in single families on farms or in rural areas. They are social and gregarious, like the Mexicans, and are likely to live in communities close to one another, even though such living may entail crowded circumstances.

"Some people think of Puerto Ricans as similar in appearance to

Mexicans. Actually, their racial background is different; they may have Indian ancestry; but they may also have European and African ancestry. They vary in physical appearance and in skin color—from fair to darkest brown, from European features to Indian and Negroid.

"There are some striking similarities between the culture of the American Mexican and the American Puerto Rican. For example, in a Puerto Rican family, as in the Mexican, the authority begins with the father, as head of the household, then goes to the mother, then from the older to the younger children in turn. A good father exerts control over his children and establishes himself as an example to imitate.

"Children are subordinate to adults and owe all adults respect, especially family members and close family friends. A father imposes respect for himself and for other adults—by punishment if necessary. Punishment may involve scoldings, beatings, withdrawal of privileges, or the destruction of something of a child's which he values, 'so he will learn to be good and obey.' In second and third-generation families, there may be more leniency and greater freedom for the children; but the father is still the final authority.

"The mother, on the other hand, is expected to keep the home immaculate; her home is *her* responsibility. If she is ill, the children or a woman relative take over the cooking and other chores; it is not compatible with the father's dignity for him to do 'women's work.'

"Both Mexican and Puerto Ricans—the older generations, at least—have their superstitions. Many believe in forecasts of the future through spirits of those who have died. Many consider destiny and good luck as determining factors in their futures.

"In many poor Puerto Rican families, diet is similar to that of the poor Mexican; beans and rice form the essential part of their main meal. Meat is scarce, except for a little salt pork, or a small amount of beef chopped in the chili or added to rice. Sometimes chicken, eggs, or stewed tomatoes are mixed with the rice. Sometimes fried potatoes replace the rice. Rarely, if ever, are salads, fresh fruits, or vegetables served. Many children of school age have never heard of or seen, much less tasted, some of the fruits and vegetables we use. Everyone, even children, consumes coffee at nearly every meal. Breakfast may consist only of coffee with milk and sugar and a piece of bread. Lunch may be no more, although perhaps a little soup and pop will be added. For every evening meal, there must be beans or rice. As with the Mexican family, the father is usually served before the others, especially if he has a male guest.

"For the Puerto Rican boy or girl, as for the Mexican, the degree of difficulty he encounters in his transition from home to school will depend partly upon the recency of his arrival in this country. For the child of Spanish-speaking parents who has lived in a large city in this country for some time, the transition will probably not be as difficult as it will if a child's parents are recent immigrants. Sometimes children, newly arrived in the United States, are assigned to a regular school class with boys and girls of the same chronological age. Thus, they are forced to compete, not only with classmates who speak a language they cannot speak, but who have gone to school long enough to attain their present grade level.

"However, all Spanish-speaking children will have problems if the school they attend is oriented toward the middle-class culture, while they are slum residents. Fortunately, many schools, particularly in urban centers, are becoming increasingly aware of this special problem. One city reports, 'from 1953 to 1957, a Puerto Rican study developed test techniques, teaching methods and instructional materials specific to the teaching of English to Puerto Ricans. The school program available to these children is based on this study — non-English coordinators and auxiliary teachers are available to work with classroom teachers, to interview new arrivals, to follow up pupils when they are placed in regular classes, and to improve cooperation between school and community. Special coaching is given Puerto Rican pupils in English — and bilingual "big brothers" are appointed to help them.'[3]

"In other schools, however, little seems to be done to alleviate the discomfort and loneliness of these children who are 'strange,' or 'different,' or 'can't even talk right.' If the teacher does not understand their problems and classmates ridicule them, it is most difficult for a child to face the school situation day by day, especially if the home is not supportive in its attitude toward education. The implication of the latter statement may be facts like these: a child's home conditions are often not conducive to study. Many homes are so crowded that the child sleeps in the kitchen or livingroom — and must study there. Before he can study or even go to bed, he must wait until adults vacate the room or visitors leave. Moreover, in homes like this, 'family business' usually takes precedence over school; parents frequently need a child to baby-sit or to do an errand — and keep him home from school. Or, he may be absent from school because he does not have enough clothes or the proper clothes to wear to school. Similar reasoning is found among many parents of poor Mexican children.

---

[3] Frederick Shaw, "Educating Culturally Deprived Youth in Urban Centers," *Phi Delta Kappan,* 1963, p. 97.

"When a child *is* in school, parents expect the child to respect the teacher as he would another adult and not bother him by talking or disobeying. On the other hand, parents expect the teacher to make the child obey, but not to punish him physically—although they may do so themselves.

"Parents and teachers may have little personal knowledge of one another. Parents are not likely to make a contact with the school; in fact, an invitation to come to school often frightens them. To some parents, it means only that the child is in trouble! However, even parents who understand that the school wishes to help them and their child may not respond to such an invitation because they are embarrassed at their own inability to speak English, or ashamed of their clothes, or fearful that they may not have proper manners, or unable to leave their small children.

The Cubans

"The Cuban immigrant or refugee child has all of the problems of a Mexican or Puerto Rican child plus those of a refugee painfully and suddenly uprooted from all that is familiar to him. In addition, a child may be separated from his family or may have lost, by death or imprisonment, one or more family members. On the other hand, though the family may be, to some degree, intact, they are probably struggling under terrific financial odds. They may have had to leave virtually all of their money and possessions in order to escape. The father and older members, though educated, may not speak English and therefore may not be able to find work commensurate with their education and background.

"Perhaps this family—or this lone child—has landed on our shores without friends or economic prospects. They must find a place to live; they must learn a new language; they must attempt to build their lives completely anew. If their heritage is mainly Spanish, their culture will be akin to that of the Mexicans and Puerto Ricans. However, Cubans may also have Negro background. When they do, they have the double handicap—of language plus racial discrimination—and a double advantage in their heritage from their Negro culture as well as from their Spanish ancestors.

"The multiple problems that the Cuban child faces make all others look insignificant by comparison. He has language problems, economic, and cultural problems—and, in addition, has probably lived through traumatic emotional experiences. He urgently needs teachers who will be sensitive to his and his family's fears and insecurities, patient and understanding if the child sometimes seems overwhelmed and unable to cope with the school situation!

Problems of the Spanish-Speaking Peoples

"Educated people are aware of problems of discrimination in our society; many, however, think of discrimination as directed against the Negro only. Mexicans, too, face discrimination—less now than formerly, I believe. I remember, when I was 11 years old, I walked into a barber shop and was greeted with, 'Sorry, white trade only.' And, just a few years ago, when a chance acquaintance heard me speaking Spanish to some friends, she asked, knowing I had an English-speaking wife, 'What I want to know is, do you speak *white* at home?' I replied, 'Sometimes I do, and sometimes I speak *brown*.' Again, last year, a man telephoned me at school to say, 'I might move into your school district, but first I want to know how many Negroes, Indians, and Mexicans you enroll.' I answered, 'Because of our location, we have no Negroes; we have six Indians, two Mexican pupils and a Mexican principal.' I never saw that man or his children! However, I am happy to add that the majority of our parents are more concerned with their principal's professional training than with his ethnic background.

"There was a time when Mexicans, in some places in our southwestern states, were consistently refused entrance to restaurants, barber shops, swimming pools, and theatres. This practice is less frequent now; but the memory left is one of bitterness. The stigma of the term Mexican has been such that some of our children grow up firmly convinced that being a Mexican is something to be ashamed of. In fact, some families refuse to claim their Mexican heritage because they desire social acceptance from the dominant culture. And, too many have heard white neighbors say to their children, 'You don't want to play with a Mexican,' or 'We don't invite Mexicans to our house.'

"Such practices, I believe, are due to lack of understanding of our culture. This ignorance has also given rise to false ideas about the Mexican people and to generalizations like: Mexicans are lazy and stupid; Mexicans are tricky, don't trust them; Mexicans are dirty; they like to live the way they do; they wouldn't know how to take care of anything better. Mexicans would rather live with their own kind; they don't like to associate with anybody else.

"Let us examine some of these statements. What can we learn from them about Mexicans? For example, what about our wanting to live with our own kind? The usual housing pattern *is* for Spanish-speaking people to live in one part of town. This is partly because they are naturally gregarious and do like to live among their friends, and partly because their language handicap makes it more convenient to live with people who speak their own language. However, many times it is also because they find that they cannot rent or buy property anywhere except in the 'Mexican section.' Various subterfuges have been used in different communities to enforce segregated housing. These range from 'gentlemen's agreements' not to sell to Mexicans to threats of violence against Americans of Mexican descent who move into Anglo areas.

"Fortunately, this situation is changing in many parts of the country today. As they become educated and manage to acquire some money, a certain segment of the Spanish-speaking population is moving more or less where it chooses, although many Mexicans still prefer not to move among strangers or to live close to people among whom they do not feel welcome, a point stressed earlier when Mexican clannishness was mentioned.

"What about Mexicans being dirty and liking to live that way? Many Mexican families where the men are employed as unskilled, agricultural or industrial workers are still bound by ties of poverty and ignorance. In most towns, there still is a 'wrong side' of something — the tracks, the highway, or the river bed — and often this is where Mexicans live. What is their section of town like? In many places, even today, there is no electricity and no sewage disposal. Streets are unpaved; some houses have dirt floors. Families of ten or eleven people may be crowded into a two or three room shack. A wood stove may serve for cooking and heating; there may be no plumbing and little furniture — often not even beds.

"*Why* do they live like this? Many families simply cannot afford anything better. The socioeconomic status of Mexicans in unskilled occupations is precarious. There is a great deal of unemployment among this group — seasonal and more permanent. The Mexican men who work in lumber mills or as agricultural laborers or common laborers often depend on good weather for their jobs; in winter, they are forced 'on welfare.' They have no way of making a better living or of obtaining better jobs because most of the men in this generation have acquired little or no education or vocational skill useful in our current industrial age. These are the Mexicans often called 'stupid' or 'lazy.'

"Some government housing projects have attempted to ameliorate these conditions and, under the federal government's 'War on Poverty,' increasing emphasis is being placed on more adequate housing for low-income families. However, such improvements take time; sub-standard housing will probably be with us for some time to come.

"Low incomes, substandard housing, poor diets, bad sanitation, and ignorance cause widespread disease among these people. Some of the more common health problems are pneumonia, influenza, diarrhea, and tuberculosis. In the towns, diarrhea may be traced to open sewage, no refrigeration, many flies, and the mother's ignorance of elementary principles of personal hygiene. These same conditions—plus con-taminated water from open irrigation ditches—plague Mexican people in farming communities with the diarrhea which still kills many babies.

"Poor nutrition, of course, is the basic reason for much illness and disease. Remember, the diet of a poor Mexican family will be beans, rice, cereals, lard, onions, potatoes, tomatoes, and a great deal of red and green chili. Many fruits and vegetables commonly used by Anglos are never eaten by Mexicans. Proteins, especially meats and milk, are sadly lacking. Very few school age children have milk; even small children drink coffee—which may be their only breakfast. This diet causes many vitamin deficiencies; it is also responsible for running noses, cracked faces, lip sores, impetigo, ear infections, and bad teeth, especially dental caries. Unfortunately, it is quite common for these Mexican children to have a mouthful of rotten teeth which cause bad odor and severe pain. Good teeth and adequate dental care is the exception, rather than the rule, among them.

"However, poverty is not always visible among the Mexicans. Their attempt to cover up their poverty is sometimes mistaken for trickery. Actually, they do not like to seek help from 'outsiders'; in times of need, they help one another. A Mexican family shares with another hungry family so that everyone has *something* to eat. In farming com-munities, no matter how poor a family is, it is customary to keep a large pot of beans and of chili on the stove—to be shared with anyone in need. Friends, neighbors, and the extended family regularly help one another out, perhaps with a sack of beans, chili, or rice. True, such diet is restricted; but it staves off hunger. Only in large cities, when many heads of families are out of work and there simply is no money to buy food is there real hunger.

Their Culture

Close Family Ties. "The concept of the extended family is important in the lives of all Spanish-speaking people, although the interpretation of this concept may vary from group to group. Its impact in the Puerto Rican culture has already been noted. Among Mexicans, immediate families are often large, and there are many close relatives.

"In northern New Mexico, family ties among Mexicans have, for years, been especially strong. Because of repeated intermarriages, in many small towns, almost everyone actually is related. Even now, it is still the accepted custom to call any relative or even close friend *primo* which means cousin. An older relative or friend is called *tio* or *tia* which means uncle or aunt.

"Family ties are close among Mexicans in many parts of Texas too. However, in large cities, particularly in California, ties are looser. One has many relatives whom one thinks of as members of the family group; but one's immediate family is one's major concern. In Arizona, the latter is also true.

"Nevertheless, in every Spanish-speaking family, relationships are intimate. Every brother, sister, first and second cousin, aunt, uncle, and grandparent plays an important part in the life of a child. The family may not actually all live together; but they try, by frequently visiting one another, to remain close to one another and bound in affection and understanding. They expect to help and support one another in times of need.

"Incidentally, in school, you may sometimes feel that the Spanish-speaking children tend to segregate themselves from the others. This is quite natural—until you help them to feel that they are actually a part of the school! Any minority group—Negroes, Puerto Ricans, Chinese, Indians—must be *won over* to the dominant culture by being convinced that they will find a place for themselves there. Given such assurance, they can accept the predominant culture; otherwise, they will cling stubbornly to their own practices and beliefs. And many Mexican-Americans, perhaps partly to protect themselves from Anglo prejudice, tend to remain very loyal to their culture and traditions, very closely bound to their relatives and friends.

"It was said that families are often large. The fact that the majority of Mexicans belongs to the Roman Catholic faith—and that their religion is very important in their lives—accounts, in part, for the large number of children in many families. Because of religious conviction or because of ignorance, some married couples do not limit their families. However, Mexicans, having a strong sense of 'family,' frequently *want* many children.

Parent-Child Relationships. When families are large, living may not be conducted in a relaxed atmosphere; on the other hand, there is seldom pressure on the children. In fact, some parents, especially among the poor, do not care when—or whether—things get done. Routine is unknown in many such families. Mealtimes may be at more or less regular times; unless Father, coming home from work, is accompanied by some of his friends! He and they may sit and visit and drink wine or beer while the family waits for dinner.

"Father is definitely the head of the house. When the family eats together, father is usually served first, and, if he has guests, they are served next. Then the family may eat. In a farming community, if father is in the fields, it is a great privilege to be chosen as the child who takes his lunch of hot beans and chili to him. Sometimes something is left for the messenger. The greatest treat of all is being *invited* to finish the meal.

"Mother has, more or less, a free hand in running the house. Money is doled out to her every day or two for buying food. She rarely makes family purchases for anything other than food. Nor does she go anywhere without her husband's permission. It is expected that he will demand an accounting of her whereabouts at all times. He, however, goes where he likes and does as he chooses.

"As women are acquiring better education and employment, they are demanding more freedom. Nowadays, many a home is the scene of stormy sessions as a husband protests sharing his authority with his wife or relinquishing his authority over her! This situation develops particularly when the woman adds to the financial support of the family—or is its sole support. Even when a man cannot secure work, she may be able to find employment as a maid in a motel, a waitress, or kitchen helper in a restaurant, or a cleaning woman, or cook in someone's home. Some younger, educated mothers secure jobs as clerks and secretaries.

"Thus marital difficulties may develop; but divorce does not usually result because of parental and church disapproval. Both sets of grandparents usually try to force the young couple to remain together. If their arguments do not prevail and a divorce *is* obtained, the grandparents ignore the matter with outsiders. They are ashamed; divorce simply is 'not expected' among Mexican people. If there is a desertion —or if a son doesn't do his duty by his children—or a daughter isn't taking care of children the way she should, the grandparents will step in and take the children away. On the other hand, parents may 'give' a child to a grandparent or aunt or uncle who needs someone to live with him. Such a child will be reared as though he were the natural child of the person with whom he is living. Sometimes, if there are too many children in a family for them to be cared for adequately, relatives may take a child who is a favorite of theirs—for a year or two—or even permanently. This practice is not considered unnatural or unusual.

"Child-rearing principles are different for boys and for girls. Fathers want boys to be '*muy hombre*,' very masculine; they teach them not to 'take anything from anyone' anywhere. They must argue and fight if necessary, whether with friends, teachers, or strangers. However, at home, they must show respect for their fathers and for all adult relatives unless they feel that they are being 'put upon,' or unfairly treated.

"At school — and everywhere else — the boys are expected to stand up for themselves and fight — to fight their sisters' battles, too, if necessary. Fighting among girls is the exception rather than the rule. Mexican girls are expected to be ladylike and cooperative. At an early age, they are taught by the mother to cook, to take care of the home and of younger children.

"Therefore, if a Mexican child, boy or girl, resents his teacher or feels that the teacher is unfair, he will probably become extremely uncooperative and do nothing he is told. Although he may not mention the situation at home, should he do so, his parents will understand and share his attitude that he must protect himself from unfairness; but rarely will they go to school to complain to the teacher.

"Younger children are often favored by their parents above older ones; but they must obey the older children. Older children, in turn, must be respectful to parents and older relatives. Children are not encouraged to talk and ask questions. Particularly when adults are talking, it is very bad manners to interrupt.

"If there is disagreement about a child's behavior or if conflicting orders have been given him, the ultimate authority lies with the grandmother — then the father, mother, older relatives, and older children, in this order. Rarely is there disagreement on a child's discipline, since a child is expected to show respect for all his elders and to mind any *one* of them. Should he fail to do so, punishment will be swift. It is usually physical and may involve severe beatings.

Strengths of the Mexican-American Culture. Some aspects of this culture are stabilizing factors for today's Mexican-American boys and girls. The culture's strengths, as I see them, are: close family ties and concern for one another; respect for family solidarity and for elders; the centrality of religion in our life; the cooperativeness and mutual assistance which have been learned in large families; and the ability to enjoy and get along with peers — even though the same experience, sometimes, also teaches jealousy of one another and competition for adult favors.

"I hope that we can preserve these strengths of our Mexican culture. Much, however, is changing in our Mexican-American way of life. Yet this flexibility is itself one of its strengths. The very fact that this culture can incorporate change as it absorbs, from the dominant culture, values which become important to us as Mexican-Americans is a fact of which to be proud.

"Many changes augur well for the future of our children. A number of parents, for example, are realizing the advantages education can give their children. They are encouraging both their sons and daughters to go to high school, and even college—although Mexican boys in college far outnumber Mexican girls, I am sure.

"The parents themselves are changing. Where formerly Mexican culture produced an easy-going type of individual whom Americans perceived as lacking in ambition, now, as more and more Mexicans secure steady jobs at every economic level—janitor, mechanic, clerk, teacher, lawyer. Mexicans are working hard and learning to be competitive in order to 'get ahead.' They see what other people have in material possessions; they want something better for their families too —and they see hope of securing it. Doing so, however, means becoming dependent on the dollar and getting to places on time—if only to collect unemployment insurance. Therefore, mañana, for many Mexicans, is on the way out! Incidentally, TV schedules have helped to develop their sense of time!

"Mexican culture, traditionally, has not been a competitive culture. However, as Mexican parents themselves have competed 'successfully' in the dominant culture, they want their children to be prepared to compete—for scholarships, good jobs and advancement, both social and economic. Children of these parents have a sense of stability; their parents are supportive and definite in their expectations—the child is to work hard and try to get ahead—as they themselves are doing. Obviously, the children of parents who are steady workers usually progress faster in school than those whose parents are unemployed or who move a great deal.

The Schooling They Need

"What is the Mexican-American child in *your* school like? Perhaps he enters kindergarten overjoyed at the idea of going to school. What if, then, he finds that he cannot communicate with other children— or perhaps he communicates with an accent? In any case, his speech is 'wrong.' Perhaps some well-meaning teacher corrects him, but does not explain to him what is wrong. With each passing day, he finds that he does more things which are considered wrong in this new environment. The children do not seem to like him or want to play with him. Gradually, this rejection makes him feel that there must be something wrong with *him;* his self-image becomes more and more negative.

"Studies have shown that, by third or fourth grade, many a Mexican-American child's motivation pattern has changed. He no longer wants to learn; he becomes either a psychological drop-out—now called a 'sit-in'—or he displays actively his hostility toward the school and becomes known as a trouble-maker. In any case, he 'loses ground' educationally so that, by the time he is in eighth or ninth grade—if he survives this long—he is educationally retarded two or more years.

Language Facility. "Is not this partly a language problem, you say? The answer depends upon the way you conceive language. Gardner Murphy once made a comment which indicated that language is so much a part of the child that, when he feels his language is wrong, *he* feels wrong. Juan's and Victor's stories emphasize this point. Victor would not speak English, even when he knew the answers to questions asked in school, because he feared being ridiculed for *the way he talked*. Juan, on the other hand, had a large vocabulary which he used constantly and aggressively—and incorrectly. Language was one of his weapons in defense of his 'self,' or rather, of the image built of himself as a bad, feisty, dirty Mexican kid. Neither was free to gain facility in his new language because his energies were absorbed in worrying about how he could combat the rejection of 'me' which learning and using the new language involved.

"In terms of language facility, Juan and Victor differ, as all Mexican-American children will, because the experiential background of each individual non-English-speaking boy or girl is different. Each child has learned what he knows in terms of his cultural inheritance, yes— but also in terms of the background of his particular family. As a concomitant of his immediate environment, he may speak his own language well; he may have a large stock of meanings and a wide variety of experiences; or a not-so-large or a meager stock.

"We know, from observation of children's problems in learning a new language, that a child's facility in a new language is most likely to develop if he communicates with facility in his own language. In other words, the child who knows his own language well will learn English fairly readily. Conceptualization, whether attained through Spanish, Navajo, German, or any other vernacular, is rather easily labeled with English symbols. For the boy or girl who has a well-developed vernacular in his mother tongue, then, learning English is the comparatively simple task of acquiring English labels for known concepts: a rose by any other name!

"However, one child may be poles apart from another in the facility he has developed in his original language. For a boy or girl with a meager experience background, numerous common concepts must be developed from scratch; he will not know them in his native language or in English. Such a child needs to know the answer to 'what is a rose?' — as did Peggy — before the word *rose* is meaningful in any language. You will have to teach the latter child very differently from the former; the latter will learn English only after intensive and extensive language activities.[4] Yet gaining facility in English is most important to every Mexican-American child! Therefore, your teaching techniques must be adequate to achieve this goal, regardless of the original stage of a child's language development.

Pride in Their Cultural Heritage. "A teacher must, however, consider another aspect of communication: how does a child's experience affect his facility in speaking or even his willingness to speak at all? Some children find it easy to talk; others find it difficult. Some have learned to be responsive to people because people have responded to them; others have learned not to respond and not to listen because it is safer to be quiet and passive.

"Now, let us suppose that a child expresses himself well and has something to talk about; then suppose that his teacher does not understand what the child is talking about, or disapproves of what he says, or indicates that he considers the child's conversation strange or different and, sometimes, what these boys and girls say or do may seem strange to you! Suppose that you talked in class about ways in which we use flowers; then you suggested that the class make drawings to show how *they* use flowers. Perhaps you found that most of the Mexican children drew cemeteries with flowers on graves. This use of flowers is important to Mexican children. Of course, there may have also been drawings of a bride or two carrying flowers and of girls in church processions with flowers on their veils. Again, suppose that, in your reading class, Mexican boys and girls told, with great gusto, a story about butchering and killing of chickens. You think, why must they be so gory? They live in a poor barrio — or neighborhood — and meat is highly prized.[5] Do you understand the significance of incidents like these? Or, do your prejudices show, as they did when a teacher who was impressed by a good drawing done by a Mexican child, exhibited it proudly to the entire class, then turned to an Anglo child who usually drew well and said, 'Aren't you ashamed to be beaten by a Mexican?' Prejudice can be pervasive and subtle.

"A Mexican-American child's self-esteem must include pride in

---

[4] Last two paragraphs adapted from Marie Hughes and George Sanchez, *Learning a New Language,* Association for Childhood Education International Bulletin 101 (Washington, D.C., 1958), p. 28.

[5] Last two paragraphs adapted from ibid., p. 18.

being Mexican. He must know who he is and know that his cultural heritage is a noble one. Many Mexican children know little or nothing of their cultural heritage. In fact, some may have never heard anything good said about Mexicans! No wonder that some of them are ashamed of speaking Spanish—or try to hide the fact that they are Mexicans. Teach these children that being a Mexican is something to be proud of, and that ability to speak Spanish is enviable. Teach them that Mexicans have contributed a great deal to American culture—especially in the Southwest. Point to the wide-spread Mexican influence on architecture, home decoration, fashions, foods, and vocabuary. Many Mexican foods—enchiladas, tacos, tamales, and tostadas—are popular. Words like *corral, burro, sombrero, poncho, rodeo, lariat, chili,* and *tortilla* are in such common usage that we rarely think of their origin. Many towns and cities have Spanish names—Los Angeles, San Francisco, Nogales, Santa Barbara, San Antonio, San Jose, San Juan, San Diego.

"Mexicans have a rich historical background which includes colorful personages like the Spanish conquistadores and the mission priests—Father Kino, for example. And who could be a more romantic figure than the great Emperor Montezuma! Many children's books and stories have been written about the Spanish and Indian ancestors of today's Mexican children. Make this historical background rich and exciting for the Mexican-American child in your classroom.

"Next, acquaint him with Mexicans who are 'successful' people. In your local community, there may be sheriffs, city councilmen, teachers, lawyers, and doctors whom the children can interview or who would visit you in school. There may be state representatives, congressmen, judges, and senators. Such people had difficulties to overcome—but they made it! These individuals are an example and an incentive for children to believe in and try for higher goals for themselves. One example of someone who conquered problems is a friend of mine, Raul Castro, currently United States Ambassador to Bolivia. Raul worked his way through high school, then went to college on a track scholarship, which meant that he was assured a job—washing dishes. In college he became a Border Conference boxing champ and a long distance runner. He earned his degree in education but couldn't find a job teaching, so he traveled all over the country, sometimes as a migratory farm worker, again as a common laborer. Next, he worked for the Immigration Service in Nogales. Then he decided he wanted to become a lawyer. Since he had no money, he went to see the president of the University of Arizona; they worked out an arrangement whereby he would teach Spanish at the University as he worked on his law degree. After graduation he became a successful attorney; later, a judge of the Superior Court for Pima County. He often tells a story about an incident which happened while he was running for judge:

Two cowboys walking down the street toward him spotted him, and just as they passed, one remarked, "I'd rather vote for a dog than a Mexican." "Bow-wow! Bow-wow!" barked Raul — and continued on his way.

He won the election and, during his tenure as judge of the Superior Court, established an outstanding reputation for his work with juvenile offenders. Then President Johnson appointed him Ambassador to El Salvador where he completed four years of outstanding service. Presently he is United States Ambassador to Bolivia.

"An ingenious teacher will think of many ways to teach about Mexico or Mexican customs: discussions and stories, songs, dramatics, puppets, and holiday celebrations when Mexican food and objects such as lariats, sombreros, ponchos, piñatas, and guitars are brought in and enjoyed by everyone. It doesn't require elaborate productions to convince a Mexican child that he has a heritage of which to be proud — or a Puerto Rican or Cuban child!

Self-Esteem. "These children must know that they are bearers of a cultural heritage esteemed by their teachers and their classmates. In like manner, they must be shown that they, as individuals, are esteemed, that they are accepted by their teachers and classmates and are important in their school life. Given this acceptance, along with a teacher's support when 'his Mexican ways' need understanding, a Mexican boy or girl will learn in school in spite of the fact that, initially, he may have entered school with apprehension, perhaps with distrust — frequently with insufficient ability to communicate with others. His acceptance in school, as was stressed earlier, involves acceptance of *all* that the child is — including his language. If he is not permitted to use his language, or is even punished or shamed for doing so, *he himself* feels the lack of acceptance. Being a Mexican and speaking Spanish make him what he is! First, see to it that you set a high value on what he is, then he can develop self-esteem!

A Good Learning Situation

"I have been stressing the fact that a Mexican child, like any human being, must feel truly wanted and 'at home' in a school situation before he can take advantage of the situation — and learn! Let me now illustrate what I mean by a *good* learning situation — an emotional climate in which a child *can* respond. Victor will tell you his story just as he told it to me last June. You will note that, just as with all-American children, Victor's success in school is due to his parent's interest and support as well as to his teachers' efforts and understanding."

I am Victor. I am thirteen years old and live with my father, mother, younger brother, sister, and baby brother. We live in the north end of town which is not the best section of town – it isn't the worst either. Most people in our neighborhood speak Spanish, but try also to speak English, and my mother says this is very important. She says that, if we are to learn to speak English too, we must practice it. Of course, this is not possible if most of the children you know speak Spanish only.

Our house is about two blocks north of the northern limits of the city. It is on Buena Vista Drive. The phrase Buena Vista, in Spanish, means good view. However, I can assure you the view is not pretty. Buena Vista Drive is two blocks long and, until recently, it was not paved. It is bordered on the west by a canal and on the east by the railroad tracks of the Southern Pacific Railroad. At last it was paved last winter when most of the streets in the neighborhood were paved. Some people say that this was done because of the efforts of our new city mayor who is a Negro and wanted his section of town paved.

We have other problems. We don't have sidewalks nor city water. The city trucks do not collect garbage in our part of town. We do not have city fire protection. However, we do have county fire protection which means that they usually get here after a house has burned down to the ground. Police protection is also provided by the county, but they too are very slow to answer a call. Fortunately, we seldom need this service.

The water that comes out of our faucet is canal water that has not been processed. It is unsafe to drink. We buy our drinking water when we have the money. When we don't, we go to the city park and bring our drinking water from there in a five-gallon can we keep for that purpose. This, of course, is not our only problem. As I mentioned before, the city does not collect trash and garbage, so Father borrows a pickup once in a while and takes the trash and garbage to the city dump himself.

The city sewer pipelines do not come into this part of town, so property owners build their own sewer systems. We have been having trouble with ours lately because it fills up too soon. Our parents have instructed us not to use any more water than is absolutely necessary. It costs $20.00 to have the sewer tanks emptied; and we need the money for other things. This, of course, means fewer baths for us kids.

I know Father worries because he doesn't make much money. When I see him worried, this worries me too and sometimes I wish I was old enough to work full-time so that I could help out. You see, it really isn't his fault that we don't live better. Father is an office machine repairman – a good one, people say. He learned his craft in Mexico; he also has a fairly good education. Both of my parents completed secondary education in Mexico. We came to this country because Father heard that one could make a better living here.

For the last two years, he has been working for an office machine store 14 miles from home. He used to work here in town; but his boss wouldn't give him a raise and he had to quit. Mother said it was impossible for us to get by on what he was earning. He likes his present job, but he isn't happy because he says that some people working in the fields are making more money than he is. What really bothers him is that some of the field workers never attended school for even one day.

This sometimes makes me wonder if an education is really as important as some people say it is—especially my parents. I mean, what is the use of all those years of hard work in school if Mexicans can't make a decent living later on?

Mother used to talk about going to work, but Father never gave his consent. He would always say that her place was in the home; we would have to get by on whatever he could earn. Nowadays with the baby, Mother doesn't even bother to ask about going to work herself.

I am glad. I don't know what I would have done, especially during my first school years here in the United States if Mother hadn't been home. It would have been unbearable to get home and find nobody to tell my troubles to—and I really had all kinds of problems.

I had been in third grade in Mexico and doing well in school. That was five years ago. That's when we moved. I have always done good in school, well almost always. I did awful that first year in the United States though. I was placed in second grade—because I couldn't do third grade work, they told me. The truth of the matter is that I couldn't do second grade work either. I simply couldn't understand the language. Imagine yourself in a Japanese classroom or a Russian classroom or in any other classroom where you hear only a foreign language. How good do you think you would do? Well, that's exactly how good I did.

I had heard English before; on the radio, on television, and from American tourists. When we were living in Mexico, I used to listen to them carrying on conversations in this strange language. I say strange because it sounded strange to me. Have you ever listened to a tape recording being played at the wrong speed? Well, that's the way English used to sound to me, something like the way Donald Duck speaks—only much faster. Now I was in this school—to learn what the other kids were learning without being able to understand one word of what was being said in this strange language.

Those first few weeks were the awfulest weeks of my life. If I could have quit, I sure would have. I guess I got by, mostly, by following the leader, that is, I did what I saw the kids next to me do. If they opened their books, I would open mine; if they closed theirs, I would close mine; if they stood up, I would stand up. When we pledged allegiance to the flag in the morning before the beginning of classes, I would try to imitate the sounds. During those days, I was always glad to go out of the room whether for recess, lunch hour, or to go home in the afternoon.

At home, I must have been the greatest crybaby in the world. I would start

crying the minute I set foot inside the house; I couldn't do anything right.
Everybody thought I was dumb. I hated the school. I wished we had stayed in
Mexico.

I guess I was fortunate in that I had an understanding mother. Father was
understanding too — and still is, but he was too busy earning a living for us to
listen to my troubles. My mother had studied English in Mexico, and so had
my father, for that matter. Both of them were aware of the difficulties encountered in learning to speak a new language.

I remember Mother would advise me, and my brother, who was placed in
first grade, not to worry, to listen to what the teacher said, and to practice
imitating what we heard; first the names of objects, sentences later. She was
constantly reassuring us that we would learn — but "it is going to take time,"
she would say. Then she would help us.

That first year, as soon as we got home from school, that is as soon as we
composed ourselves enough from the frustrating experiences in school, she
would ask us simple questions, using the best English at her command.
Questions like "what is this?" while holding a book or a pencil for us to
identify. We were coached into answering "this is a book" or, perhaps, "this
is a pencil." This would go on for about an hour every day including Satur-
days and Sundays. She used only a few objects at first, then added more. She
made us talk in sentences. As soon as we learned a certain sentence (sentence
patterns, she calls them), she would go into another one. She kept adding
something new as fast as we learned whatever she had introduced before. This
practice helped us a lot.

In the evening, right after the dishes were washed and put away, she would
start us on our reading lesson. Our reading lesson would consist of trying to
read what we had learned to say orally. After a few months of this, we went on
to our school readers. As I said before, her pronunciation was awful at first,
but improved with time — and so did our school work.

I was, also, very fortunate in having such understanding teachers at school.
I will always be grateful to Mrs. Jones, my second grade teacher, who would sit
with a small group of us for 30 minutes every day — 15 minutes in the morning
and 15 minutes in the afternoon — and would help us with our English.

It must take much patience and understanding to work with non-English
speaking groups like ours. I remember that, of the seven kids in this group,
four of us didn't know a word of English when we started; the other three could
understand a little — but not much. Poor Mrs. Jones, she would work and work
with us for weeks and weeks just to teach us to produce a single sound correctly. I don't mean that she wouldn't teach us anything else. She did — much,
much more.

There was this kid, Pablo is his name, who tried so hard for weeks to say
book but kept on saying *bok*. Finally he learned, but the trying must have been
very frustrating for both Pablo and Mrs. Jones.

I did much better than Pablo. As a matter of fact, I did much better than most of the kids in this group because Mother took such a deep interest in my troubles and was willing and able to spend all of those many hours helping me and my brother.

Most Mexican kids are not that lucky. Take for instance Pablo. Pablo is small, dark-skinned and looks as though he's always hungry. No one speaks any English in his home. Pablo had, at this time, two older sisters and an older brother and two younger brothers. Pablo's family lived about two blocks from where we live—on the "wrong side" of Central Street and I used to visit him often. He was and still is one of my best friends. At this time, the family lived in a two-room house with no running water. When I say two rooms, I mean that there was a kitchen and a bedroom. For those who had beds, they slept three in a bed. Toilet facilities were outside toward the back of the yard in a shack which served the dual purpose of garage and bathroom. The reason for saying all of this is because I want to make it clear that their living conditions were very crowded, to say the least. Pablo's parents are strict; he and his brothers must play near home—on the unpaved street or in the vacant lot next door. Imagine *their* Mother trying to teach those kids anything with so many people talking and moving around the house—and an old radio that is never turned off. Neither are Pablo's parents educated like mine. His father is a caster in a local pottery factory. He wants Pablo to stop school as soon as possible to go to work. Neither parent can read or write. I know—because every once in awhile they bring their letters for my parents to read for them. My parents also answer their letters for them. Poor Pablo, he still has a difficult time in school! Some of the kids think Pablo is dumb because he doesn't do very good in school. If they only knew the problems poor Pablo has! At first they used to tease him—until one day he got pretty fed up at being teased and beat up a couple of his worst tormentors. They quit teasing him after this. As a matter of fact, he has many friends nowadays, probably because he is good at sports.

By third grade, I did better in school. That is, I did better in everything except those subjects in which I was supposed to participate orally. Our teacher was Mrs. Green and she also was very kind and understanding just like Mrs. Jones had been the year before. She never asked me a question which would require more than one or two words to answer. By then, I could understand quite a bit of English and could speak more than I dared to because I did not want to be made to talk in front of the class. Often I knew the answer the teacher wanted; but I preferred to play dumb rather than to try to answer in my limited and awkward English vocabulary. Some people don't understand how difficult it is to try to converse in a foreign language when you're just learning the language. There are also a few who find it amusing when they hear a person who is beginning to learn the language try to say something in this new language. Some will laugh and make fun of you. Because this happens often in school, the only safe thing to do is to play dumb and just not talk.

As I said before, Mrs. Green was a very understanding teacher and would explain to the class the problems we Mexican kids were having in trying to learn English. Most of the kids were very understanding and helpful too. But, still, it was safer to play dumb—and this I did for a long, long time.

I remember the time Superintendent Packwood visited our room. He went around the room looking at what we were doing. It was during arithmetic and most of the kids were working on their problems. I had finished mine. Arithmetic has always been easy for me. I was reading ahead in my reader. When Mr. Packwood came to where I was, he asked me to read for him, which I gladly did. Here was my golden opportunity to show what I could do, I thought. After I finished reading the page or two which he had me read, he asked me to tell him what I had read in my own words. Of course, I couldn't do it. Not because I didn't know what I had read but, as I said before, because I was afraid I wasn't going to find the right words to express myself intelligently. Besides, everybody was listening. I don't know what he thought of my inability to re-tell him the story in my own words; perhaps he thought I didn't know what I was reading. I have often wondered.

My fifth grade teacher was Mr. Smith. Mr. Smith is one of my favorite teachers, even though I am no longer one of his students. I will never forget the way he was always asking me questions which I had to answer because they were questions which he knew I *could* answer. As I look back to my year in fifth grade, I realize that asking me those simple questions was his way of encouraging me to participate in class discussions. As the months went by, I became increasingly active in class activities. Toward the end of fifth grade, I had lost most of my feeling of being ashamed to talk in class. My command of the English language improved by leaps and bounds after I gained courage really to try to talk. My school work improved much more than it had the year before. Toward the end of the year, I was one of the best students in class. Mr. Smith was very interested in all types of playground activities and would encourage us to participate. This participation did much to develop my confidence in the use of the English language. You see, when you are playing ball, and you want one of the players to throw the ball so that you can put somebody out, you simply holler "throw the ball" without worrying about your pronunciation. We played lots of games that year; so I practiced my English without really thinking about it.

This has been my best year yet, with Mr. Ross as my sixth grade teacher. I excelled in everything from the very beginning of the year. My language handicap has almost disappeared. Mr. Ross told my folks recently, at a teacher-parent conference, that I was one of his best students. I think he meant it because he gave me mostly "A's" and "B's" on my report card.

I was master of ceremonies for the program we gave for our parents toward the last of the year. Yes, I am proud of myself—but mostly because my parents are happy and proud of my accomplishments.

However, my problems are not over. I have had problems of a different kind this year. I guess when one problem disappears, another takes it place. About a month ago, during the lunch hour, some of the Mexican kids cornered me.

There were about five of them. Their leader, a boy they call "Punky," did all the talking: "I hear that your eyes are turning blue," he said. "What do you mean?" I asked. "Well, my boys tell me that you are very smart and that you always have the right answers for everything. You know what I mean. You just don't want to talk to us ignorant Mexicans. You think you are too good for us." He carried on like this for a while. Since I didn't answer him back — frankly, I didn't know what to say — he started to shove me around. Lucky for me that Pablo had seen what was happening and had run and told Mr. Ross. When they saw Mr. Ross coming, they quit shoving. They were taken to the office. Later, I heard they had been kept after school.

I know this isn't the last of it. They haven't bothered me since, but I know that, one of these days, we are going to meet somewhere. I only hope somebody will be around to help me.

"Victor's story ends with a dramatic example of one major difficulty we have in developing leadership among Mexican people: namely, their lack of support of someone who does get ahead. Unfortunately, jealousy from other Mexican-Americans is not unusual. Reasons for this are complicated: they include the fact that some Mexicans see themselves as of little worth, thus have little hope of personal success; many fear competition and resent the person who dares to compete; and finally, in many large Mexican families as stated earlier, children must compete for their parents' attention, thus they learn jealousy of one another early.

"Perhaps, because Mexicans are often forced into competition in their homes, many do not like to compete elsewhere unless they are fairly certain that they can come out ahead. You will notice, in school, that Mexican boys will compete in athletics as long as they think they're good, but they quickly lose confidence and enthusiasm when things don't go so smoothly. For example, during fifth, sixth, and seventh grades, many Mexican boys have a natural advantage over Anglo boys because of their early rate of maturation. After this time, however, their advantage is gradually lost because Anglo boys usually become larger than Mexicans and, as they gain coordination as well as strength, they often do better in athletic competition than the Mexican boys. The latter simply drop out of athletics when this happens.

"Similar behavior is evidenced in those Mexicans who have dropped out of life's competition, for some reason, yet are jealous of any neighbor who gets ahead. They say *quiere hacerse mejor* which means, literally, 'he wants to make himself better'; but, it is used by those jealous of their contemporaries to mean 'he wants to be better than I am.'

"Such behavior is due to fear and envy, as I said before. However, fear and envy, like jealousy, are based on a poor self-image. The Mexican who acts in these ways feels worthless; therefore, he lacks self-confidence; or feels that he cannot do the things his competitors have accomplished. One of the most important tasks facing our schools and our Mexican-American leaders is to try to change the negative image many Mexicans have of themselves and to replace it by pride in their Mexican background.

"An initial step toward this goal is for Mexican children to learn in school about the many contributions made by Mexicans to American culture and to become acquainted there with leaders in our country's politics, business, education, journalism, law enforcement, music, and artistic endeavors—people who proudly proclaim their status as Mexicans. Thus the Mexican-Americans now growing up will gain a positive image of themselves; they will know *their worth* as representatives of our Mexican-American culture.

The Teachers Spanish-Speaking Children Need

"Victor's most pressing problem was learning English. Victor relates poignantly how it feels not to be able to communicate—he could not speak, listen or comprehend what was happening to him. He makes clear, too, how long it takes to become accustomed to another language—how surprised, resentful, and discouraged a child can become at his slow progress and how a new language must be *used* continuously day after day, week after week, month after month—even year after year—before a child feels safe in using it—or comfortable enough to venture its use publicly.

"Victor lets us know what teachers can do to help; do not expect rapid progress or become impatient, irritable, or discouraged. Do not force the child to speak; he will withdraw into complete silence. However, if the teacher encourages him, praises each small effort, draws him into conversation about something important to him, helps him to speak with a few other children, especially if those children too are struggling with a new language, then gradually, the child may gain the courage to speak in front of a group. He can be particularly encouraged to do so if, as one of Victor's wise teachers did, he is, at first, asked questions which he can answer in one word.

"Not all of your boys and girls will, after a few years, be able to preside as master of ceremonies in a school assembly as Victor did. However, each one can learn that you believe in his abilities, respect his worth, are interested in listening to *him,* and willing to help him to make the most of what he, as a person, can be.

"The importance of teaching Spanish-speaking children to communicate cannot be overemphasized. Not every child's language problem will be as acute as Victor's—but some will find learning English even more difficult than Victor did. In future meetings with some of your colleagues who are experienced in this area, you will be discussing techniques used to teach English to bilingual children.

"I shall close by summarizing the major problems faced by the culturally and economically disadvantaged Spanish-speaking child in our schools today:

1. Inability really to communicate in English. I am sure that you understand the implication of my phraseology; not one of you will be fooled by the child who can read—or say—words he does not understand. You will remember that, until a boy or girl knows the meaning of what he is reading or saying, he does not know a language and cannot communicate.

2. A poor self-image resulting generally from the fact that he has been made to feel ashamed of his cultural heritage.

3. Poor food and clothing.

4. Poor health or malnutrition.

5. Poor housing.

"However, the *most* serious problem this child can encounter in school is a teacher who is blind to his difficulties, who dislikes him as a person, and who makes no effort to break the barriers which separate him from the life of the school. Today, an increasing number of teachers sincerely want to help these children—or I would not have been invited here. Many of the more experienced teachers in your school have already developed effective methods for 'getting through' to these children.

"To those of you who are less experienced and feel baffled, let me make some concrete suggestions:

1. You *can* understand that each child has problems.

2. You *can* become familiar with the particular problems of each child by learning about *his* background and home conditions.

3. You *can* go out of your way to emphasize communication in the classroom—between you and the child, the child and others with similar problems, the child and the class. If the child has particular difficulty in observing, listening or speaking, you *can* help him. Your colleagues, will, in future meetings, give you specific suggestions—and methods they have developed.

4. You *can* help the child to feel that he is an accepted, acceptable, and worthwhile individual. You can raise his self-esteem and consciously foster pride in his cultural heritage.

"Are you disappointed that I have no panacea for your problems with these boys and girls? *Teaching* is a complicated process; it involves knowing many theories, methods, and techniques. Yet *learning* takes place in a relationship between one individual and another. If you can develop a relationship in which learning is possible, you can successfully reach and teach disadvantaged children! A Spanish-speaking child will work hard *for* you if he feels that you are *for* him; he will work *against* you if he feels disdain or lack of understanding. It is hoped that you will teach him: to feel worthwhile as a person, to know who he is as a Mexican and to be proud of this heritage, and to communicate what he knows effectively — in speaking, reading, and writing. After he has been taught this, he will be better equipped, intellectually and emotionally, to solve life's problems and to profit from the opportunities that will become available to him."

CHAPTER 5

Juan Is Going to Be in My Room!

"I knew it! The thing I most dreaded all summer—Juan Chavez is going to be in *my* room! When Mr. Jackson handed me my class list for the new year, the name *Juan Chavez* might as well have been lit up in neon lights, the way it stood out from the rest. Yes, that's the way I felt about Juan in September!" Thus Mrs. Branson began the teachers' meeting at which she had agreed to discuss Juan. She continued her story,

"The previous year I had watched this child. How could anyone help watching him? He was the constant center of storm on the playground—running, yelling, galloping, shouting, fighting, kicking. As soon as Juan appeared, chaos descended—little girls fled screaming if he looked at them. Boys went running to tell the teachers, 'Juan is fighting again.' His greatest delights were either vigorously pounding everyone within reach or being pounded himself. And he was only a first grader then!

"Juan's teacher last year had the sympathy of all of us. She was so patient with Juan. None of us could understand it—but she actually seemed fond of him! She would admit, though, that his attention span was nonexistent and that he was a constantly disruptive influence in the classroom because he pestered the other children *all* the time.

"How can you be so patient? What do you mean—'He's really a sweet child?' How on earth can you even *stand* him? I know *I* never could." His last year's teacher heard such comments a hundred times!

"And now he's going to be *mine?* What on earth am I going to do? He's too much for anyone! A problem child? Juan Chavez is the absolute epitome of the term: 'Everyone in his neighborhood knows that dirty, feisty Mexican brat!'

121

"Then, I tried to think of Juan in a different way. The day before school began, I still didn't know what to do about him, but I had found out some things about him which helped me to understand what made him behave as he did. And then I thought: maybe he's grown up some during the summer and settled down a bit! Oh, I know that's just whistling in the dark—but it helps to start off with a positive attitude!

"In the past, I've found that, if I kept a day-by-day record on a child, sometimes I could find a clue as to *why* he behaved as he did. Since I hadn't come up with any better idea, I tried this with Juan. I began by writing down what I had recently learned about him."

WHAT I LEARNED ABOUT JUAN'S BACKGROUND

Juan is a seven-year-old boy from a Mexican family. Though he acts like a demon, he looks like a small Italian cherub. He has enormous brown eyes and an infectious grin with two deep dimples. The other boys in class are all taller than Juan; so are most of the girls. But his short body is very sturdy, his muscles well developed, and he is much stronger than his size would indicate.

His clothes usually come from the school clothing bank or from some relative. Occasionally, he will have a new pair of shoes—when his toes are far enough out of the old ones. His clothes rarely look as though they had been washed—and often he doesn't either. In fact, some dirt is so ground in, especially on his hands, that it is probably a permanent part of his skin. When his hair gets very shaggy, his mother puts a bowl on his head and gives him a most distinctive haircut.

There are 13 children living with Juan's mother in a three-room shack. At the moment, Juan's father is in jail for non-support of his family, and they are on welfare. Apparently, family conditions are seldom good. Twice during last year, Juan's father was put in jail for beating his mother and chasing her with a knife. This was printed in the local paper. In between these episodes, his father seems to live at home and work as a laborer, sporadically and as little as possible.

The family diet consists largely of beans and tortillas, with candy and cakes when they have money to buy them. The home is so overcrowded, dirty, and depressing that Juan's mother spends as much time as possible away from it. The children run wild. She doesn't care whether they go to school or not. His sisters, in the sixth, seventh, and eighth grades of our school, attend, on an average, two or three days a week. They say that they stay home to baby-sit (when the truant officer checks on them). Actually, they don't like school and prefer to watch TV. One brother, three years older than Juan, has had a terrible reputation for behavior all through school. Juan's oldest brother is a high-school drop-out and has been in trouble with the juvenile authorities. The younger ones—in first, second, third, and fourth grades—often come to school sick—or with drippy noses and coughs. In the winter, all of them wear ragged sweaters which they are always losing. A favorite reason for missing school in the winter is, "I ain't got no boots."

The children in Juan's family are accustomed to hearing Spanish spoken at home. Juan *can* speak some English, although his vocabulary is limited, and he has difficulty in pronouncing many words. But Juan has no hesitation in speaking—or shouting, I should say—and he makes himself understood very well! In fact, communication with him is one-sided; he does the talking— you listen. Juan has never learned to listen to anyone or anything! Perhaps, just to survive at home, he has to be constantly aggressive verbally as well as in actions.

JUAN'S FIRST DAYS OF SCHOOL

First day: Juan wouldn't stay in his seat. He was continually in motion— walking around, talking and laughing loudly. He pounded the boy behind him because the boy touched his desk. He had a fight in the bathroom; he started three fights in line when we were going in or out to the playground. He twisted a girl's arm. He got out of line and tried to force his way into a place he wanted. I said that we were going to have to learn better manners so that we would have a nice room in which to work and enjoy ourselves: then he was requested to go the end of the line. He went—protesting loudly all the way that he didn't do anything; it was all another boy's fault!

Second day: I'm sure that Juan's attention span is less than five seconds—it is gone before I finish speaking his name!

The Principal came to get Juan and Bob for fighting and for beating a first-grader on the playground. They were both paddled. Both promised to behave themselves.

Fourth day: Juan had to be told not to write his name on someone else's paper; he erased the original name and handed in the paper as his finished work.

Also, all in one day, he had to be told not to throw pencils, not to pound people, not to choke them, not to knock things off other people's desks on purpose, and, of course, not to wander around, and not to shout so loudly.

WHAT I LEARNED FROM OBSERVATIONS OF JUAN

"Talk about a challenge! During that first week, I was thinking that either I find a way to reach this boy or I abdicate my authority and let him take over the classroom. He talked incessantly, mostly in a shout or roar. His unbounded nervous energy was manifested in undesirable attempts to make everyone notice him all the time."

Observing: Whatever comes within range of two or three feet from wherever Juan happens to be distracts him. Whether or not it has anything to do with him or with work he is supposed to be doing, he calls it to the attention of everyone with a loud bellow, "Hey, look! Bob is shewing gum!" "Hey!

Lookit! There's a bug. He's gonna get you, Kathy!" "Hey! Who put this paper on my desk? It ain't mine. Is it yours, Roy? John, is it yours? I'm gonna tear it up and throw it away 'cause it ain't mine." On the other hand, Juan observes nothing beyond his personal sphere of operations.

Listening: Juan's attention span is so short that, even if I stand right in front of him and try to explain something, it doesn't penetrate. I was explaining the function of a placeholder in math the other day. After the other children had begun to work independently, I went to Juan's desk and asked if he could tell me why a placeholder was used in the problem. "What placeholder? What's a placeholder? I never heard about no placeholder." I showed him on his paper where the placeholder was—"Do you see this little box, Juan?"

"Hey! Lookit! There's my pencil on the floor!"

"No, it isn't your pencil because you have yours in your hand."

"Where? Here? Oh, yeah, here."

"Now, please look at this, Juan—"

"You mean that box?"

"Yes, that's what I mean. Now the reason for this—"

"Kathy ain't doin' her work. She's lookin' at me. Quit it Kathy!" He tried to hit her.

"Juan, if you don't listen to me, you won't be finished when it's time to go out to play—and we want you to play with us. So get busy now!"

"Busy? Who? Me? O.K., O.K., I'll get busy. What do I do? What am I s'posed to do? How can I do it if I don't know how?"

"That's exactly what I've been trying to do, Juan—help you to know what to do." He finally listened long enough to grasp the idea.

Speaking: This is one area in which Juan unquestionably has no difficulty. His vocabulary is limited and his pronunciation weird, but he has absolutely no hesitation, ever, about putting his thoughts into words. On the contrary, he talks all the time about everything in as loud a voice as possible. He can't bear not to have everyone hear what he has to say.

Reading: Juan can't settle down or focus his attention on the book long enough to keep the place, although he is always demanding his turn to read. He does know quite a few words, even though he usually pronounces them incorrectly. This doesn't faze him; he just makes excuses when you try to correct him— and doesn't listen to the correct pronunciation! If I can keep him still long enough to read a whole sentence, his comprehension is usually good. He enjoys anything humorous; he laughs loudly and frequently. He also is constantly poking, punching, or kicking the other boys—all in good fun!

Relationship to Other Adults: Mostly, Juan ignores grownups unless he wants them to notice something. Then, it is absolutely impossible to ignore him. He is not afraid of anyone as far as I can see!

Social Activity: Juan wants to be with other children all the time. He loves to pound on everybody in sight; and he doesn't mind being pounded back. His idea of a good time is to run up to a crowd of children, throw himself on one or two of them and drag them to the ground with him—laughing uproariously all the while that he is kicking and pounding. He doesn't understand why other people frown on his fun!

With the exception of a few rough boys, the other children don't like the way he plays; but they don't seem to dislike him personally. On the playground, most of them try to keep out of his way whenever possible; but, in the class-room, they are quite willing to be friendly and to help him if he wants help. I wouldn't say, however, that he has any *good* friends.

The things that bother *me* the most about him are:
1. His attention span is almost non-existent;
2. He doesn't know how to listen;
3. When out of my sight, he is inevitably fighting;
4. In the classroom, he is a constant source of annoyance and interruption for the other children; and
5. He won't obey.

Well, that's a pretty grim list. To be fair, I'd better list his good qualities.
1. Great energy,
2. Keen sense of humor,
3. Enthusiasm about anything he likes,
4. A good mind. (He can think and reason if he tries.)

He reminds me of a miniature tornado! If I can just find a way to harness that tremendous energy or to turn it into acceptable channels—

I've thought and planned and stayed awake nights considering those five things about Juan that bother me most. His attention span and inability to listen should improve if I start to train them. He certainly isn't the first child who has had to learn to listen! And one reason for his short attention span, I think, is that he's immature for his age. Both these areas should respond to treatment if I can do something about his behavior first.

Why does he fight and yell and bother others all the time? Well, the obvious reason is that he desperately needs attention. He seems to need it so badly that he doesn't care whether it's approval or displeasure which he incurs. Wait a minute—how do I know he doesn't care? Did anyone ever give him approval—or even notice anything nice that he does? He's just been that "dirty Mexican brat" whom no one could stand! Displeasure seems to be the only kind of reaction he knows how to invoke. Maybe, just maybe, he could be trained to learn how to be noticed for the nice things he does. He might learn to like approbation better than the negative attention he gets now. Anyway, it's worth a try. He is about to be noticed anytime he does the smallest thing right!

That brings me to the last problem—he won't obey. Well, has he ever learned how to obey? Has he been told exactly what was expected of him, then had someone check to see whether he did it and reward or punish him accordingly? I doubt it. I imagine that, in his home, he constantly has people order him to do things—he is roughly in the middle of 13 children—but I wonder whether anyone ever follows through to see if he obeys. I'll have to be sure that I do.

Just because I plan to give him attention and approval when he does things the right way doesn't mean that he is automatically going to obey me or do what I want. So, along with praise and attention, he is going to get a large dose of firmness. He is going to learn that I mean business when I tell him to do something; he is going to find out that I check to see if he has obeyed me. If he has and has done his task well, my genuine approbation will, I hope, teach him, eventually, that there is more pleasure in obedience than in disobedience; and that listening to directions and doing what you are told to do earns a reward worth the effort of trying!

Classroom Observations from the Third Through Ninth Weeks of School

Third Week of School. Juan has been doing nothing; he will not stay in his seat. In one hour of independent work yesterday, his total accomplishment was to write his name on *one* paper. Since he had been told that, if a certain paper was not finished by recess, he would have to stay in and do it, he stayed in and did it. He still seldom listens to directions. However, I have begun praising him for anything possible that he does right, if it's only getting his desk cleared off first. In this case, I announce to the whole class, "Do you notice how fast and *quietly* Juan got ready? I wish you could all do that well."

One morning in the reading group he shouted, "Can I read, huh? Can I? Can I?"

"No, I'm sorry, Juan, you are being too noisy. If you keep the place and stay quiet, I will choose you in a minute." – – – – "Do you have the place now, Juan?"

"Oh, huh? Yeah! Here it is—just a minute."

"I'm sorry, you still don't have it, so it can't be your turn yet. My, I like the way Paco and Joe are keeping the place. That's why they know so many words." This elicited smiles from Paco and Joe.

Juan said, "I have the place, too. See, I have it right here."

"Yes, I'm glad you do. Now it can be your turn to read. – – – – That was a good reading, Juan. Did the rest of you notice the way Juan knew that hard word, *here*."

Paco said, "I knew it, too."

And Joe chimed in, "Me, too."

"Yes, that's because you keep the place all the time."

Fourth Week. Juan is beginning to do a little work; but he tries to convince me that it's *all* finished.

"I finished all my work."

"That's fine. Juan, did you do your arithmetic paper?"

"Yeah."

"Where is it? I don't see it here with the others." (I knew he hadn't done it.) Juan put his finger on his chin and looked at the ceiling in an attitude of puzzlement. "Oh, uh, oh, yeah." (He opened his desk.) "Here it is!"

"Fine, now you get to work and finish it, please. O.K.?"

"O.K."

The next day: I have a regular policy of giving directions for our seatwork the first thing in the morning. I have two exceptionally bad listeners, so I alternate in having them repeat the directions. "Now, Juan, can you tell us what we are supposed to do? Just in case somebody doesn't understand it?"

"Yeah, you said to do our equations first 'cause you might 'rase the board."

"That's exactly right. I'm so pleased that Juan is getting to be such a good listener. He used to have trouble listening – but he's getting better all the time." He beamed with pleasure.

Fifth Week. Juan is trying to finish his work. He comes to show me every time a paper is complete. I always praise him and urge him to finish another one. Sometimes he does – but sometimes he just plays. On Friday, we had a math test. He sat for half an hour and did *one* out of 48 problems. (I knew he could do them.) I bawled him out and said he would *have* to do better if he was going to belong to our class of good workers. That afternoon, he got 100% on a test.

I have discovered that I must maintain exactly the right balance between praise or attention and firmness. He certainly needs to know that I mean business! I am generous in my praise of his good work; but I expect the work to be done – correctly too.

I'm trying hard to build a good relationship with him so he will know that I like him; but I want also to have him know that I won't put up with disobedience. Whatever I say I'll do, I *must* do. I had to remember this the other day: He played during work time; I told him to do his work like everyone else or he would have to take it home. He took it home but didn't bring it back the next day. I was going to overlook this when I overheard him bragging to another boy, "Ha! Ha! She told me to take my work home and do it – but I didn't do it, and she can't do nothing about it!"

I waited until recess; then, as we lined up to go out, I handed Juan another paper to do and said, "Please take your work from yesterday to the office and do it while we go to play. If you can't work when we do, you can't play when we do either."

He took the paper and did it. I praised him for finishing it and said, "Next time I know you'll work when we all do so we can have a good time together."

"Yeah."

Sixth Week. Juan is beginning to want to be noticed for keeping the place, for good work, and for other positive behavior. If I don't notice him, he reminds me. "Look! I have the place."

"Yes, I see, Juan, I'm very pleased with the way you've been keeping it lately. Your reading is much better, too. If you all (in the reading group) keep doing such a good job, I'll ask Mr. Jackson to come and listen to you read."

Paco whooped, "Oh, boy!" and Juan said, "Can I be first when he comes?"

"We'll see, Juan."

One afternoon, Juan brought in a caterpillar on a leaf. "Can we put it in the jar so it can hatch like the others?"

"Yes, you may put it in." I try to give them a variety of experiences in class in order to develop their powers of observation.

October 3: Juan still plays roughly; he either pounds people or lets them pound him. At recess this morning, I cautioned him, "Juan, please don't be so rough; someone will get hurt."

"O.K."

Yet he wasn't out of my sight before he began again—throwing people on the ground and hitting them. There haven't been two consecutive days since school started that he hasn't jumped on someone as we line up!

I don't like his fighting and I try to discourage it, but I can certainly understand it. At home, he either fights for something he has and wants to keep, or his older brothers take it away! His father—when he's home—even encourages the children to fight each other—or anybody else.

He himself whips the children for any kind of disobedience or talking back—or just because he's drunk. He also beats Juan's mother when he has been drinking. So, of course, Juan thinks it necessary to fight constantly—someone smaller, someone his own size, or even someone bigger (if he thinks he can win). Violence is the only way of life he knows; and he's far from convinced that our way at school is better!

The other day, Juan said, "Teacher, will you keep this little flashlight I got, for me?"

I said, "Why don't you take it home, Juan, so you won't lose it?"

" 'Cause Mario will take it away from me," he said, matter-of-factly. "He always takes my things if he wants 'em." I kept it for him.

October 4: Juan was exceptionally good all morning. (The first time since school started!) He kept his place in reading, didn't talk unless it was his turn, and finished all his work. I was very pleased and praised him. Even the other children noticed. Laura said, "Juan's really being good today, isn't he?"

I said, "Yes, he certainly is, and I'm very proud of him."

Then, just before afternoon recess, he began throwing his pencil. He hit a little girl in the head with it. Yesterday I had warned him about throwing pencils. (He'd been doing it for several days previously.) I told him that I would have to have him spanked if he didn't stop it, because it was dangerous.

I said, "Juan, what did I tell you yesterday about throwing pencils?"

"You said you would have me spanked if I didn't stop it."

"Yes, that's right. I hate to have to do it because you were such a good boy this morning, but you just can't seem to remember how dangerous this is. So I guess we'll have to go down to the office and help you to remember."

As we started out the door, he said, "Am I gonna get paddled?"

I said, "Well, that's what I said would happen if you didn't remember, isn't it? I don't know how else I can help you remember, because you don't pay any attention when I tell you."

"I'll 'member. I will."

"That's what you said yesterday, but you didn't remember today."

"Am I gonna get paddled lots?"

"No, you have been a very good boy today and I am very proud of you. I'm going to tell Mr. Jackson what a good boy you have been and how pleased I am with you. You will get one swat to help you remember—not to punish you."

When we walked into the office, Mr. Jackson automatically reached for his paddle and began to frown. (Juan has been a regular visitor in the office for a long time.)

I said, "Mr. Jackson, I would like to tell you what a good boy Juan has been today. He has followed directions, finished all his work, and done everything I asked him. I am very proud of him."

"That's very good to hear, Mrs. Branson. I like to hear things like that about my boys."

Juan broke in nervously, "I ain't s'posed to get punished—only just, I need to 'member."

"What do you need to remember, Juan?"

"Not to throw pencils and hit people."

"Well, how do you think I can help you remember?"

"You could give me just only one swat and I could 'member all right."

"Is it all right with you, if I give you one swat to help you remember?"

"Yeah. It's O.K. with me."

After the one swat was administered, Juan turned around, rubbing his seat, "I'll 'member now."

Mr. Jackson smiled, "I think you will, Juan. I'm certainly glad to hear how much your behavior has improved."

Before Juan went home today, I complimented him again on his behavior.

I am most pleased that Juan trusted me enough to go with me calmly today and to believe what I told him. I absolutely *had* to do what I had said I would; yet I hated to ignore his good behavior—because it's still rare.

October 5: When we finished our reading group today, Kurt, Juan, Joe, and Paco didn't want to go. Paco said, "Aw—let's read some more."

Juan said, "Can't we read one page more? We hardly got to read very much." (The first spontaneous evidence of his interest in learning!)

"I'm sorry, but it's time for the next group to come. Maybe tomorrow we'll have a longer time to read."

October 6: Juan is absent today—about once or twice every other week he doesn't come.

October 8: I was explaining that Norma was absent because she had broken her ankle. I showed the children which part of the foot is the ankle. Juan's eyes widened and he said, "Did her foot fall off?" So we talked about how Bob's hand didn't fall off when he broke his wrist—that only the bones were broken inside.

After reading groups, I was about to tell everyone to clear their desks and fold their hands. I said, "Now—" Juan broke in, "Please don't tell me what to do again. I know—and I'm *so* tired of hearing the same thing."

I said to the class, "Juan is as tired of hearing me say something as I am of saying it. So, if you all watch Juan, you will know what to do and I won't have to tell you." Everyone quickly followed Juan's example. He sat straight up with his hands folded.

"Should I have gotten angry with Juan for his remark? He was telling the truth. He *was* tired of hearing it, and I *was* tired of saying it, so I used the opportunity to give Juan legitimate recognition. He just can't be handled like the other children in the class. First, you have to make up your mind not to get upset or be shocked by his behavior. Then, if possible, turn the child's statements or actions to your advantage. You can—if you are on your toes and think fast!"

Eighth Week. Juan is restless again this morning. At reading group he kept interrupting with irrelevant questions—"Can I pump up my football at recess, can I, huh?"

After reading group, he went to his seat, then raced to the back of the room to get his math paper which he had left on a table, then raced back to his seat. On the way, he tapped everyone he passed on the head. He flopped into his seat and began to work. In a few minutes, he came back to me at the reading table—which is against our rules when another group is reading—and showed me his math paper. "Are they right? All of them? Did I miss any?" I told him it was a good paper and I was pleased that he could do his work now (because he often doesn't do it if he isn't in the mood). I sent him back to his seat to finish his other papers. He hopped up to visit Joe. I told him to go back to his seat. In a few moments, he went to sharpen his pencil; on the way back he stopped to tell me he had only two more papers to do. Why was he so jittery?

Maybe something happened at home to disturb him. I don't ask him what has happened—I just prepare for the worst and try to smooth things out a little.

Sure enough, after school today, Mario, Juan's older brother, came to see me. (We have been friends for several years and he occasionally visits me.)

"Hey! You know what Juan did yesterday? He stole a quart of my Grandpa's beer from the refrigerator. He and some other guys—little ones like him!

They went out behind the shed and drank it all. Boy! Were they sick! Juan got real dizzy and vomited most all night. Was Grandpa mad 'cause he didn't know who took that big bottle!"

"Did you tell him who took it?"

"Boy, not me! Juan knows too many things about me — you know — bad things! I can't never tell on him or he'll tell on me. Like he knows about when I put a rock on the railroad track and the train ran over it; and he seen me stealing stuff from the liquor store. I don't dare tell on him.

"You know what else Juan did? One day last week we was at church. Juan was upstairs in the choir loft and he was spitting over the railing on some guys down below that he didn't like. Right on their heads! My Grandpa caught him that time — and pow! He really hit Juan in the head so he wouldn't do that no more."

"Was that a nice thing for Juan to do — what did you think about it?"

"Well, the fellows he spit on were always calling him a dirty Mexican brat and beatin' him up. You know, people are mean to Mexicans around here. I don't blame him. Sometimes I have to beat guys up myself to make them leave us alone."

October 17: We were ready to stop one lesson and start another. Juan said, "Oh, oh — I can tell — time to clean off our desks." He whisked everything inside his desk.

To the class, I said, "That's right. I'm so pleased that Juan is watching carefully and doesn't have to be told all the time."

Juan straightened up in his seat, with a big grin on his face.

October 20: It was time to listen to instructions on seatwork. All the other children were in their seats with their hands folded. Juan stood up in front of his desk with his hands folded.

"Juan!"

"What's the matter? My hands are folded."

I pointed to his seat. He laughed and sat down. (He loves to tease me or anyone else.)

I had just explained that we would write one equation in each square on our paper. Juan said, "Do we write four equations in one square?"

"Juan wasn't listening today. Who can tell him how many to put in one square?"

There was a chorus of, "one!"

To the class, I said, "You know, usually we are all good listeners, and Juan has been getting better all the time, but today we had to waste too much time getting started. Tomorrow I'm sure we will all be ready to listen right away." (Whenever I have to correct or reprove Juan, I try, at the same time, to say something nice about him.)

During the reading group, Juan came to the word, *happy,* and was trying to figure it out. I said, "How would you feel if Mr. Jackson said we wouldn't have school today?"

"Glad!" Then he clapped his hand over his mouth. "Oops! I mean sad."
I laughed and said, "Well, I wouldn't feel sad. I'd feel happy."
"Oh, happy? You would?"

October 21: The children were trying to define *subsets* in our math class.
"I know! I know!" shouted Juan.
"What are they, Juan?"
"It's when you have two numbers — some over here (he illustrated with his hands) and some over here, and you can put them together and have some more and take them away and it doesn't make any difference."
"Good for you, Juan. That's the right idea."
"What did he say?" asked Laura and Bob.
"He said, if you have two smaller sets and (I illustrated with some books) put them together, you can make a larger set. Then you can take the larger set apart again into the two smaller ones and we call them subsets."
Juan beamed. "Yeah, that's what I meant."

Afternoon: I had to leave the class in the music room for a few minutes. When I returned, Juan and Bob were sitting on the floor in front. The music teacher said they had both misbehaved. When we got back to our own classroom, I said that it was too bad that some of us forgot our manners sometimes and made people think that we didn't have good manners in our room. I added that I was sure that, next time I had to leave, everyone would remember to use his best manners. Juan *is* better about obeying me — but he seldom behaves equally cooperatively with other adults.

October 21: I asked each child in the reading group what they had eaten for breakfast.
Joe said, "I had an egg."
Kurt said he had eaten cereal, and Paco said, "Fried 'tatoes and chili."
"What did you have for breakfast, Juan?"
"I didn't have no brefuss. I wasn't hungry. It was too late, anyways."
"What did you eat yesterday for breakfast?"
"Some beans."
"Did you eat tortillas with them?"
"Yeah."
"You know, I like tortillas and beans, and so does my family. They always like for me to fix them."
"Do you know how to make tortillas?"
"Yes, I do, but I don't think mine are as nice and round as your mother can make them."
"Yeah, she makes good ones."
"How many of you eat tortillas and beans sometimes?"
All the hands went up except Kurt's.
I said, "Maybe one of you could bring a tortilla so Kurt can taste it and see why we like it."
This evoked a chorus of, "I'll bring one!" "No, I will!" "I will!"

I said, "Well, if more than one of you can bring one, we might share them with the people in the other reading groups who have never tasted any."

October 22: Juan, Joe, and Paco had all brought tortillas, so we broke them in pieces and shared them with everyone. I had brought some jam to make them appealing to children who hadn't tasted them before. We talked about how nice it is to try different foods that our friends like, and that often Mexican children like to eat tortillas instead of bread. One of my Hopi boys volunteered to bring some *Piki*—the Hopi bread made from corn rolled in paper-thin sheets. His cousin said he would bring some, too. I said I'd have one of my Navajo friends make us some *fry bread;* and we'd have a real tasting party on Monday.

Ninth Week:
October 25: Well, we had our bread-tasting party this morning. It was fun. One Hopi boy forgot his bread but Bryson remembered and brought three rolls of *Piki* made from blue corn. The children were fascinated by the color, and everyone tasted it. It is very brittle and a little sweet. I had brought some *fry bread* which the Navajos make by dropping squares of dough in hot fat, and letting it puff up and turn brown (very much like Mexican *sopapillas*). I put a little bit of honey on each small piece and distributed the pieces to all the children. The bread was a great success. We talked about how different kinds of bread are good and how nice it is to have so many different kinds of friends who can help us learn about different things—in the hope, of course, that "Mexican brats" and "dirty Indians" would gradually be perceived differently by their Anglo classmates!

October 26: Today was difficult. It began with Juan calling out, "Can I read first? I want to be first." I had already asked Paco to begin.

"No, I'm sorry, Juan, you are too noisy. If you can be quiet for a minute, you may have your turn."

Almost at once, Joe said, "Juan is kicking me!"

Juan laughed and said, "No, I ain't. My foot is just on his chair."

"Well, please put your feet under your chair."

We went on reading. Kurt was stuck on a word. Juan yelled, "I know! I know! It's *new*."

"Thank you, Juan. I'm glad you know it; but I would like it much better if you could remember to raise your hand as the others do."

The one bright spot: During our math seatwork this afternoon, Juan said, "I looked and looked and I don't see *equations* on the board anywhere, but I see some on my paper. How come?" Juan has trouble with many words, but he loves the word *equations*. When it is written on the board, he always tries to be chosen to tell what the word is—and he never misses it. So now I told him.

"That's very good thinking, Juan. You *are* doing some equations, but I wrote *missing addends* on the board instead of equations. I wanted to see if the class knew what that phrase means."

During our afternoon reading, we couldn't read in our regular place. We were also using small benches instead of chairs. Juan grabbed one end of a bench and slid two boys together, laughing uproariously all the time. When I reproved him, he said, "O.K., O.K., I have the place now, see?"

Two people read. Then I chose Juan. "Juan you may be next because you are quiet and keeping the place." In one line, we had the word *wants* and in another line, the word, *wanted*. Juan said them both correctly.

"How did you know those words, Juan? How could you tell which one was *wants* and which one, *wanted?*"

" 'Cause you showed us 'bout *wanted* when we started, and I could see how it looks. And I just know *wants* cause I know 'bout the *s.*"

"That's very good, Juan. I'm most pleased with the way you are paying attention. You're getting to be a good reader." This *is* progress!

Later in the afternoon, the class went to the art room. Juan kept talking in a loud voice, so the art teacher could not begin the lesson. I said to the class, "Why do we have to wait?"

Juan said, "I know. I'm making too much noise. Right?"

"Yes, that's right. Can you remember your manners now?"

"Yes, O.K."

We made Halloween masks. Juan kept putting his on and trying to scare people. He went to the big crayon box, ran his fingers through the crayons and pretended they were money. "I'm rich, rich!" he shouted. Then he jumped on Paco and twisted his arm behind him.

"Juan, would you please take the wastebasket around so we can put our scraps in it?"

"O.K. I will."

"Thank you, Juan." Rather than reprove him repeatedly, I have learned to put him to work. At the end of the day, during spelling, we were changing beginning consonants to form new words.

Juan yelled, "I ain't had a turn! Why don't I get a turn?"

"You are too loud, Juan. If you can be quiet for a minute, you may have a turn." He calmed down.

I guess we're making progress. Juan does try to cooperate—in his way. But just when I think he is settling down to work, we have a day like today when I have to keep after him every minute! Of course, when school started, every day was like this! This is better, but it's still quite a strain to live through a day like this! However, Juan tries to work—sometimes—because he does want to be praised for doing his work. Though he still will attempt to get out of working and try to make me think he has finished! Also, most of the time he will mind *me* now; but he misbehaves for the art teacher and the music teacher constantly to see if they'll *make* him mind. I hear, too, that the minute he is out of my sight, he does as he pleases.

October 27: Another day when Juan has had to assert himself: "Hey! I see *equations* on the board! I see it today!" He ran up and pointed to the word. "Here it is, see!"

As math class began, he shouted, "I don't got any counting sticks."

I gave him some. "I was going to give you both sticks and crayons — as soon as your turn came."

"I can use sticks? Crayons too, if I want?"

"Yes, you can count any way you like."

At reading group: "Can I be first? I want to read first."

"Yes, you kept the place so well yesterday, and were so quiet, you may be first."

Juan read one page.

"That was very good reading, Juan."

He kept right on reading the next page.

"All right, Juan. That's enough for now. Stop reading, please."

He didn't.

"Juan, will you please stop teasing us, and let Paco have his turn?"

"O.K.," he laughed.

During the afternoon, we had a vocabulary test. I pronounced the word *kitten* and said, "A kitten is a baby cat."

Juan said, "I know, *kitten* don't start with a copycat letter *c* like *cat*."

"That's right. That's very good thinking, Juan."

Later we came to *cat*.

"Now it starts with a copycat letter, huh?"

"Yes, Juan, it does."

A little later Juan tried to read *Fun with Our Friends*. He read, "Fun with" — and got stuck on *Our*. I said, "It means it belongs to us."

"Oh — *Our?*"

"Yes, that's right."

"Fun with Our — what's that?"

"What do you call the people you like?"

"Family?"

"That's good thinking again, Juan. You know it begins with *f*, but these are people like Paco and Kurt that you play with. What do you call them?"

"Friends?"

"That's right."

After recess, we continued with Juan's reading group. Juan plopped down in his chair. "Where's Paco? I don't see him nowhere." He threw his arm around Kurt, "Come on, let's go on and read without him." Kurt began. He got stuck on *friends*. I said, "Maybe Juan remembers that word. It means people we like to play with."

"I know! Family! No — no — that's not right. I mean *friends!"*

"Good, Juan."

Kurt was stuck on another word. Juan raised his hand. I called on him to help and commended him for raising his hand instead of shouting. He smiled at me, then suddenly looked me over and yelled, "Hey, you got rocks around your neck!" (My necklace.)

Juan's Halloween surprise: Juan was very excited about the Halloween parade to be held this afternoon. He talked incessantly about it during reading group—but he did remember to raise his hand occasionally.

Then came time for the parade! All the children had some kind of costume for the parade—and the masks that we had made in art. Juan had no costume and refused to wear his mask. "I don't like it. I ain't gonna wear it. I ain't gonna be in the parade." I knew how he felt—the only one without a costume!

Suddenly, Mr. Jackson appeared in the doorway of our room, and beckoned to me. "I have one costume that a lady brought by for any child who doesn't have any, a gorilla costume. But it's a small size. Do you have any children without costumes?"

"Yes, Juan. He is small. Maybe it will fit him. He would love it."

"All right. Let's see if it fits him."

"Juan, would you go with Mr. Jackson, please?"

Juan slowly approached the door, dragging his feet and obviously expecting the worst. You could almost see him going over his recent crimes and wondering which one Mr. Jackson had found out about.

In about five minutes, he came roaring back into the room, dressed as a gorilla. "Hey! I bet you thought I was gonna get paddled, didn't you? I bet that's what you thought, huh?" His relief was evident.

"No, Juan, I knew what Mr. Jackson wanted you for. What did you think he wanted?"

"I thought I was gonna get paddled, but I didn't! He gave me this keen gorilla suit! I get to keep it—I think."

When the parade was over, he said, "Maybe I'd better sheck (check) with Mr. Jackson, and see if I get to keep it, huh?"

"Yes, I think that would be a good idea."

He was back a minute later. "I *do* get to keep it, he said!"

"That's very nice, Juan. Did you remember to thank Mr. Jackson?"

"Yeah. I did."

Are My Methods Working?

It sometimes seems to me that I'm complimenting Juan every other minute; but if I don't, his behavior takes an immediate turn for the worse. He wears me out sometimes; but I'm beginning to understand how his teacher of last year felt. He is a very lovable child. Loud, naughty, boisterous, but lovable! He is basically kind, has a keen sense of humor, a good mind and boundless energy!

Classroom Observations: November Through May

November 2: Juan read a whole page without a mistake. He is using phonics more all the time—especially on beginning consonants. When he was stuck on a word, I said only, "That's our new word."

"I know. I know. Don't tell me!" He sounded it out slowly — "It's *there!*"

"Good for you."

November 8: It was very cold today, but Juan wore only a thin sweater. I asked him if he had a jacket. He said no, so I sent him to the nurse, who gave him a warm jacket which had been donated to our clothing bank. She told me later that she hated to see what happened to the clothes given the Chavez family. They "just get dirtier and more ragged until they are thrown away. Once in awhile, some get washed. But they have a lot of used clothes given to them, so it's easier to just throw them away after awhile! I'm sure that the socks Juan's wearing today could stand up by themselves."

I called Juan's reading group to the table. He came back first. "Ain't nobody gonna read but me?" He grabbed his book, then shouted,

"Somebody took my marker!" He put his head under the table. "It ain't under here." He found it on the floor.

"Can I read first?"

"No, Juan, it isn't your turn. Kurt hasn't read today."

"Oh, shucks. I want to read."

Later it was his turn. He did well. When I told him to stop, he said, regretfully, "That wasn't very much turn!" He really seems to enjoy reading now.

November 16: I said, "Someone is talking."

Juan — "It ain't me. I ain't talking, am I? It ain't me *this* time!"

"No, Juan, it isn't you."

Later that day, another teacher sent him to the office for fighting in the boys' bathroom. When he came back, after being punished, he looked like a thundercloud. "I'm quitting school! I'm moving at noon! I ain't ever coming back!"

The children were horrified. Kathy said, "Juan isn't coming back to school any more!"

Kurt spoke up, "That's right. That's what he said."

"Juan isn't happy right now, but he'll feel better later, and then he'll want to stay with us. Now we'll just leave him alone and not bother him until he feels better."

He sat, staring straight ahead, with his arms folded.

In a few minutes, I made a point of asking him to turn on the lights, then later to erase the board. In a little while, he began to participate in class again. After lunch, he was late in coming back to school. But he did come in — and I relaxed.

November 17: Juan seems very upset about something today (it could be his punishment yesterday). He crumpled his seatwork and threw it in the wastebasket. "I ain't gonna do it," he said for all his neighbors to hear. Two or three of them came to tell me.

"I think he will do it after awhile," I said. "We all know that we need to do our work so we can get ready for third grade. Juan knows that, too."

Then Juan took Donna's seatwork and brought it to me with his name on it. I had him change it. "Juan, I know it's not yours." (Donna is in our top reading group and has very different seatwork.) "Please stop teasing Donna." (Although I knew perfectly well he was trying to get out of doing his own.)

A little later, he brought his wrinkled paper to show me.

"See, I done half of it."

"That's fine, Juan, I'd like to see it when it's all finished."

A little later — "I'm done now. I think it's all right, ain't it?"

I checked it quickly. "Yes, it is. That's fine, Juan. You didn't make any mistakes."

I've learned not to make an issue of Juan's misbehavior unless absolutely necessary — or it immediately gets worse. I ignore it when possible. Most important, if I try to place a positive interpretation on what he did, he is likely to cooperate with me. Of course, I cannot overlook any behavior which could be dangerous to the other children. But if the issue involves doing his work on time or being loud or noisy, usually I can soothe his feelings and, gradually, a positive attitude develops. Sometimes he actually comes to believe he *wants* to do what I want him to!

Patience? It takes absolute, unlimited patience to handle this boy. I don't always have it, if it's been a hard day; but I'm learning that I'd better use as much of it as I can possibly muster! Of course, it's tiresome, having to praise and notice him all the time. Sometimes I think I won't be able to stand it another minute! Then he does something funny or kind, and I relax and see things in perspective! Some days are better than others. I usually can tell as soon as he arrives in the morning what kind of day it will be. If we're in for trouble, I try to prepare for it. But the bad days are getting fewer. He knows I like him — but he also knows that I will be firm with him. I seem to have convinced him that I mean business so that now he usually minds me promptly. And he's getting to like the firmness — in fact, to depend on it because, as a result of my insistence that he do something, he is finding out that he can do things.

November 29: Juan dashed in after having been out for a week and a half with chicken pox.

"I'm back! I'm back! See, I'm back! You know why I didn't come?"

"Yes, I know. You had chicken pox. We all missed you."

"Well, I'm back now."

When we gathered in our reading group, he asked eagerly, "Can I read first? I ain't read for a long time. Can I read now?"

Juan was given first turn to read. He read very well. I said, "I guess Juan stayed home and ate reading pills when we all thought he was sick. He is such a good reader today."

He laughed. "I did practice sometimes." (So he's really become interested in learning!)

He raised his hand several times to help someone. Each time, I praised him, "I wish we could all remember to raise our hands the way Juan does."

November 30: "Can I read? Can I read, huh? I got a good loud voice. I can read loud."

"Yes, I know you can read loud, Juan."

"Can I be first today?"

"All right, you may be first because you are the first one to have the place."

Afterward, I said, "Do you know, Juan, you read so well today, I think you can go read to Mr. Jackson?"

"Can I go now?"

"Why don't you practice a story first? Choose one you like, and I'll help you with the words. Then you can be sure you know them."

"Can I practice now?"

We were finished with our reading; so I took a few minutes to listen to him. Then we went down to the principal's office. Fortunately, Mr. Jackson had a few minutes right then to listen. Juan was nervous on the first page. He gripped the book tightly and missed some words he knew. Gradually, however, he relaxed and read much better. Mr. Jackson praised his efforts. On the way out, Juan said, "Can I read to Mrs. Brown today?" (Mrs. Brown was his teacher last year.)

"I'll ask her as soon as I see her, Juan. Whenever she has time to listen, you may go."

She was able to hear him this afternoon after school.

December 1: "Yesterday, I didn't miss no words when I read to Mrs. Brown."

"Yes, she told me. I'm very pleased with you. Did you read to your mother or brothers or sisters last night?"

"Naw. They didn't have time."

In reading group that afternoon, we ended with Paco's having only a few lines to read. I said, "Paco, you got cheated today because you only have to read a few lines, so you may be first tomorrow."

Juan laughed. "Paco got sheated! Did you hear that, Kurt? He got sheated. That's funny! He gets to be first 'cause he got sheated." I must work with those children on the *sh* and *ch* sound! Spanish-speaking children always have difficulty with these.

December 2: All during the year, I have tried to emphasize the contributions to American life of various cultures represented by children in our room. Since it is getting close to Christmas, we talked today about different Christmas carols and Christmas customs. I explained to the children about the Mexican custom of "Las Posadas" where a group of singers pretending to be the Holy

Family go from house to house seeking "a room in the inn." At each house they are turned away, to be accepted at last at a prearranged place where refreshments are served. We dramatized "Las Posadas" as our music teacher helped us learn the song "Vamos Todos a Belen."

December 3: Yesterday, we had group IQ tests. The result of Juan's tests were an IQ of 80 on the verbal and 95 on the non-verbal. Of course, I question such "results."

December 6: Juan wanted to sit in a different seat from his assigned one. He tried out a new one. "Can I sit here? It fits me better." His feet were several inches off the floor.

"I like you better over here where you can help me."

"But I can see the flag better over here for Pledge of 'llegiance."

"All right, you may sit there today, if you can be very quiet and a good worker."

"O.K., I'll be a good worker."

A few minutes later — "I'm a good worker. See, I'm good. I got good manners, and I ain't talking, am I?"

December 7: Juan was in the seat he had chosen the day before. "See how good I am? I got good manners, don't I?"

"Yes, I noticed your good manners, Juan."

When we were reading, Juan began the word *called,* but couldn't figure it out. "Boy, they sure put funny words in this book, don't they?"

"Yes, some are pretty funny all right. This one means he wanted Dick to come — so he did what?"

"Called? Is that it?"

"Yes, that's exactly right. You are a very good thinker when you use your head."

"I didn't hardly miss none, did I? I read pretty good, huh?"

December 8: Juan came running back to the reading table and skidded into his seat. "Oooops! I fell down!"

"Yes, I see you did. Now please write your name on your workbook page."

He hid the workbook under the table. "I can't find it. Where is it? Do you know where it is?"

"No, I don't, but you do, and I'm afraid you can't read until you find it. Paco, you read first."

Juan pulled the book out and found the place — but knocked his chair over. "Paco pulled my shair out!"

"No, he didn't. He isn't even close to you. We are reading now, and I'm afraid that, if you can't get ready to read, you will have to go back to your seat." He sat up at once and began to keep the place.

As we read a page silently, Juan said, "What's this word? Paco, what's this word?" Kurt said, "I don't know it either." Juan shouted, "I can't hear!"

"Do you know why you can't hear? It's because this group is making too much noise."

"I know. I know. May I read? May I read? I know where—may I read?"

"I'm sorry, but I have to choose someone who is quiet."

"I'm quiet, ain't I?"

"I'm afraid not, Juan; but you will be in a minute." A little while later when he had quieted down, I chose him to read. He did very well. "I read good, didn't I?"

"Yes, it was very good. A little later, he was talking again. I said to no one in particular, "You know, I like the way Paco always keeps the place. I never have to remind him."

Juan immediately found the place, and said, "I'm keeping the place nicely, ain't I?"

"Yes, I'm very pleased, Juan. You are doing just what you should."

"Paco's doing good, ain't he?"

"Yes, he is, and so are you, Juan."

December 14: Juan brought me a Christmas card which he insisted I open. I thanked him and put it up above the blackboard where everyone could see it. Then he plunked a butterfly pin down on my desk and said, "Here. You want it?"

It was old and obviously used, but prettily colored and shiny. I thanked him and pinned it on my blouse. He went around pointing it out to the other children. "See, I give it to her."

December 16: Four grades went to the Christmas program in the gym. Juan kept standing up in front of his chair. The third graders behind him couldn't see. I asked him to come to the end of the row by me.

"Why? How come? What did I do?"

I explained that if he couldn't see, since he is the shortest one in the class, he could stand up in the aisle near me when the program began.

Juan seemed to have little understanding of Christmas traditions—songs or stories. He kept asking questions, "Are they gonna sing? Are they gonna have a act? Hey, look! Here they come!"

"Yes, I see them, Juan, but we must be quiet so we can hear them, too."

"Look, those guys with the sheep got spears!" (Shepherd's crooks.) The wise men appeared. Everyone was quiet. Juan said loudly, "They got a treasure shest! What for?"

"When is the play gonna start? Is this it?"

"Hey, look! They shanged the walls (the sets). "She's just pretending to sweep, huh?"

"Is that a boy in that dress?" (The innkeeper.) Then, when the curtains closed, he said, "Is that all? Ain't there no more?"

Afternoon: On Tuesday, we had wrapped the ceramic dishes which we had made for our mothers' Christmas presents. Because I didn't choose Juan to be one of the first four to come to the table where I was helping them wrap, he wouldn't come at all. I didn't force him to. I wrapped his present for him after everyone had gone home. Yesterday, I told the children to take the presents home. Juan said, "I ain't wrapped mine yet."

"I wrapped it for you, Juan."

"Who? You? Oh."

Today, he told me that he had dropped his present on the way home and it had broken. I had made some extras for emergencies. I said, "I'll give you one of these I have left."

"Is it fried?" (Has it been fired in the kiln?)

"Yes, Juan, it's all done and ready to take. We'll wrap it now."

"Oh." He doesn't know how to express appreciation, although he obviously was pleased at my concern for him.

December 21: Juan said, "Do you got girls at your house?"

"Yes, I have two girls."

"Any boys?"

"No, I don't have any boys."

"I know why you don't got any! 'Cause you got enough here at school! Huh?"

"Yes, I guess that must be why." The implication was "And I'm one of them." I am getting through to him!

January 3: "Hey! You're back! I'm back, too!"

"Yes, I see you are, Juan. It's nice to see you again after vacation."

He handed me some polished stones. "Here, if you want 'em."

"Thank you, Juan, they're very pretty." I began to take roll.

Juan—"Did you notice our row? How good it is?"

"Yes, I did. I wish all the rows were as good as Juan's row."

He seems very happy this morning. He has a new shirt and a bowl haircut. I told him how nice he looked.

A few moments later, when I was in the back of the room, he shouted, "Hey, I finished all my work!"

"That's good, Juan, I'm very pleased with you today. You are behaving very nicely."

"Yeah, I am, ain't I?"

January 4: I remarked after lunch that several people didn't seem to have finished their reading seatwork.

Juan said, "I finished."

"Where is your paper?"

"Up there." He waved at my desk.

"I can't seem to find it." I looked at him. We both knew that he hadn't done it.

"I'll look." He dug in his desk, then walked over to the wastebasket, which was full. He put his finger on his chin, looked at the wastebasket, and said, "Well, 'magine that! How do you s'pose my paper got in here?" He began to dig in the trash. Clear at the bottom, he found his paper. He retrieved it. "I better do it."

"Yes, I think you had better."

He did it.

Later in the day, we had a special celebration. At Christmas time, the children had become so interested in the different ways that different people celebrated Christmas that they began asking about other customs and holidays. We had already tasted the foods of other people. We decided next that, once a month, we would have a special day to learn interesting things about the cultures of our classmates. We are planning, for the future, a Hopi Day, a Chinese Day and, most important of all, in Juan's estimation, a Mexican Day.

Today we began our series with a "Navajo Day." We have learned in music class, to sing "Brother John" in Navajo. So our celebration began with this song. Then I read from "Navajo Stories." On our bulletin board, I had displayed several excellent drawings and paintings done by Navajo ex-pupils who are now sixth or seventh graders. These pupils have won awards at the Junior Indian Art Show held each year at our local Museum. After I had read the stories, we talked about the pictures. Then the children tried to make "Indian" pictures of their own as we listened to tape-recorded Navajo songs. These were recorded for me by some seventh grade boys and girls, who were too shy to appear before us in person, but consented to sing for me alone at home and to allow me to tape the songs. One boy played a drum accompaniment to furnish the rhythm.

"Mr. Gonzales had emphasized to the teachers the importance of teaching Mexican children about their cultural heritage; he talked of the close relationship between their self-esteem and their pride in being Mexican. I know how right he is! I saw, dramatically illustrated, in Juan's behavior today the effect of such study."

February 8: The great day has arrived—our Mexican Day! Juan has asked me at least once daily, since our Navajo day, if I'm sure we're going to have a Mexican one next. I have been assuring him that we were. Actually, I hadn't planned to have it so soon, but Juan and Paco and several of the others were so excited at the prospect that I moved it up to get peace and quiet! For several weeks, we have been reading stories about Mexican children and Mexican customs. Our bulletin board is decorated with colorful pictures and Mexican travel posters. Our art teacher has helped us make our own papier-maché and crepe paper *piñata*—a gorgeous, multicolored burro which I filled with wrapped candies, gum, and small toys from the dime store. This magnificent object, suspended from the ceiling, has been the center of attraction all day. All day long, Juan has shown it off to anyone he could drag to the door to look at it.

"Hey, Mrs. Brown! That's our *piñata!* We made it our ownself! We're gonna bust it pretty soon. Boy, am I gonna hit it hard! Whammo!" (He illustrated with an imaginary stick.)

We've made quite an occasion of this day because there are more children of Mexican background than any other in our classroom this year, and also because I am more familiar with Mexican food and customs and better able to help in this cultural area than in others.

The children all arranged to have lunch at school. Two mothers, Mrs. Sanchez and Mrs. Gomez, came in to help me serve tacos, tostados, and Spanish rice, which they had prepared beforehand. Mrs. Sanchez told the class how to fix this food.

Yesterday, Juan, Paco, and Joe had gone to invite Mr. Jackson to have lunch with us. "Be sure to tell him what kind of a lunch we're having, boys."

When they returned, I asked Juan what they had told him.

"We said, 'We came to 'vite you to eat lunch with our class tomorrow — it's gonna be Mexican food 'cause tomorrow is 'Mexican Day' in our room. Did you know that?' "

"And what did he say?"

Juan shouted, "He said, 'That's very int'resting'; and were we sure he was s'posed to come, and we said, 'Yeah, we came to 'vite you so you'd know.' "

Paco chimed in, "And he said he wouldn't miss it for nothing, and he's really coming!"

After we had eaten our food and cleaned up our room, we all sang "Brother John" (Hermano Juan) and "El Rancho Grande" in Spanish for the two mothers and Mr. Jackson. Juan always sings loudly and enthusiastically (if he likes the song) and he certainly could be heard today! Then Mr. Garcia, from the sixth grade, and another teacher, both dressed in serapes and sombreros, came in and played their guitars and sang several songs for us.

Next, we played a word game on the blackboard. I wrote numerous common (to us here in the Southwest) Spanish words on the board for the children to guess their meanings. I divided the class into two teams and made sure there were Mexican children on both teams, so neither team would have an advantage over the other. I used such words as *burro, lariat, corral, frijoles, tortillas, tacos, tostados, rodeo, tomatoes* and *chili.* I always gave the non-Spanish speaking children the first chance to guess a word's meaning. The game ended in a tie and everyone was happy.

The highlight of the afternoon was the breaking of the piñata and the scramble for the surprises! I need not describe the excitement! I am worn out after it all! From the children's point of view, Mexican Day was an unqualified success.

Notes at the End of February: I haven't been making many entries lately because Juan has improved so much in the classroom. He really seems to be trying to work and do what is expected of him — at least three or four days a week he will finish all his work. And I never fail to notice his effort. Once in a while, though, he reverts to his old behavior patterns. I still have to be on the lookout for regression — although occasionally I relax a little. (One day, when I was ill, he behaved abominably for the substitute.) He will challenge any new authority. He minds me very well and will mind Mr. Jackson; but he still doesn't usually mind teachers on the playground. We haven't been able to convince him that he is supposed to obey them, too. Oh well, who expected miracles? In class, he had only one really bad day this month. He was wound up like a top. He ran, shouted, poked, and refused to work. The next day he was back to normal — his new normal, that is!

March 7: Today was one of the few days Juan has had money to eat in the cafeteria. He was sitting next to a Navajo boy who had just come to us from the reservation. Ben is a new first grader; he speaks *very* little English, but he tries hard. Ben picked up one of the damp dishtowels we use to wipe the tables, and with an impish look in his eye, said, "Wet dopper!"

I said, "No, Ben, that isn't a wet diaper. It's a clean cloth to wipe the table."

Juan spoke up, "Smell it, Ben. It don't smell like a wet diaper."

Ben held it up to his nose and inhaled strongly. Still teasing, he said, "Phew! Wet dopper!"

March 23: The children were reading silently, after the new words had been introduced. Juan suddenly began to count out loud. "One, two, three, four, five, six, seven, eight, nine, ten — ten more pages." He went on, "I ony got to read once. It's my turn again."

I said, "I don't want to hear anything while we read to ourselves."

"The party's over, huh, teacher?"

"Yes, it is. We have to work now."

After we had finished our reading, Juan suddenly asked, "What is the Golden Rule, anyway?"

"It just says that we should treat other people the way we want them to treat us. For instance, it means that, if you wouldn't like Kurt to kick you under the table, then you shouldn't kick him the way you just did."

"I didn't kick him hard!"

"Would you like him to kick you?"

"No."

"Then you shouldn't kick him at all."

April 13: Juan came quietly back to the reading group, sat down, and was ready to read. I commented on his good work habits. We have been working for some time now on the pronunciation of *ch*. Juan sometimes says *sh* and sometimes manages to say *ch*. Today he said, "This is *sh*ildren — is that right?"

I said, "*Ch*ildren" — and showed him with a mirror how to use his tongue to say the *ch* correctly.

"*Sh*ildren? *Ch*ildren?"
"That's right, Juan, you are getting better all the time."
He said, "*Sh*erry Street — *Sh*erry Street?"
"*Ch*erry Street."
"Yes, *Ch*erry Street, is that right?"
"Good for you. Yes, that's right."
"*Sh*erry?"
"No, *Ch*erry."
"Sherry — *Ch*erry."
"That's right. It takes a lot of practice to be able to say it right."

"Sometimes children have become so accustomed to their way of saying certain sounds that they really cannot distinguish the different sound the teacher is trying to teach. If a person said to you, "Here, tune this piano," you would probably think he was out of his mind. Most of us couldn't tell if the instrument were sharp or flat. The Spanish-speaking child finds himself in the same predicament when, for example, he is asked to distinguish between a short *i* and a short *e*. To his ear, they sound the same. His ear must be trained to hear the differences and similarities just as most of us would have to be trained in order to tune a musical instrument properly.

"It is very common for a Spanish-speaking child to say *heet* for *hit*, *leave* for *live, heem* for *him,* etc. However, the mispronunciation most common in Mexican children is the substitution of *sh* for *ch: shop (chop), shimney, shair.* This is probably due to the fact that English-speaking people use their tongues a great deal in articulating words, while Spanish-speaking people place a much greater emphasis on the lips.

"For example, examine your pronunciation of *ch*. Stand in front of a mirror and watch yourself as you say *children*. The tip of the tongue is pressed against the back of the teeth, effectively shutting off the passage of air from the throat. On the other hand, if you pronounce *shildren,* the tongue is not held against the teeth and does not interfere with the breath which goes across the tongue, between the teeth, and out through the protruding lips. Therefore, I had to show these children by example, and by looking in a mirror, where to put their tongues. This particular incorrect speech habit can be overcome through practice."

April 15: Juan looked up from his reading. "I can say *shair.*"
"*Ch*air."
"*Ch*air!"

"That's perfect, Juan! You do it exactly right!"

He leaned over to whisper in Kurt's ear, "Chair, chair, chair, chair."

Kurt complained, "Teacher, Juan's buggin' me."

"All right, Juan, your pronunciation is good, but Kurt doesn't want to hear it any more."

A little later, we were reading aloud. Juan came to the word, *Cherry,* and pronounced it exactly right. He looked at me to see if I had noticed. I remarked. "You got it just right this time, and I didn't even have to tell you. Now, Bob, you say it."

"*Cherry.*"

"Good, you try it, Paco."

"*Sherry?*"

"No, *Cherry.*"

"*Cherry.*"

"That's very good." I explained to these boys again that they had special trouble in saying *ch* because they were used to speaking Spanish and didn't use the *ch* sound. I said how nice it was that they could speak two languages. Paco said, "I can say lots of Spanish words."

"Yes, I know you can, and so can Juan and Bob (Roberto). You have to be very smart to be able to speak two languages."

"We have talked many times about the abilities of children in our class to use different languages. Some can speak Navajo, some Hopi, several Spanish, one Chinese, and—for a couple of months—we had a girl who had just come from Austria.

"The whole class learned a few words in each language and we had learned at least one song in each language represented in our classroom. We consistently tried to emphasize everyone's special cultural contribution to our class. The children themselves called to my attention each other's different abilities and backgrounds and suggested ways in which the class could utilize them. Such a response from the children has reemphasized for me what Mr. Gonzales said earlier, namely that a child of a cultural background different from that of many of his classmates is helped tremendously to feel accepted in school if he learns that his culture—and he—are respected by his classmates and are interesting to them. This experience has certainly helped Juan to become 'ready' to learn. My final entry demonstrates Juan's present attitude."

May 18: Juan came up to me, "Can our reading group be first, huh?"

"Yes, I think so."

"Oh, boy! I love to be first! You know why? 'Cause I really like to read."

WHAT HAS JUAN LEARNED THIS YEAR?

"I don't think more entries are necessary. We did both manage to survive this year—Juan and I. I couldn't say which of us learned more. There's no denying that it was a strenuous year! Yet it was enjoyable. I wouldn't have believed when it started that I would really be sorry to see Juan leave with the rest of the class, but I'll miss his happy grin, enormous energy, and very prevalent, but lovable personality.

"When I think back to the beginning of the year, there are some real differences apparent between Juan then and now":

Observation: Juan's range of observation has been broadened to include all the happenings in our room, anything he can see from our windows, and everything along the way to and from school, though I'll have to admit—the less it has to do with work, the more he notices it! And he still calls it loudly to everyone's attention!

Listening: This is one area of real progress: Juan's attention span has increased tremendously. I can't take all the credit; I think part of it was maturation. He was really still a baby in many ways when he came to me! However, part of it *was* training. At first, several times daily, I had him repeat directions to me or tell the rest of the class what was said. My using these techniques made him begin to listen. I tried also to remove distracting influences whenever he needed to concentrate on work. Most important, patiently, day by day, I tried to give him a reason for listening: by praising him instantly whenever he listened, or kept his place, or knew what I had said.

Speaking: This was one area in which Juan had absolutely no difficulty—in spite of his limited vocabulary, poor pronunciation and bad grammar. He still uses incorrect forms; but he knows and uses many more words correctly. Some of our language lessons have been especially effective: he is very careful about helping words, about saying, "My brother and I"—and he has accomplished the herculean task of being able to pronounce *ch!*

Reading: I am proud of Juan's accomplishments in reading. He has read a junior primer, a primer, a first reader, and well into a second reader—as well as many small, easy story books. His last statement speaks for itself as to how he feels about reading. He loves it! Mr. Jackson sat in on several of our last class periods and commented on Juan's improvement.

Relationship to Other Adults: Juan is much friendlier to adults than he used to be; but, I'm sorry to say, he still doesn't admit that many of them have any authority over him! He still gives the teachers on the playground a hard time. He does behave a little better for the art and music teachers.

Social Activity: A social individual, Juan has always been and will always be — as are so many Mexican-Americans! Juan does display his enthusiasm for people in more socially acceptable ways now. He seems to realize at last that we just *do not* jump on little girls, pound them, kick them, or twist their arms, although he still loves to chase them and hear them scream. Maybe someday he will stop being rough with boys, too, but I'm not sure about this. He now has two or three boys that he plays with most of the time — but he likes absolutely everybody!

"Juan will never be a quiet, relaxed child — it just isn't his nature! He still reminds me of a miniature tornado! His tremendous energy and drive have not been harnessed; they were only temporarily diverted into acceptable channels. What will happen next year? Maybe he'll do even better — maybe he'll revert to his old behavior. Only time will tell — "

WHAT HAS MY EXPERIENCE WITH JUAN TAUGHT ME?

"Mostly, I think I've learned about the power of emotions — both his and mine! Next, I've learned how inextricably intertwined one's emotions are with one's language, one's cultural background, one's health, one's socioeconomic status and the way one has been perceived by other people.

"Juan behaved badly when — and because — other children and adults, including teachers, expected him to be nothing but a 'stupid, dirty, feisty Mexican brat.' Juan seemed stupid in school, partly because his level of language development was not adequate to the school's demands (though the language he possessed was certainly used in volume), but mostly, he seemed stupid because his mind was not on his work! His mind was occupied with his concern about how to fight back at people who humiliated him through the low expectation they held of him. Juan was not free to learn while he was bound by these emotions. Emotions are necessary to life and health. Normally, emotions function to give pleasure, to warn of danger, to draw people together, or to disturb a person to the extent that more adequate methods of meeting situations are developed. However, society — and schools — sometimes create too much emotional pressure. When a child is unable to handle his emotions positively, he develops ways of protecting himself. Schools must carry the responsibility for a child's emotional maladjustment if they make requirements which the boy or girl cannot meet; or teach curricula that do not serve his needs; or have grading systems that destroy his sense of security; or teachers who use fear and humiliation as a means to motivate learning.

"Put yourself in the place of the Mexican or Indian boy or girl.

Like Juan, Victor, and Peggy, each one may come to school "knowing some English" or he may be barely able to communicate. If, because of his looks or his language or his behavior, his classmates consider him strange or peculiar, what is his response—uneasiness, fear, withdrawal, aggression? How can he be expected to accept the group's ways—or want to learn about them and their language—if they make him feel that *he* is inferior or unacceptable and that his own language is 'bad'?

"On the other hand, if the child who comes to school friendly and outgoing finds friendly people in this new kind of world, people who accept him as uniquely himself, even though different in some ways—language among them—he will want to try the school's new ways and be like these friendly people. If he is given support and encouragement, he becomes comfortable enough to practice these new ways even though he makes mistakes. Gradually, he grows confident that he can manage himself in these new situations. When he knows that he has been accepted, then he will enter into learning activities with eagerness—as Juan, Victor, and Peggy did.

"Such a boy or girl acts differently from the one who is not accepted. The latter loses confidence in himself; he may appear hostile, uncooperative, aggressive, boastful, or sullen in learning activities because he has found it unsafe to enter such activities; he feels that he must protect himself from a world he has not found good and from people who have been unfriendly to him.

"Each child has *learned* his behavior patterns, whatever they are. Some of them he learned long before he came to school. In any case, he will behave in school in whatever way he has learned to behave. And he will be able to change his behavior only after he has developed relationships with people which convince him that his former behavior no longer fits the facts in this new school situation!

As Mr. Gonzales has emphasized, the Spanish-speaking—or any non-English-speaking child—is, first of all, a child! Each boy or girl, in pre-school years, is exposed to a wide range of human relationships: he may be accepted and cherished in his family, taken matter-of-factly as another addition to a large family, 'put up with' or actively rejected. He may be an only child or one of many siblings. Like all children, he wants to learn things; he wants to go places and do things. Depending upon the language background of his parents, the amount and kind of verbalization to which he has been exposed and the experiential background his parents have been able to provide, he comes to school with a large, medium or small background of meanings about his world.

"The non-English speaking child will be different from his classmates to the extent that he is cut off from the larger society in the community — isolated in Mexican Town, Chinatown, Brewery Gulch, on the Reservation, across the tracks, or in Little Puerto Rico. When this happens, he is well aware of the fact that his culture and his language are not those of the larger society! Moreover, he knows accurately the way in which that larger society views his culture and that of his group. Whether society's attitude is subtle or blatant, it is readily conveyed to a child. Even though a child only partially understands the causes of discrimination, every boy or girl from a minority group senses the status position his group holds in the larger society.

"A teacher needs to understand a boy or girl's view of the world because upon it will depend a child's response to learning. Coupled with understanding must be a teacher's personal acceptance of the child. Acceptance is not readily described: it comprises words, gestures, smiles, a twinkle of the eye, a pat of the hand, the appreciation of a joke, the quick sympathy when things get tough, silence when only silence can serve, words of encouragement when these are apropos. Acceptance tells a boy or girl, in many ways, *you are important. You count because you are you.*

"Acceptance of a non-English-speaking boy or girl is not easy for some teachers. Their irritation may be unconscious or it may be due to frustration, as it is when a teacher has a large class, and then a family of children who cannot speak English enters! The teacher's feeling of inadequacy, of "what do I do now?" may, at such a time, become translated into irritation at the child.

"In addition to understanding and acceptance, an effective teacher of culturally disadvantaged children must also exemplify mastery of a variety of teaching techniques, skill in adapting appropriate methods to the range of eventualities these children present and wisdom in assessing a child's emotional and intellectual development as well as his language development. The concern of this effective teacher is less with teaching a child English *as such* than with helping him to fulfill his potentialities — to learn to think, to acquire tools for thought and to use these in developing concepts, in communicating ideas and in solving problems.[1] Learning English can be a natural consequence of the child's becoming educated, but the two are not synonymous. Whether the child does learn at all depends on whether he is *free* to learn. For the teacher who has accurately determined a child's total needs and has

---

[1] Paragraph adapted from Marie Hughes and George Sanchez, *Learning a New Language,* Association for Childhood Education International Bulletin 101 (Washington, D.C., 1958), p. 32.

effectively created the kind of school environment in which the child
can believe in himself and in his potentialities, a child like Juan, Victor,
and Peggy will try to learn and his teacher will be truly educating him."

After finishing her talk, Mrs. Branson distributed to the teachers a
useful list of commonly used Spanish phrases to help them effectively
communicate with their Spanish-speaking students:

LIST OF SPANISH TERMS

please	por favor
sit down	siéntate
listen	escúchame
let's eat	vamos a comer
let's go play	vamos a jugar
let's go to recess	vamos a recreo
let's go in line	vamos en linea
let's go home	vamos a la casa
write (command)	escríbe
tell me the word	dime esta palabra
come here	ven aqui
what's the matter?	¿ qué pasa?
school	escuela
teacher	maestra (feminine)
	maestro (masculine)

CHAPTER 6

Tony Goes to School — Again

When the problems of Mexican children had been discussed at the faculty meeting, one faculty member had asked, "What about those Mexican youngsters whose families are migrant workers? Migrants concern us most — even annoy some of us — because the children never stay long enough for us to teach them anything. Maybe if we knew more about migrant workers — the Anglos and Negroes as well as the Mexicans — we'd be able to do a better job with their children. Can anyone help us to get to know something about them?

Mr. Jackson had agreed that children of migrant workers did, indeed, have special problems. Only that morning, he said, he had talked with Mrs. Allen, the school psychologist in the district, about one boy, a migrant child of Anglo-Mexican parentage, who had briefly been in this school. "Mrs. Allen told me Tony's story. I think hearing it directly from her at the next faculty meeting might help us better to understand these children's behavior."

Now, here was Mrs. Allen — explaining to the faculty that she had recorded, with Tony's permission, a conversation with him. As Tony told his story in his own words, she said, he would dramatize better than she could explain what problems a migrant child lived with, and what he hoped for from his school experience. Mrs. Allen suggested, "After listening to Tony, let us discuss the needs of the Tonys in our schools and plan, if possible, specific ways of helping them." She continued, "Let me briefly introduce Tony, just so that you can hear his voice and his most immediate problem. Then I'll tell you something of Tony's background so that the balance of our recorded conversation will be more meaningful." Mrs. Allen started the recording.

"Yeah, I'm back here," Tony spoke without enthusiasm, "got back 'bout two and one-half months ago—but I ain't doin' nothin'. That's what you want to talk to me about, I guess. Well, I don't know *why*. I just can't work in this school."

"Can't work here? Let's talk about that some more," Mrs. Allen's voice said. "But first I wanted to tell you that I'm so glad to see you back. I hadn't known you were in town or in this school. In fact, when you left Central— about ten months ago, wasn't it?—I thought you said your Father was taking the family to California to pick grapes."

Mrs. Allen stopped the recording and began her explanation to the faculty. "As you know, Tony is a migrant child, one of approximately one million migrant workers who cross state and county lines as harvests peak. Nimble-fingered families—whites and Negroes from the South, others of Mexican descent from the West and Southwest— furnish the stoop labor which picks crops for a New Jersey or Imperial Valley lettuce grower, a Pennsylvania tomato grower, a Texas sugar beets grower, or a California grape grower. Numerous families still ride their—or their employers'—rickety trucks, live in them or in un-hygienic work camps, eat questionable meals, and often are forced to neglect their children's health, upbringing, and education.

"Exploitation continues to be the lot of many migrants, although state and federal laws, including minimum wage coverage of a small number of farm workers have alleviated conditions somewhat. Never-theless, migratory workers endure the degrading environment of poverty. And, since many are on the road between October and May, children are placed in a succession of schools—if they go to school at all.

"Tony has been in school 'off and on,' as he told me. He has been in and out of various schools in our district within the last two years. While Tony's parents are working in nearby fields, they camp their truck-trailer wherever they can procure space. This 'residence' de-termines the specific school for which Tony is eligible."

Mrs. Allen smiled as she explained that she had "seemed to hit it off well" with Tony the four or five times she had talked with him previous to this conversation. Tony had told her a great deal about himself. Tony's mother had, some years ago, come from Tennessee to California with her husband to work in the lettuce fields. But things had not gone well and, one day, her husband had "just wandered off." The wife did not have money to return to Tennessee, so, several months later, she had married a Mexican. He was Tony's father. But that marriage had not worked out either and Tony had learned from his mother to dislike intensely "those dirty, fighten', stupid Mexi-

cans"; he hated his Mexican name and insisted on being called Anthony, the name his mother had given him—"though kids call me Tony
and so does Pop." His mother did not want him to "grow up stupid
like those Mexicans," Tony had told Mrs. Allen. Therefore, "when
we're near a school, she always sends us kids to school. Pop couldn't
care less."

In addition to Tony, there was a "baby sister" and seven-year-old
Bill who, according to Tony, was a "very tough little guy" who had
been in trouble with the police several times. One of Tony's main
worries was that he would "really beat up that brat because he makes
me so mad." Tony dreaded being left in sole charge of Bill and his
sister at home. Yet this happened daily.

In fact, Tony spent all of his out-of-school time caring for the
younger children. Consequently, he had no friends. "I ain't got no
time for any," he had told Mrs. Allen when she had asked him about
friends. He continued, as tears came into his eyes, "I had only one
friend in my life—my Grandpop down south. But he died last year. I
miss him. Ain't nobody ever understood me like my Grandpop. Now
he's gone."

Mrs. Allen paused. "I believe that we can resume Tony's story
now." She turned on the recording and Tony's voice said,

"Yeah, we went to California. Pop kept us kids out of school the whole
year too. That's the kind of bum he was."
"Why did he do that?"
"First we all worked the fields—then he got fed up with how they treated us.
So he just got drunk—and we started moving. Aw, that's the story of my life!
I'll bet 'ya I've been all over these United States—all—all over the place. You
name it, I've been there. We even went up to Alaska one time"—he paused.
"But you're back here now?"
"Yeah, Mom liked it here, so when Pop walked out, she drove the trailer
back here—I don't know for how long though"—
"Your father walked out"—
"Yeah, in one of his drunk spells"—
"Where is he now?"
"I don't know and I don't care. He kept hitting me. I'm glad he's gone. Mom
says maybe I can go to school awhile now. Only not this school—I can't work
here"—
"What do you mean, you can't work here?"
"I just get in trouble here. Everyplace I go, they pick on me—in Physical
Education they pick on me—in class, they call me names—on the playground,
they make fun of me."
"You know, Anthony, when I first met you—at Central—you were having
lots of trouble"—

"Yeah, I know, I was all shook up."

"You were shaking and nervous and very upset—but you worked your problems out. Remember, the few times after our first talk that I saw you, I asked, 'How are you coming?' and you said, 'Just fine.'"

"Yeah, but that was Central. That was the best school I ever was in. All I need is to get back there. But we couldn't get into the trailer camp in that district. I told Mom I didn't like it here and asked her to try again to move us, but she just said, 'That's tough. You're going to stay where you are.' But I can't work here!"

"I know. Your teacher says that you just sit in class. She says she can't pass you"—

"I know. I don't blame her. She's got a lot on her hands—34 kids, 20 of us boys. It'd be better for her if they was mostly girls. She won't pass me, I guess—and Mom has so much trouble—she's afraid she'll have to go to the hospital *again*—and there's a new man Mom is marrying and he don't understand me. If I don't pass—and I'm afraid I won't—he's going to beat me, just like Pop did. He's a big man, a very big man."

"You stiffen, just the way you did when you talked about your Pop—"

"Yeah, I like this guy in a way, but I'm afraid of him. He seems a mighty big man to mess around with—"

"Does he drink?"

"Oh no, he's not a guzzler like Pop. He drinks some, but he don't ever get drunk. You know, its O.K. to take a drink, but not get drunk like my Pop. But he's going to whip me if I don't pass and Mom'll get all upset and end up in the hospital—"

"Well, Anthony, what can we do about this? Can we help you to pass? At Central, you were doing good fourth grade work. I just talked with Mr. Hall there about you this morning and he said, 'I can't understand that he's not passing. Anthony was doing such good work in my room.'"

"I wish you'd tell Mr. Hall, if he don't understand—I was coming along good there 'cause I was with *him*. I would've passed there. But here it's just nag, nag, nag. The reason I'm not doing good here—it's mostly the kids—they bug me and I just can't get to my work, I— I— just sit"—

"Do any of them play with you?"

"I tried to play with poor Jack Spache. I go with him because the guys are always teasing him. I can't stand to see nobody teased and not have no friends."

"You can't stand to see anybody teased?"

Anthony shook his head negatively.

"Is this because you've been teased yourself?"

"I understand their feelins', 'cause I always had problems, I guess—and no one understands me—my Grandpop did, but he's dead now—and Mr. Hall did—"

"Did you feel Mr. Hall understood you?"

Anthony shook his head affirmatively and began to cry. "Yeah, with Mr. Hall, I was gettin' better and better. I would've passed there, but here I ain't gonna. I just know it. I can't work here. They just criticize me" —
"The boys criticize you?"
"Everybody."
"Over at Central, you got to know the Physical Education teacher — and you began to like him too, I think. What about the Physical Education teacher here — Mr. Myer?"
"Oh, he's a MAN. He don't understand me. When I first came here, I was scared of him. I still am" —
"You're still afraid — "
"Yeah, I hate PE — I can't keep up with the other guys."
"Lots of times one can't keep up with people, Anthony."
"Yeah, but they laugh at me 'cause I'm no good at PE and I can't lift weights good. You have to pass tests here. All the kids can do the tests. They lift weights good. — "
"You can't lift weights?"
Anthony shook his head. "So the day of the last test, I took off — I just skipped school. I can't stand to have everybody laugh at me. Besides, I was afraid I was going to hit that one guy, Roy, that was always on my back. I remember a long time ago, I hit a boy in the face real hard. It was terrible. When I get mad, I lose my temper. Then I hit with a terrific amount of hardness."
"This happens when you get mad?"
"Yeah, I get pressure inside and my veins go all out of whack. It happens sometimes when I get mad in the classroom too, when they bug me. I just feel like I want to punch them in the nose. My Pop taught me how. He used to be a boxer" —
"You said your Father used to hit you?"
"All the time he kept hitting me. I think of him a lot — of him hitting me. If I'm trying to whip a guy in a fight, I start thinking he's my Pop — and the kid looks just like my Pop" —
"In a fight, everyone looks like your Pop?"
"Yeah, everything gets blurry — and I don't know what I'm doing. I just pound on the other kid. Guys say I turn all kinds of weird-looking colors."
"Do you get in many fights?"
"Not too many, any more. I've got to stay out of them 'cause I lose my head and have all those feelings. If a guy says today, 'You couldn't lick a wet noodle,' I'd walk off — 'cause if I'd ever light into him!!"
"Do you ever fight with your brother Bill?" Anthony had gasped, "Oh no!" I just let him beat on me 'cause he's little. I'm afraid if we really fought, *he'd* start looking like Pop. When I was six years old, I swore I was going to kill Pop. I swore it."
"When you were six years old?"
"I said, 'Mom, I'll kill him for you. I'll kill him for you' — and ever since then,

I've wanted to pound the hell out of him. I still think I will if I ever see him again. Then I'll be big, big enough to go up against him and beat him to death just like he did Mom" — and Anthony started to cry.

"He beat your mother" —

"With his fists, just like he did in the boxing ring!"

"Where was she?"

"In the house, right in front of us kids" —

"Is that when your Pop left?"

"No, he just went in the bedroom."

"In the bedroom?"

Anthony nodded his head. "He was drunk" — pause — "all the time."

"That was hard on you."

"I couldn't stand him beating Mom that-away. One time when he was beating Mom, I took a iron skillet at him. I couldn't get no other weapon; I'd'a got a gun if I'd been bigger. I wasn't very big then, but I was really mad. I swung the skillet and went for him!"

"Your mother — "

"She screamed. She knew I was going to hit him. That's the time he threatened to send me to reform school. I worry that I might go to reform school 'cause I got a really bad temper when I get mad — and my feelings, they hurt easy — "

"You're working on your temper though."

"Yes."

"I think you're learning to control it."

"I guess so. I used to fight like crazy — when I was little. At other schools, I used to always get swats for fightin'. I remember those fights — if I ever see those kids again, I'm goin' to get 'em! I often think about 'em when I'm sitting in class — "

"When you're not doing your work in your room?"

"Yes, that's what I'm doin' — just thinking, thinking, thinking — holding my temper, but things bug me something terrible!"

"*Things* bug you?"

"Yes, I think about my Pop and these guys here and how I want to get them. And about my Grandfather laying there in that stupid box — that coffin. I can remember every detail, even the sound of the footsteps the people took." (Anthony started crying) "For two whole days people came — and he just laid there — and he looked awful. His house was all changed too. I used to stay there a lot. It wasn't much — but to him and me it was a mansion. He understood me — and now he's gone."

"You really miss him."

"Yes, he stood up for me. I felt safe with him."

"Have you felt safe since?"

"Not very much — only with you and with Mr. Hall. (Anthony was still crying) And now I don't have Mr. Hall and you ain't here enough and Grandpop's dead—and I can't go to Mr. Myer. He's a MAN and he don't understand. Mr. Hall would—he's like my Grandpop—I'm not trying to say Mr. Hall is old—"

"I understand. You're comparing their personalities."

"Yeah, he's nice and understanding. Grandpop was too."

"You know, Anthony, Mr. Hall is going to teach in summer school. When I was talking to him this morning, he said he'd like to have you with him in the program this summer. Maybe you could go to summer school to finish up your fifth grade work if you feel you simply can't do it here."

"Whoops, Mr. Hall this summer!—Oh but gee, I have to go to Tennessee! My Mom's takin' us. I'd sure like to be with Mr. Hall though."

"You felt Mr. Hall helped you?"

"Mr. Hall seemed just like a father—(Anthony tried to control his crying) a father—the right kind."

"Just like a father—the right kind. I don't think you could say anything nicer about anybody."

"And I had to move—because of the Pop I had! I wish I could go back. In Mr. Hall's room, I felt calm. He wouldn't let them tease me. Course, he had a smaller class. I understand my teacher here; she's got an awfully big grade. Mostly boys—that's the whole trouble—too many boys for her and for me. If we didn't have so many boys, there wouldn't be so many to tease me."

"Maybe you *could* go to summer school with Mr. Hall. Do you want to ask your mother about it?"

"I could talk to Mom. (Pause) No, I know I gotta go to Tennessee. I sorta want to go and I sorta don't. There just ain't two of me."

"Your mother is going to take you to Tennessee?"

"Yes, she's going to take us in our old trailer, she and Daddy."

"When you say Daddy—"

"This is my new Daddy, I'm going to have—Jim, in other words."

"The one you said you were afraid of sometimes?"

"Yes, only it's not him I'm afraid of about the trip—it's Mom. I guess I'm really afraid we won't come back here. Mom's been in the hospital, you know. Maybe she'll want to stay down there with her folks. That is, if Jim gets work. If not, we'll be on the road again."

"You said your mother had been in the hospital. Is she home now?"

"Yes, but she's still all shook up! Like last night—I was tryin' to do some homework. Everytime I start to work at home, one of the kids will start doing somethin' or makin' noise. In that old trailer, noise sounds awful big. I just got started good on some problems and that brat brother started screaming. I blew my temper. I started shaking—I was all nervous—I yelled in his face 'SHUT UP' so loud that he jumped back and fell on the floor. Mom leaped at me and slapped me in the face."

"Your mother slapped you"—

"Yeah, she didn't mean to hit me in the face—she's just shook up!"

"You were shaking too?"

"Yeah, she did it because I was real nervous and she wanted to slap me out of it. Maybe she didn't feel well—and all the noise got her."

"Yes, you said she'd been in the hospital. What did she go to the hospital for?"

"Some junk to be worked on. She won't tell me what it was."

"Who took care of the younger children while she was in the hospital?"

"I did most of the time. The hours I was in school, we had to hire a baby-sitter for my sister. The money we was saving to spend for lunches here at school we had to put out to pay the baby-sitter."

"Your mother's back home now?"

Anthony nodded affirmatively.

"How do you get money now—for food?"

"Mom has some money, but I can't have money for school. I make sand-wiches for lunch with whatever we got."

"You still have feelings of wanting to hit your brother and sister when they get hard to manage and you are alone with them?"

"Yeah, the other night, Mom and Jim went out for a beer. That bratty brother of mine started it and the kids were givin' me a hard time. I lit out for him—I wanted to kill him—it's the maddest I've ever gotten! All at once, I knew I'd blow up if I didn't get out of there. I ran outside. There, on our trailer steps, was a little guy named Frank—sitting. He's a two-year-old; he lives near us. I sat him in my lap—he's as precious as can be. He was the only thing I had to cling to—(Anthony was sobbing)—he helped me. He's only a little bitty guy, but he helped me."

"You could love him?"

Anthony nodded his head as if to say, "That's it!"

ANTHONY BLINKS A RED LIGHT

When the recording ended, Mrs. Allen said, "Let me describe Anthony and tell you some more about him—so that we can begin to understand why he feels and behaves as he does. Anthony is a bright, handsome, blonde fifth grade boy who, in his own words, has been all over these United States. I had first met him last year, a year before this recorded conversation took place. He was also in fifth grade then. Since he was not doing fifth grade work, his teacher, Mr. Hall, wondered if he should be moved to a homogeneous group working at a fourth grade level of achievement where academic pressure was no factor. To secure advice, Mr. Hall sent Anthony to me for testing. The test results were not nearly as important as the conversation Anthony and I had. It uncovered Anthony's pre-occupations and anxiety—also, his positive feeling about Mr. Hall who, informed about Anthony's problems, agreed with me that he could help Anthony more than any-one else."

Mrs. Allen went on to explain that, at the time of the first conversation, Anthony's mother and father both "worked crops—from sunup to sundown," Anthony took sole responsibility for his brother, then six years old, and his sister, three, not only each morning, but also each afternoon until the parents came home. Often, he prepared dinner too. Every evening, after dinner, the parents would "go for a beer," leaving Anthony, again, alone with the smaller children. Anthony told Mrs. Allen of his inability to manage the children, particularly his brother. Anthony had to spank him several times to keep him from running away and getting into trouble.

Anthony had serious guilt feelings about hitting the child. Yet he had "to fight the brat," he said, even to keep order in the trailer which apparently was "a homemade job—kind of camper on a truck base." Finally each evening, he'd manage to get the kids in bed and asleep; then he'd "pick up the mess" and try to sleep himself. But he never slept much; he was "afraid there all alone with those kids on my hands"—and he had nightmares.

His grandfather had died a few months earlier and Anthony, his mother and the children went to Tennessee to the funeral. The casket was brought to the grandfather's home and friends came to visit. Anthony was in the home for a night and a day before services were held. Back here, with this recent death on his mind, he'd lie awake in bed in the trailer, waiting for his parents to return. The "bed rails" of the improvised cot on which he was sleeping in the all-purpose living-eating-playing-sleeping section of the trailer would remind him of the handles on his grandfather's casket. He would begin sobbing in grief and fear; he felt deserted both by his parents and by his grandfather.

After Mr. Hall heard Anthony's story, he went out of his way to support and encourage the boy. He coached him individually in his academic work; he gained his confidence, listened to his home problems and tried to help him. Mrs. Allen had several opportunities, in the next weeks, to talk further with Anthony and, gradually, he seemed to become less tense about his problems. His work improved until he was actually functioning at fifth grade level in Mr. Hall's classroom.

Several months went by with no "red lights blinking" from Anthony. Then suddenly, the family left for California. Now Anthony was back—again in fifth grade—in a different school in the district. This school's students come mainly from above-average income homes. Anthony managed to function for about a month. Then he "blinked a red light."

Anthony began skipping school on Physical Education days or hiding out during Physical Education class. Simultaneously, his fifth grade teacher reported that he was no longer doing anything in the classroom, not even his reading assignments. For written work, he turned in blank papers. His teacher stated that, although his classwork had been poor ever since he entered her room—"at first, he at least seemed to try. Now he just sits. You can't pass a child who won't even make an effort." This was the background for the recorded interview with Anthony.

WHAT IS ANTHONY "UP AGAINST?"

At first, when Mrs. Allen was told about the problem in Physical Education, she had hoped that Mr. Myer might be able to help Anthony. However, it became evident, in conversation with Anthony, that he could never identify with Mr. Myer. In fact, Mr. Myer typified, for Anthony, one of his serious emotional conflicts. Anthony had had a father who was strong, but who used brute strength to hurt other people. Anthony had seen his mother hurt by his father and had been hurt himself. Therefore, he hated brute strength—yet he wanted it. Consequently, anyone who typified, to Anthony, a STRONG MAN was someone to be feared—also someone who would not understand him and his feelings!

The anger and hatred which his father's treatment of his mother and Anthony had built up in Anthony made him yearn for the strength to avenge himself. As he grew, he gained this strength; and he learned how to fight. Everytime he fought, however, all the anger and hatred came out; he wanted to kill. It was his father whom he wanted to kill and he began seeing his father in everyone whom he fought. These experiences so frightened him that he dared not use his strength to fight anyone because he feared that he might "let loose" his hatred and anger—and actually kill.

These worries, anxieties, fears, and angers are "bugging" Anthony so that he is not able to keep his mind on his school work; his energy is drained by the effort of keeping his temper—his hatred and anger—under control. Anthony is a bright boy—capable of doing good work, yet unable to study. Nor will he be *free to learn* or to use his intelligence while his feelings keep him from concentrating on his classwork. Let us try to understand what he is "up against." The teasing of his classmates and the difficult behavior of his younger brother have reactivated his conflict between his desire to fight and avenge himself—and his fear of the consequences of his uncontrolled anger and hatred. His mother's illness, his loss of his grandfather and Mr. Hall have intensified his fear of being alone, deserted by the only people with whom he had a meaningful relationship—he felt "safe" with Mrs. Allen, she was happy to know, but she "wasn't around enough."

What did these explanations suggest to the faculty? What insight did they give into reasons for Anthony's behavior? Mrs. Allen guided a discussion in which the group considered, first, the fact that Anthony is deprived of a father. Anthony desperately wanted—and needed—"a father, the right kind" with whom to identify. The new "Daddy" was "too strong to mess with," someone who would beat Anthony if he didn't pass. To a large extent, the group concurred, boys and girls learn what it is to be a man or woman by modeling themselves after their parents. But Anthony cannot copy his own father or his step-father since they represent to him brute force which arouses such anger and hate in him that he dares not even contemplate the results should these feelings "get loose"—and they might if he responds to the teasing of his classmates. Remember, he said to Mrs. Allen, "my feelings hurt easy." He is so absorbed in—"bugged by"—these fears that he cannot do his schoolwork.

Second, the group emphasized: through parents' unselfish, de-monstrative concern for a child, a child learns that he is wanted and loved and secure. Anthony is deprived of this concern, one of a child's basic emotional needs. Yet Anthony is, unrealistically, expected to supply it for his younger siblings when he has never had it himself—and to supply it under circumstances which assume more maturity than a fifth grader has—and more control than a child with his particular emotional conflicts should be expected to have. No wonder that Anthony is physically tired and emotionally exhausted—in no condi-tion to learn!

Not only is Anthony deprived of emotional security, the group noted, he does not even have physical security. He has no adult to look after him at night; therefore, he lives with fear and panics at the thought of his nightmares. Instead of having a baby-sitter, as many children would at his age, he *is* the baby-sitter. Because of his mother's illness and the lack of money, he does not even have the security of knowing that he will have good food and regular meals. He doesn't even know where he will go to school from one month to another, what city or state he will be living in! In fact, the entire family pattern changes from time to time; when his Pop walks out on the family, and his Mom finds a new Daddy. The only constant thing is liquor; it's all right to "go out for a beer"—just so you aren't "a guzzler" or "stay drunk all the time!"

A faculty member summarized, "If I didn't know what might happen to me tomorrow and I was hungry besides, I don't think I would con-centrate on my studies either."

"Anthony is deprived of freedom too," someone emphasized next. Like many culturally disadvantaged children whose homes are so inadequate that they have no place, inside or outside, to play, Anthony is imprisoned in a trailer with, as he says, "screaming brats." He is not free to do as he wishes before school. His parents have already left for work; therefore, he must awaken, dress and feed the children, take the sister to a baby-sitter, then get himself and his brother to school — and the latter can be a task of no small dimensions! After school, he must get his sister and, in addition, see that the brother gets home — an even greater trial than getting him to school! Then he must "mind" the children until his parents return from work — and, often, start dinner, too. After the evening meal, he baby-sits again while his parents "go out for a beer."

Anthony never has time free from responsibility, free to think or even to rest; seldom does he get even a good night's sleep. He cannot go home with a boy-friend or even linger on his own way home to play with friends. Chronologically, he is in "the gang" age, yet he hasn't time to cultivate even a single friend. He will never know the freedom of childhood.

One faculty member concluded, "No wonder *things* bug him!"

"Nor will he have an opportunity to develop the self-confidence which is gained through accomplishment," was the next point made in the discussion. He is accomplishing nothing at present, either in classroom learning or in Physical Education where he is humiliated and teased because "I can't keep up with the other boys here."

How can he! With his home responsibilities plus the family's "change of address" pattern, he has no opportunity to *be* with, much less identify with and learn from boys and girls of his own age! He does not belong anywhere — in a family, a school, a church, or a community! He feels worthless and useless. Like so many disadvantaged boys and girls whose parents are migratory workers, he is part of the "poverty's harvest of failure" in our country.

Mrs. Allen summarized the faculty discussion with: "The demands which face a boy or girl like this, at home and at school, often seem, to him, to stretch into a seemingly endless string of failures. His experiences have been inconsistent or non-supportive; he has had no opportunity to learn the competencies necessary to his adequate functioning as a person. The ill effects of these failures are not confined to specific learning. As the behavioral scientists say, we become what we practice. In other words, Anthony thinks of himself as in a situation where he practices only failures; therefore, he will begin to see himself as a failing person. Continuous failure gradually destroys even ability to learn."

WHAT CAN HIS SCHOOL DO FOR ANTHONY?

The danger, for Anthony now, lies in this further development of a sense of inadequacy and inferiority. "If he despairs of his tools and skills or of his status among his tool partners, his ego boundaries suffer, and he abandons hope for the ability to identify early with others."[1] In this, Anthony is not unusual. Teachers who work with culturally disadvantaged children report that, in school, these children, more than others, are frustrated and more often become apathetic or rebellious when they cannot succeed at school tasks.[2]

Essentially what Anthony hopes for from his school experience is "An educational program which will insure meaningful growth, provide a sense of attainment and accomplishment, help youngsters understand and face their limitations as well as their strengths, provide for healthy attitudes toward school and society, and generally turn the indifference or antagonism of the disadvantaged child into acceptance and understanding.[3]

To what degree can his hopes be realized? Much of Anthony's motivation for learning will come from his drive to enhance his self-concept through achievement or to protect it by avoiding failure. Will his teachers recognize this fact? Those who do will adjust demands made on him to his particular competencies, rather than gear them to group averages. Anthony will be given opportunities to develop a positive view of himself. His home cannot provide the kinds of experiences necessary for this type of learning; therefore, Anthony's only hope is that the school will develop compensatory strategies through a program of stimulation appropriate to Anthony's capabilities.

What this means, in the school as a whole, we shall discuss in the last chapter. The emphases especially pertinent to Anthony follow. *What one teacher did* for Anthony was basic to his becoming able to learn: with Mr. Hall, he felt safe; he had feelings of being liked, wanted, accepted. Within this relationship, Anthony developed sufficient confidence not only to try new experiences; he, also, was able to get along with his classmates, was free to concentrate on his schoolwork, even

---

[1] Erik, H. Erikson, *Childhood and Society* (New York: W. W. Norton and Co., 1950), p. 227.

[2] Benjamin Bloom and Allison Davis, *Compensatory Education for Cultural Deprivation* (New York: Holt, Rinehart and Winston, 1965), p. 47.

[3] Harry A. Passow, *Instructional Content for Depressed Urban Centers: Problems and Approaches* (Columbus: Ohio State University Press, 1964), p. 23-4.

became successful in it. When Mrs. Allen asked him how he was coming along during the time he was with Mr. Hall, he had said, "Just fine!"

However, with children whose problems are as complicated as Anthony's, even the best *teachers will need support and encouragement*—and specific *help* if they, in turn, are to support and help the Anthonys. Specialists in child development and adolescent psycology—counselors, social workers, psychologists, and psychiatrists should be available to consult with teachers. They should visit in classrooms where they can observe, listen, learn, and come to understand what it *feels* like and what it *is* like to be a teacher of these children. Gilbert Wrenn says that no other teacher in the world has a more difficult task than that of the American teacher because, here, effective teachers become *involved* in this process of learning to understand and help a child.

But teachers cannot carry such responsibility alone: some of these children need information; some need counseling; some need assistance with health problems, with jobs, or with family situations. True, such assistance from specialists is expensive and time-consuming. But it is necessary. Anthony appraised its effectiveness when he said to Mrs. Allen, "And you ain't here enough!"

Finally, to turn the indifference or antagonism of a disadvantaged child into understanding of the importance of learning, teachers must realize that whatever is done for Anthony in school must be characterized by a *genuine concern for the way he and his people see their lives.* An educational program which is to provide meaningful growth for him, to develop healthy attitudes toward schooling and toward society must be one in which Anthony recognizes that he is attaining ends important to him, moving towards goals he and his family have envisioned as desirable. To migrants, their world[4] is one of sunrise and sunset, seeds becoming plants, plants becoming fruits or vegetables to be harvested on farms or plantations scattered over the nation. They manage their lives by *their* standards—the obligations and challenges of their world. Some of them have deliberately chosen their way of life: faced with alternatives of the ghetto or the relief rolls in an urban setting, they have determined that "following the crops offered a better life"—"It's hard, but we can do as we know to, and it's better on you than being in the city, sitting yourself on the stairs all day."

These people are not clinging to what little they have out of vain

[4]Remainder of material in this chapter adapted from Robert Coles, "What Migrant Children Learn," *Saturday Review,* May 15, 1965, p. 73 ff.

contrariness or inherited foolishness. True, some migrant families feel that they have little need for education. Hundreds of thousands, however, want a better life *as they know life*. They want steady work at higher wages, a chance to live in homes that are theirs, on land they know, near towns and people they know. As did Anthony's mother, many of them picture their children going to school some day, learning those numbers and letters which—they vaguely know—lead to an improved kind of existence. But what comprises improvement? School and society together must face this question. If we really wish to help these people, we can.

"I want my child to go plumb through school, but if he does, then what will he do?" a parent asks. This parent and child want to find *a sensible connection between what happens in school and in their lives*. Evolving an educational program which will make this connection, one which will ensure meaningful growth to these children, is the problem facing the school and society.

Not only must the educational program be established on the basis of the needs and lives of these people, school organization itself must be modeled on their habits and interests. For example, mobile teaching units could go to these people; it scarcely makes sense to expect people chronically on the move to respect the primacy of town schools. Perhaps regional networks of schools, many of them mobile, could evolve—all staffed by teachers knowledgeable about the customs and concerns of the rural poor and of the disadvantaged, whatever their ethnic and cultural background.

Moreover, migrant children need books and lessons centered around a life that is real to them. Their special language, their ways of dressing and eating and getting along with one another, must be understood and taken into consideration in their schooling—even as our ideas and habits inform the spirit of our middle-class, neighborhood schools.

Most important, however, is real, not transitory, interest in the welfare of these people on the part of business, labor, and government; interest permanent enough and inclusive enough eventually to supply small, diversified industry to employ them. Each year, farm machinery displaces more of them. If these migrant workers are not permanently to swell the ranks of the unemployed, they will obviously need jobs the year round. And, for these, they will need education and training.

Obviously, their needs—for work, for better living conditions, and for knowledge, both for their children and for themselves—"cannot be considered separately—Society must be equal to the total task . . . Many incredibly poor farm families are made up of tenacious and willful people. Theirs is the tragedy of inner strength—consolidated

and tested by a hard life — in search of its own fullfillment. As a nation
founded essentially by farmers and built to its present greatness by
wanderers, can we continue to deny many migratory farm children
their reasonable future without losing, at the very least, a good deal
of our own self-respect?

CHAPTER 7

How Do We Teach These Children?

"There are thousands of children like Tony, Juan, Peggy, and Victor in our schools, children from a variety of cultural backgrounds. Many are bilingual. Yet in many schools, their special problems have been given too little attention." With these words, Mr. Jackson was closing the meeting at which Tony's story had been told. He continued,

"It has been said that the bilingual child is the forgotten child of American education. Here these children—Mexicans, Puerto Ricans, Chinese, Eskimos, Indians, and others—live in an English-speaking country and, if they are not to be socially and economically handicapped throughout their lives, they must learn to speak, understand, and read English well!

"Learning a new language is, however, only one aspect of the school life of these children. Miss Begay and Mr. Gonzales made clear that Indian and Mexican children live in a completely different world from that of their Anglo classmates. So do others—our migrants and our Negro children, for example. All of them need contacts with, experiences in, and understanding from the new world in which they must learn to live, the world of the dominant white middle-class culture which prevails in our schools.

"Some educators have called all these children culturally deprived. What an inadequate term! Those children whose behavior and values do not conform to the dominant 'American' patterns are by no means deprived of a culture, as Miss Begay and Mr. Gonzales emphasized. But they *are* at a cultural disadvantage as they attempt to make the transition to the school's culture. Pinpointing their problems improves our comprehension and understanding of these children. Hopefully,

169

this will result in our realization that these 'disadvantaged' children do not wish to be labeled as different. All groups share this aversion. These boys and girls wish to be like other people – to become a part of the mainstream of our culture. How can we help them toward this goal in spite of language barriers, cultural differences, and a set of values unfamiliar to us?" Mr. Jackson paused.

"This was certainly an aspect of teaching neglected in my training," Mr. McMann, a first-year teacher volunteered. "We learn about children, but the ones described in our textbooks, the ones we are acquainted with – and teach in our College Demonstration School – are mostly from approximately our own economic level, middle-class in background and culture. When we actually begin teaching, we find that many children don't fit this category. Yet our readers and workbooks and picture books are usually aimed at this first group; they are the ones who 'fit' into the school.

"The other children look at the pictures too – but you can't say to them, 'This is the way life is. This is the way things are done.' They know that isn't so. Their lives are not like that. So a new teacher keeps asking – where do you begin with these children? What do you try to teach them? In fact, how do you build up a relationship in which they'll *accept* you and trust you to teach them? Mrs. Brown and Mrs. Branson certainly proved to us, in their stories of Peggy and Juan, that it could be done. Then, too, we've learned much from Miss Begay and Mr. Gonzales who have helped us to understand Indian and Mexican children – although I have Negro children and others in my class who have many problems too.

"I wish I knew more about *all* of them. I guess what I'm asking is whether some of our experienced teachers could now summarize what we've been learning. Perhaps they could discuss, as a panel, exactly what they do to teach all these disadvantaged children successfully. Especially, I'd like to have them emphasize techniques for working with the bilingual child, as Mr. Gonzales suggested."

Mr. Jackson was obviously pleased. "You have asked many good questions, Mr. McMann. I am happy when teachers want to learn about these children and sad when they argue that they'd rather not have them in class because these children don't want to learn. 'How can I help him if he doesn't *want* to read?' I've had teachers ask me.

Mr. Jackson continued, "If *you* can't help him, who can? On the other hand, if you *do* learn to understand him, you'll help him because you'll be interested in him. Many of these children have never had anyone *personally* interested in them. They'll sense your interest and respond to it. They'll want to please you – and they'll learn. But it takes effort—continuous hard work from the moment the child comes into your classroom until you pass him on to someone else. You relax and he'll stop progressing. I see some of our experienced teachers nodding. They certainly *are* the ones to answer your questions about how you teach these children and where you begin. Suppose we ask them to share their experiences with you in another meeting?"

All the new teachers responded with enthusiasm.

Mrs. Brown began the next meeting by explaining, "Today, several of us who have taught in this school for a number of years are going to talk as a panel with Mr. Jackson about our experiences with these children whom we've been calling, in our meetings, 'culturally and educationally disadvantaged.' The three of us, Mrs. Branson, now teaching fourth grade, Mr. Salas, the sixth grade, and I, the second grade, have learned to know a great many Indian and Spanish-speaking and Negro children—and a few Chinese. The suggestions we shall discuss and the lists we have made available to you can be adapted and applied to these children at all ages and grades. We may draw examples from one group or the other; many of mine will be from my experiences with Indian children. However, what I say about them, I know from experience, will apply equally to other culturally disadvantaged children. We'll be talking informally—and we're going to feel free to interrupt one another."

THE PANEL DISCUSSION

One teacher on the panel began by emphasizing the fact that a culturally disadvantaged Indian child might enter school at any grade— "Although more and more of them are coming to school at an early age, there are still some who are 'hidden' by their parents—kept out on the ranges sheep-herding. Then they come to school at 10, 11, or 12 years old, knowing no English. This situation occurs, too, when a Mexican child of migrant workers first enters school—or when a child has recently come from China or Puerto Rico or Cuba. Obviously, such a boy or girl cannot be placed with first graders. Therefore, any one of us may face this basic problem, 'How do I communicate with the non-English-speaking child?' "

What Does "Learning a New Language" Mean?

The discussion went on. "And the problem of communication is not confined to what we used to designate a 'language problem'; in other words, the question is not only whether the child knows English. It is rather 'What English does he really understand?' As we interpret the problem in this manner, we include our urban and rural poor, both Negro and white. Mrs. Brown, you recall, spoke of a child from the Tennessee mountains whom her classmates could not understand."

"Mr. Gonzales was well aware of this dilemma! Remember his discussion of the Mexican child's language facility? We've thought about this language problem a great deal, too, and we're going to share our thoughts and conclusions with you.

"Many teachers are confused about what is actually meant by *learning* a language. This confusion is due partly to the fact that we do not always distinguish between being able to say words and being able to handle concepts. Words are merely symbols for manipulating concepts. They can be parroted; but understanding concepts depends on experience. If you have not experienced the concepts represented by the words, the words are obviously meaningless. You don't know what you're talking about!

"All useful language, then, is based on experience—and, as Mr. Gonzales said, children's experiences vary widely. One child may have a wide variety of experiences (and resultant concepts) and have labels —or a vocabulary—attached to them. We say that such a child is fluent in a language. Another child may have the concepts, but have comparatively few labels—or words—attached to them; we say that he seems bright, but has a poor vocabulary or that he can't seem to express himself. Another child may have a narrow range of experiences, few concepts, and few labels attached; we may say he has delayed speech—or that he has been overprotected; or that he is retarded; or that he is culturally deprived, like our urban and rural poor children! Another child may say or even read many words; yet he has a narrow range of experience and has merely learned words by rote—but they have no meaning to him.

"Let's apply this reasoning to the child who must learn a second language. If the child has had wide experience, a good understanding of his own language, and is fluent in the symbols (words) of his own language, then his problem in learning a new language is a comparatively simple one—Mr. Gonzales described it as replacing the Spanish, Chinese, or Navajo symbol with the English one. Such a child is truly bilingual and, rather than being handicapped in learning a new language, he usually sees the process as a challenge—as would you and I if we set out to learn Spanish!"

"That is—may I hasten to add—unless society has complicated the situation! Every child who does not speak the language of the dominant culture faces the fact that he is cut off from the larger society because his language is not theirs and/or his group's culture not theirs. Mr.

Gonzales discussed the fact that such a child's social development must include his coming to terms with his background—with the particular subculture in which he has lived in his preschool years. How he feels about being Indian or Mexican or Negro will, certainly, be affected by the way that his new environment, the school, judges his culture. We shall consider in detail, in a few moments, the implications of this situation. Let us confine our present discussion to the child's *intellectual readiness* to learn a new language. What do I mean by this term?

"We have said that a child's experiential background determines his language facility and the stock of meanings with which he comes to school. These are affected, too, by the type of receptiveness a child meets within his family, especially from his parents, brothers, and sisters. Do they encourage him to talk? Do they listen to him? Do they take his questions seriously and, by answering them accurately, extend his vocabulary? Do they encourage him to use language to get for himself the things he wants?

"Some children I know have never really had to use language; they merely point to what they want—or they get a brother or sister to ask for it! Others have not found language useful. They 'ask and ask' for something; whether they get it or not depends more on the parents' mood of the moment than on their language facility. Still others have experienced little communication of any kind in the home; they just grab what they want. Moreover, all of these disadvantaged children, I find, need to learn to talk with adults. Most of their experience in speaking has been with their siblings or playmates. When there has been conversation with adults, these children have usually been talked *to,* not *with.* They have been told to be respectful and obedient— or they have been scolded—or adults have 'yelled' commands at them. Such relationships do not invite expression of a child's own ideas or encourage growth of his vocabulary.

"The child with a true language handicap is the child who has a narrow range of experiences, few concepts, and a small store of symbols—in other words, the child who cannot express himself well in any language, even his native one. Such a child does not understand ordinary relationships—like big and bigger, better and best! To complicate matters, some of his symbols of communication—the words he uses—come from two languages, English and his native tongue. But, when he is well-versed in neither, this kind of bilingualism merely adds to his confusion in using either language. Our task with him is: first, to develop clear concepts in one language or the other, then to attach definite symbols to these concepts. How do we proceed?

"A teacher of Mexican migrant workers' children explained the process in these words: 'All language development is based on experiencing.' Especially for the young child, experiences should be direct and personal. From experiencing results the development of concepts. These concepts, in turn, must be labeled with words.'"

"In a deprived environment, there is no opportunity to go through this process; the child has few experiences—few things to see, to feel, to manipulate, to play with—consequently, few concepts of the kind that will be useful in school. Therefore, when he comes to school, he uses and understands comparatively few words. Remember Peggy's first weeks in school? With a poor vocabulary and a sparsity of concepts, a child cannot think well either. After all, concepts are the tools of thought. Incidentally, this explanation accounts for the fact that such a child frequently does poorly on school intelligence tests.'"

"You are saying then, that before a culturally disadvantaged child can equal a normal child of his age and potential, he must acquire meanings or concepts. I agree. These develop only through 'make-up' work in experiencing; he needs a wide variety of experiences. After—and only after—his teacher has done remedial work in teaching him conceptualization can the child take the next step: to acquire facility in manipulating meanings through symbols and words—through reading words and using them in speech. A child will read and speak voluntarily and correctly *only after he knows what he is talking about* or what his reading words mean. Peggy's and Victor's stories certainly emphasized this point! Obviously, the effective teacher of disadvantaged children does more than 'teach them English!'[1] "

"Yes, Mrs. Brown's story of her year with Peggy makes this very clear: the manner and degree to which a child expresses himself—in speech, reading, or writing—depends upon the facts and ideas he has to express. The wealth of intake determines the quality of output. A good school experience will provide boys and girls with many intake opportunities—with new facts to acquire, new avenues of experiences, new relationships to explore, new occasions for communication—all opportunities which will enrich ideas and expand vocabularies.

"As children gain meaningful concepts, feel the desire to express them, and experience encouragement and success in doing so, they are mastering the skills—of reading, writing, and speaking—necessary to implement their purposes. They next progress to learnings of a higher order, as did Juan, Peggy, and especially Victor: to sentence mean-

---

[1] The section adapted from George Sanchez, "Significance of Language Handicap" in *Learning a New Language,* Association for Childhood Education International Bulletin 101 (Washington, D.C., 1958), p. 25–30.

ings, structural analysis, sensory images, whole-part relationships, relationships by association—and insights into their emotional reactions toward the total process of learning a new language. For these children, such a range of accomplishments in a second language is a triumph indeed!

"So let us never forget that disadvantaged children you teach—even those who presumably know English—will have problems of communicating with you and with their classmates because they do not know the *language you use* at school—or the words found in their readers. These symbols simply do not have enough meaning for them to communicate in English with confidence and facility!"

Language? Or Feelings About Language?

"There are other reasons why children may have what seem to be 'language problems' in school. Some Indian, Spanish-speaking, Chinese, or Negro children are hesitant to talk because what they know about and can talk about does not seem to fit into what the teacher and their classmates expect of them. They are baffled in this new environment, uncomfortable or ashamed because they do not fit in. Consequently, such boys and girls may become the hostile, problem children. Or, they may just sit in your classroom; they won't talk; they can't read; they don't even seem to listen. Some teachers can't reach them; so they think them sullen—or lazy—or mentally retarded."

The panel was "going strong"; one person could hardly wait for another to finish. They kept on interrupting one another in order to add to or expand on an idea—"When the real problem is that such boys and girls have some deficiencies upon beginning school which are not shared by children who come from the predominantly middle-class culture! Much has been written lately about the problems of these culturally disadvantaged boys and girls. Many schools have been trying to understand what these children are 'up against,' so that teachers can develop ways of working with these boys and girls which will offset some of their disadvantages."

"In a study in Pennsylvania, educators found that these children were deficient in seven areas important to school success. The areas were: the child's

1. Inability to understand or use the language of the school;
2. Inability to concentrate or listen beyond very short periods of time;
3. Social insecurity;
4. Apprehension of the school and its components;
5. Inferior training in pre-requisite visual or auditory discrimination;

6. Unfamiliarity with scheduling and order;

7. Lack of intrinsic and extrinsic motivation to succeed.[2]

"Isn't it interesting that Miss Begay and Mr. Gonzales mentioned each of these areas as they discussed the Indian and Mexican child's school problems? It is noteworthy, too, that, of these seven deficiencies, three are clearly communication problems and the other four are directly related to communication; for example, the boy or girl will not speak if he is apprehensive in his school surroundings; or if he does not feel socially acceptable; or if he does not care about succeeding in school."

"In other words, a child's feelings are powerful determinants of what he learns in school. If a child feels unhappy, fearful, or hostile towards a teacher, he cannot identify with that teacher or want to learn even the new language represented by the teacher. Unfortunately, some teachers are not favorably inclined toward disadvantaged children. And this feeling of theirs includes even children whose school achievement is good! The teacher's negative image of the disadvantaged child, in turn, is reflected not only in a child's inability to learn in the classroom, but also in his behavior and in his lowering of his self-image. Studies have shown that children quickly sense and accurately perceive a teacher's lack of confidence in them or his rejection of them."

"Yes, all of these feelings result in what the Pennsylvania study calls 'social insecurity': a composite of feelings bound up in the phrase 'they don't like *me*'—or 'they don't like *who I am*.' Because a child learns who he is in his family, rejection of him means rejection of his family and all that it represents—its language, its culture, and its values. Mr. Gonzales, you know, impressed upon us the fact that a child's desire or willingness to learn a new language—and the school's new ways—is related to the complex of experiences, and their affective elements, with which, as a member of a minority group, he and his family view the world and the world views them."

"You are saying that since language is directly related to the total development of an individual, any attempt to deprecate his language strikes deep at the inner core of his personality. If a child is made to feel that his language is inferior, therefore not to be spoken in school, *he* feels inferior. If a Pablo or Juan has to tell his friends, 'Don' let 'dem hear you speakin' Spaneesh. We go to da offeece, get swat, swat ven ve say one teeng in Spaneesh,' then the prejudice against Pablo and

[2]"The Program to Reduce Dropouts in the Schools of Pennsylvania," Phase I of a Three-Phased Pre-School and Primary Operation, Department of Public Instruction, (Harrisburg, Pa. 1963), p. 17.

Juan and their friends implied in such school rules is certainly not conducive to building up enthusiasm for learning English. In fact, so
blatantly do such rules spell rejection of the child that all learning is
blocked!"

"Just how powerful feelings of rejection, whether related to language or to cultural differences, can be in blocking a child's learning
was illustrated in Juan's story and in Anthony's attitude toward school.
Should any of you meet a Juan or an Anthony, keep in mind, that, however he behaves, he has learned those ways. They are the only ways he
now knows to protect himself—and his self-esteem. Before he can
change his pattern of behavior, he will need to develop a different set
of relationships with people; he will need to have enough positive experiences with people to convince him that it is safe to learn new ways
—their ways."

"Or their language! Remember that a child will need acceptance and
support as he tries to learn new concepts, as he attaches the proper
object, action, property, and relationship to an appropriate word; he
will need time to discriminate between new sounds he hears; he will
need many opportunities to use those sounds—it is one thing to pronounce the words of a new language from a reading lesson, but quite
another to use the new language in general conversation! (Have you
tried speaking Navajo—or Chinese—or Spanish?) He will need supple-
mentary practice with pictures, stories, experiences—the kind of practice Mrs. Brown gave Peggy! Most important, he will need the understanding of his classmates. They may wonder about what the teacher is
doing with him and think, 'funny way to read!' as did some of Mrs.
Brown's pupils. However, children can and do learn—from their
teacher's attitude and example—that everyone is different and that
consequently, different people in the class learn in different ways.

"I suggest, therefore, that a teacher's *basic assumption* be that the
culturally disadvantaged child, regardless of age, *needs help in learning to communicate before he can be taught to read.* Given this
assumption, the teacher knows where to begin with the child: with the
three aspects of communication—listening, observing, and speaking.
These are basic to the development of language skill. Without them,
there can be no reading—in fact, no communication."

Teaching Listening

"May I interrupt? I agree with you. Therefore, I want us to be certain to ask a question. The study quoted emphasized that one of the
deficits with which this child comes to school is inability to listen.

This may sound peculiar to some of us. Can't everyone who isn't physically deaf listen if he wants to — and tries?"

"Many teachers assume that everyone *can* listen. On the other hand, teachers are fully aware of wide differences in listening ability in each of their classes. Many teachers also assume that listening is only a question of will — or 'wanting to listen.' You've heard teachers complain, 'He just *won't* listen.' Does the complainer ever wonder why he *won't* listen? Could it be that he has never been taught to listen?

"What do I mean? Isn't listening dependent on ability to hear? Of course, but listening is not a *mere* physical process. To be able to listen, a boy or girl must perceive and understand what he hears — he must be able to relate to it. To understand how this comes about, remember what you know about mental development: a child learns in the intimacy of the care and affection given him as an infant. The skills, habits, and attitudes he learns early in life are learned in concrete, meaningful situations — through actual experiences. As sounds become meaningful, because they signal the fact that something pleasant is about to happen — perhaps he is about to be held and fed — a child learns to listen for these sounds. As people who are meaningful to a child talk to him, their words gain meaning; thus, he learns to listen to them! By listening, he also learns to imitate sounds around him. His parents' smiles and encouragement reward his attempts to listen and to imitate what he hears. Such a child keeps on listening and trying to talk because these are ways of securing approval from important people in his environment.

"The culturally deprived child may not have had such opportunities to listen, much less to talk. His parents may have been so absorbed in the task of providing the necessities of life for a large family that, like Anthony's or Juan's parents, they had neither the time nor the inclination to give the child individual attention, to listen to or to talk to the child about anything. Besides, it may never have occurred to them that there was any need for such attention or any benefit to be derived from it."

"In fact, I should like to emphasize that the culturally deprived child might actually have learned *not* to listen. If he lives, as many do, in a crowded trailer or one or two-room house, often with an 'extended family' of grandparents, uncles, aunts, and cousins sharing the home along with his parents, brothers, and sisters, the child is forced, in pure self-defense, to 'tune out' many of the noises around him. (Anthony speaks of this necessity.) With so many people crowded into a small space, the only way a child can achieve even a small measure of privacy is to ignore much that is happening around him and blot out as much sound as possible. Result: he dulls his powers both of listening and of observing, since listening with comprehension involves both these aspects! Yet without these skills and habits a child cannot learn—"

"Yes, listening, like reading, is a complicated learning process. Careful, thoughtful listening is fundamental to everyone's learning— the pre-schooler, the fourth grader, the high school, or college student. Moreover, it is important not only in school, but in out-of-school life. Everyone is constantly bombarded with a multitudinous variety of sounds and words to many of which a response is expected. How a child learns to respond to these auditory signals, then, is an important factor in the manner in which he makes adjustments throughout life.

"Obviously, school time *must* be devoted in every classroom to teaching skills necessary to good listening! Every child can benefit by improving his listening habits—but the culturally disadvantaged child who doesn't know how to listen and cannot learn on his own will profit most. How can a teacher help children learn to listen?"

"Just to be certain that hearing is taken into consideration, a child's ears should, of course, be checked by the school nurse if there is any question of ability to hear. After all, listening constitutes three-fifths of communication, according to research—therefore, the school must know whether a child is able to hear! However, mere *ability to hear* does not insure that the meaning of the sounds or language is 'taken in' or understood. A child may listen and hear sounds, but he will not 'take them in' if he literally does not understand the questions or directions he hears. Plainly, in this case, he will not know what the teacher expects of him."

"May I suggest, you seem to be saying that the teacher who is trying to help children learn to listen needs to ask himself questions like these:

1. How do I know whether a child is listening? Teachers must remember that listening is never just the absence of talking!
2. If a child seems not to be listening, is this daily behavior, frequent, or rare behavior? Ability to listen will vary from child to child and from situation to situation—as it does even with you!
3. If a child seems unable to listen, what do I need to know about him? Perhaps he has never learned to listen; for example, Miss Begay emphasized the fact that Indian children are taught to look and to imitate rather than to listen, to question or to follow directions. Perhaps the child in question has had comparatively little experience in listening to and speaking with adults;

he may have spent most of his time with his brothers and sisters and his play-mates. Perhaps his parents communicated with him only briefly as they gave him orders or scolded him, as in Juan's case. Hence, the child now pays more attention to his classmates than to his teacher. Perhaps the child is not listen-ing because he "has other things on his mind," as Anthony did. Bear in mind that the poor listener has learned his behavior; his teacher must teach him dif-ferent habits.

"How do you teach a given child to listen? There is no single method. However, basic to all a teacher does will be his ability to do what Mr. McMann called 'building up a relationship with a child' so that the child will trust you to teach him. If a teacher is to be successful in building such a relationship, he must be genuinely concerned about the child and able to communicate personal interest in him as a human being in whose growth and development the teacher wishes to be in-volved. The building of such a relationship takes time, patience, under-standing, and ever-growing ingenuity in sensing when and how a child needs support and when and how he needs encouragement to move forward."

"The process of building a relationship with a child may have once seemed to you new teachers somewhat vague and abstract. You wanted to know *what to do* with a particular child. Mrs. Brown and Mrs. Branson tried to answer your questions by sharing with you their stories of Peggy Blackgoat and Juan Chavez. They kept daily anecdotal records for a year; they wrote up these records of their relationship with a Navajo child and a Mexican one. As they discussed the records with you, you realized, I am sure, that here was a demonstration of the growth, development, and results — if you will — of a genuine teacher-child relationship."

"To return, then, to our original question 'how do I teach a child to listen?' Our first assumption will be that each teacher is able to de-velop in his class a favorable atmosphere for listening. Obviously, such an atmosphere will be one in which a child like Peggy or Juan will learn that, by listening, important personal needs will be satisfied; for example, that he or she will gain acceptance and response from his teacher and classmates, and a feeling of achievement.

"Next, we have distributed to you a list of specific *techniques* which some of us have *used* successfully in *helping* boys and girls of all ages to *learn to listen*. Each of you can adapt this list to the age-group you teach. Need we say that these will be useful to you only when the teacher is aware of the need for listening? We don't teach what we don't know — or practice. Sometimes, in our zeal to teach, we our-selves do not spend enough time listening.

"Children will learn to listen to you if you have courteously listened to their remarks and shown interest in them. Avoid the 'brush-off' — and do not attempt to write or do something else while children are talking to you. Give them your undivided attention if you expect their undivided attention when you are talking to them.

1. Provide a setting for listening. The room should be quiet and the desks clear of unneeded objects so that full attention can be given to listening to what you have to say. For small children, requiring hands to be on desks and each child to be reasonably erect in his seat enhances the possibility of his listening.

2. Do not begin talking until the pupils are ready to listen. If you ask a question, call on a boy or girl only after the question has been asked, not before. In this way, everyone will listen. Do not repeat the question for the person who has been called on unless the question needs to be rephrased because, although heard, it has not been understood.

3. When a boy or girl talks, do not repeat what he has said. No one will listen to him if the pupils depend upon you to rephrase, or improve upon, someone's words. On the *other* hand, do not allow boys and girls to do something else, like drawing while they are listening. They cannot do both simultaneously; they are only wasting time.

4. Do not expect boys and girls to listen to you if you are standing behind them. They must see as well as hear; preferably, all the senses should be involved in the listening process. Sight, touch, taste, sound, and smell can make listening meaningful. Listening is not an isolated experience.

5. Give boys and girls experience, not only in listening, but in recording what they hear. Help them to listen to something, perhaps a news broadcast or a pupil's report on some assigned topic, to take notes and then to compare what they have heard with the original. The teacher takes notes along with the group, both to set an example and to assess adequately what the boys and girls have heard and reported.

If this method is followed as boys and girls give their own reports, improvement in their efforts is almost immediately apparent. When a pupil knows that he is expected to give constructive criticisms on form, content and organization of each report, he listens to others' reports more carefully and works on his own more zealously. The day may come when the boys and girls hear things the teacher misses! Two cautions: do not expect children to listen for too long a period of time, particularly not after a long seatwork period. And do not abruptly interfere and trick any group into listening to something *you* want them to do when they are deeply engrossed in some project important to *them!*

6. Make up games which require listening to simple but specific directions such as "stand up" "sit down," "hands on head." "Simon Says" is a possibility.

7. Make up games which require attention to detail. For example, "I am thinking of something in our room which is brown. It is square. Shall I give you another clue?"

8. Make a "toy chest" out of a shoe box. Provide a set of cards with "toy words" on them — wagon, ball, car, train, doll, boat, etc. Give each player four cards. The teacher holds the toy chest. He calls for a toy and says, "I wish I had a toy that begins like bat." The player who holds a card beginning with the right letter says, "I can make your wish come true." He reads his card out loud and puts it in the toy chest. Your ingenuity can apply this idea to categories of all kinds — from animals to space flight!

9. Look for any opportunity during the day to listen to identifying sounds just for fun; for example, Is it a helicopter or a jet? Or, with primary children, at going-home time, say "All of those whose name begins with the same sound as 'duck' may go."

10. Make several sets of word and picture cards. In each set, put six or eight rhyming words together with one or two that do not rhyme. As the teacher says each word in a group, he asks the boys and girls in turn, "Does this rhyme with the others?" If it does, the pupil puts it into a pocket on a chart — or a pile on the table. If it does not, he puts it into the joker pile.

11. Use riddles as an opportunity for careful listening as well as for fun.

12. Make up riddles based on analogies between living and inanimate things; for example, "It has two hands but no arms" (clock), "It has teeth, it says 'zzz,' but it cannot eat" (saw), "It has four legs, but it cannot walk" (table). This technique not only involves learning to listen; it also helps prepare boys and girls for figures of speech — and is especially applicable to preadolescents and adolescents, who eagerly invent their own sets of analogies!

13. Establish a regular policy of giving directions only once. Make the directions simple and definite.

14. Give only one direction at a time as you work with boys and girls. In a primary reading group, for example, say, "Find two words that begin with *B*." "Put your finger on a word that ends with *T*." "Frame a word that means somebody's pet." "If you can find the name of a girl on this page, read it out loud."

15. Check listening ability by asking questions about a story you have just read: "How many girls were in the story I read? Did the wolf eat the sheep? How many brothers does Johnny have?" This is *necessary* with all age groups!

16. Read aloud poems with content and mood especially suited to imaginative drawings; for example, Laura Richard's *The Monkey and the Crocodile*. Tell the boys and girls that, after they have listened to a poem, they are to draw pictures which the poem makes them see. Read the poem several times if necessary.

"Each of us could discuss with you specific reasons why we developed each of these particular techniques. Not having time, we'll use one illustration: establish a regular policy of giving directions only once and of making them short and clear. We feel that this way of working with culturally disadvantaged children is most important in training them to listen. Why?

"As we said earlier, we have found that often these children, in their crowded homes, have learned to shut out or disregard much of the verbalization that goes on around them, particularly the quarreling of young children, the 'yak-yakking' of adults in the household, and the TV or radio turned to the loudest possible volume in some homes. Adults in these homes, in turn, have learned not to expect a response from a child until they have repeated an order or given a direction several times, raising the volume of their voice each time. In other words, many of these children have learned not to respond to an adult voice until it has reached a certain pitch and volume.

"We suggest that teachers *retrain children's listening habits* rather than fall into the trap of giving repeated directions on an ever-rising decibel of sound! Therefore, give directions once in a well-modulated low speaking voice—but not a monotone! A monotone + an expressionless face = a bore and discourages any response.

"So far, we have said that: *learning to listen precedes learning to read* and that *listening can be taught* to culturally disadvantaged children. *Learning to talk also precedes learning to read.* In fact, the rate at which a boy or girl learns the new language, is able to imitate the new words, and to use them with meaning in conversation will determine the progress he will make in reading."

Teaching New Words and Concepts

"Culturally disadvantaged boys and girls *can* learn to talk the language of the school. They will learn new words in two ways: by imitating words and by learning their meanings. Frequent repetition of a new word is necessary; this involves imitation of the teacher's pitch, stress, volume, and rhythm as he or she uses the word. Do you recall Mrs. Branson's teaching Juan to say *children* and *cherry?* In addition, meaningful experiences must be linked with the word.

"Words become meaningful as boys and girls develop skill in observation. Such skill involves interpretation of the messages children receive from their five senses. A child's senses help him to make contact with the world. Every child's world is full of an endless variety of interesting things: but the child needs help in developing, first, awareness of things, then, familiarity with them. As a child learns to make contact with the world, his teacher teaches him to interpret messages he receives from his five senses. The child's world becomes increasingly meaningful to him as he becomes increasingly skillful in interpreting these sensory stimuli and labeling the new concepts with words."

"How does the wise teacher utilize a pupil's five senses in this process of learning a new word? We *look,* and what can we see? How big is it? What color it is? Will it hurt us? We *listen,* and what do the sounds tell us? Do we hear a happy sound? A sad sound? A scary sound? A warning sound? If we close our eyes, how can we tell what it is? We *feel.* Is it soft? Hard? Square? Round? Sharp? We can't see it, we can't hear it, or touch it? Now what? Let's *smell* it. How does it smell? Sweet? Strong? Unpleasant? Good? There's no smell? We can *taste* it. Is it sour? Salty? Bitter? Sweet?

"In other words, teach a boy or girl new words through direct contact with his environment. Depending upon the pupil's age, use toys and other familiar objects such as play telephones; supplement with visual aids such as picture cards, puppets, films, teaching machines, or experience charts. Thus, as you teach a pupil to observe and to describe his environment, he finds that there are sights and sounds and tastes and smells he has never before encountered. If his encounter with these new things is pleasant and satisfying, you instill in him a desire to learn more about them — to enlarge his stock of meanings. A culturally disadvantaged boy or girl may never have wanted to learn before because his environment was unpleasant; now he finds a different world outside his circumscribed sphere."

"With a culturally disadvantaged boy or girl, a teacher can *never* assume that he understands words just because they are common words or because they represent familiar concepts. If a boy or girl has never seen or tasted honey, how can he understand a story about bees and honey? The word 'rug' means nothing to him if he has never seen one on the floor of a home. He may have seen one in a theater, but this gives no conception of the way it is used in a home. An Indian child, in fact, is likely to have used what we call a rug as a blanket. Perhaps the teacher reads about an ant. Everyone knows what an ant is — or do they? Some boys and girls may understand that the wife of his uncle is an aunt — although Navajo children who are a part of an extended family may have difficulties! To distinguish between *aunt* and *ant* and to know the latter as a little red or black insect, they need to relate to each of these words through experiences and examples. The teacher must constantly be on the alert to show a child, to explain, to have a child experience meanings of new words.

"When abstract words appear — in conversation or reading, a pupil's difficulties mount. A boy or girl confuses *across* and *around?* Well, why not? A teacher can help: have the children demonstrate by walking *around* the table and crawling *across* the table. Or perhaps it is raining outside. The teacher can take the group to the window to look at the puddles. If they are big, we can go *around* them; if they are small, we can step *across*. In the next day or two, to reinforce these meanings, the teacher has the boys and girls look *across* the room to see what is there; then they all look *around* the room—and then they talk about the difference between the two words.

"Such understanding is basic if a boy or girl is to develop a stock of accurate ideas or concepts about the world in which he lives. As the pupil integrates words and ideas or concepts, he develops his tools of thought."

"This process is familiar to you. How could *you* think except by beginning with your immediate experiences, recalling them and reflecting on their meanings; giving names to things, actions, and issues involved in them; and appraising the total in terms of concepts and values which you understand and accept as important to you? When a child reacts in these ways, he can possess the world in a new way; he can integrate what he says and does; and he is able to exert influence over his own behavior and over that of others. As a child learns to communicate with himself, then he becomes capable of planning his actions—and of evaluating a plan before he puts it into action! Bear in mind this process as you tell the Juans and the Anthonys to 'think before you act.'"

Teaching Observation and Meaning

"I'm so glad that you pointed out these fundamentals in the teaching process: that we proceed from observation to meaning to thinking. The examples given suggested to me that this might be the logical time for us to give you a list of activities which we have found useful in helping culturally disadvantaged children *to develop* their powers of *observation*. However, as we have specifically pointed out, we see these, not as a set of techniques or 'gimmicks,' but as tools to be used in the hands of sensitive teachers who want to enhance boys' and girls' understanding and comprehension of language so that these children may develop tools of thought and grow in their ability to learn control of themselves and of their environment. Here, then, is our list, to be adapted to any age group—limited only by your ingenuity:

1. Bring into the classroom a variety of objects the boys and girls can see, feel, smell, and taste: for example, various fruits and vegetables—samples of many different kinds of fabrics, materials, minerals—pictures of objects or processes—dependent on the age and interests of your pupils!

2. Collect pictures of objects that are used together such as knife and fork, shoe and sock, pencil and paper, tie and shirt, dress and belt, hammer and

nails. Paste one of each pair of associated objects in an envelope at the bottom of the chart. Teach the boys and girls to match the objects. This suggestion can be adapted to the interests of any age group.

3. Make a seasonal bulletin board which will emphasize sensory images. For example, under the heading *Fall is Here,* place subheadings: *We See It—We Hear It—We Feel It—We Smell It—We Taste It.* Have the children draw or paint pictures to illustrate the subheads. Encourage them to bring real leaves, flowers, seeds, etc. to put under appropriate headings.

4. Make two posters. Paste a happy face at the top of one and a sad face at the top of the other. Let children cut out happy and sad faces. Talk about them and let the children tell why those they cut out belong on either the happy or sad poster.

5. Start a class scrapbook with headings like: *Things We Like to See—to Smell—to Taste—to Hear—to Touch.* Let the boys and girls cut out pictures from old magazines and make their own drawings for the scrapbook. Let older children make individual scrapbooks planned around subjects which interest them.

6. Start a chart called *"What Would You Find?"* For example, draw—or paste a picture—of a refrigerator on a piece of oaktag. Let the boys and girls collect pictures of things they would find in a refrigerator and paste these on a chart. This idea can be adapted—for a clothes closet, a playground, a classroom, a fire station, a specific room in a house, etc.

7. Describe for a child a familiar person, such as another child in the classroom or another teacher—or a familiar thing such as an article in the classroom or a piece of playground equipment. Have the child "guess who" or "guess what."

8. Read a story aloud and let the boy or girl tell what happened first, next, and last.

9. Scramble the letters of new words learned in a story. Have the pupils rearrange them in their original order.

10. At the end of a story, let each boy and girl draw a picture and tell about it.

11. Take your pupils on field trips. The airport, zoo, firehouse, post office, supermarket, a house being built, a highway being repaired, a farm, a dairy, a ranch, a sawmill, a factory, a nature trail, City Hall, a science museum, a theatre, a fruit orchard, or plant nursery may be new experiences to many culturally disadvantaged boys and girls. Be sure that you help them to know what to look for before the visit; then check to see what they can tell you afterward. To make their report vivid, you might adapt the chart mentioned in item 6.

12. Let boys and girls participate in simple science experiments: for example, teach them to observe the differences between plants growing in sunlight and in darkness—or to observe and describe the process of water evaporation.

"So far, we have said that *careful listening and keen observation are the bases for meaningful learning of new words.* Effective *listen-*

ing habits *can be taught* to a child; his *powers of observation can be built up.* We have discussed *ways* in which attentive listening, analytical listening, and appreciative listening habits can be developed. We have given examples of *techniques* which will encourage children to observe carefully and accurately."

Encouraging Speech

"As a boy or girl learns more and more words, he begins to feel more 'at home' in the school situation. He responds to the teacher's encouragement to use these new words; he begins to talk. His first responses may be single words—or two or three-word sentences. In some cases, his pronunciation may be strange. Note how Mrs. Brown managed Peggy's first attempts at conversation! The important thing for a teacher to remember is that there is little point in trying to teach reading until a child can use words in sentences—and sentences in conversation. Just as *learning to listen precedes learning to talk,* so *learning to talk precedes learning to read.* A boy or girl can learn to read no faster than he can learn to understand and use the new words he is daily encountering."

"Speaking is an integral part of learning and of life. Yet, in this area, the culturally disadvantaged boy and girl shows the greatest deficiency. His lack of experience in speaking correlates with his inability to listen and to observe because, in his home and background, comparatively little verbal communication takes place; and people seldom bother really to listen to one another. It is difficult for these boys and girls to express their ideas, since most of them have never learned that they had any ideas which anyone considered worthy of attentive listening."

"Consequently, it should not be surprising that some of these children are loath to speak even though they may be learning—and understanding—many new words. Even Victor, in spite of encouragement from home, was loath to speak in school! Moreover, each child's language development will depend on factors other than his cultural background: for example, his intelligence, his temperament, his motivation to learn, and his degree of security in the classroom situation."

A panel member who had been intently interested in this discussion interrupted, "I am glad that you mentioned the child who is loath to talk—and I don't mean the Victors who, gradually, will gain confidence to do so! I mean that, sometimes, a teacher feels that he has run into a blank wall; a certain child simply doesn't *want* to talk! Let the teacher who thinks this look at the situation from the child's point of view. Perhaps no one ever considered this child's remarks or opinions worthy of listening to before; why should he assume that this new adult in his life really wants to hear what he has to say? Perhaps, at home, he has so often been told to 'pipe down' that he is convinced that his ideas are worthless.

"A teacher's primary aim must be to build up this boy or girl's confidence that he does indeed have something of value to say. The teacher daily encourages him to express his ideas by making opportunities to talk with him alone or in a small group—before and after school, in the halls and on the playground."

"Possibly the child needs help in putting into words what he wants to say. Sometimes, a boy or girl simply doesn't know how to *begin* speaking. He fears that the other children might laugh at him, that what he says might not be what he really meant to say, that he does not have the words he needs or that he does not use them correctly. Do you recall that Victor, even after several years in school, poignantly expresses feelings like these?"

"May I interrupt? One fear you mentioned—of being shamed—especially influences the Indian child. Remember that he comes from a culture which uses public shame as a method of correcting the child. He would far rather not speak at all than take the risk of someone laughing at him. In fact, it is not unusual for an Indian child to fail to answer a question asked him in a class discussion. Even if he knows the answer, he may not venture the possibility of being wrong. However, outside of class, if he were alone with you or with a small group with whom he felt comfortable, you might find him ready to speak.

"Children of Mexican extraction will usually answer in class, but the reply may be 'I don't know' if they would rather not talk. Negro children are generally individualistic in their reaction to a request to speak, depending on their environmental backgrounds which are usually more varied than those of the other children being considered here."

"Perhaps we should add that a minority of children may hesitate to talk because they have speech defects. The problem of speech defects, whether organic, functional, or emotional in origin is an entirely separate problem from the one discussed here. We are concerned with the communication problem of the culturally disadvantaged child who, because of deficits in his background, has used his speech equipment sparingly, when he has used it at all. We are considering techniques and activities designed to help him to overcome his *communication* problems.

"Teaching culturally disadvantaged boys and girls how to speak clearly and how to express ideas effectively, however, doesn't mean that a teacher sets apart a period in which 'we learn to speak!' On the contrary, throughout the school day, these boys and girls should have opportunities to talk on any subject that interests them — opportunities to describe, narrate, demonstrate, or dramatize — whether this speaking takes places informally or in connection with spelling, science, arithmetic, art, writing, or reading! Note how Mrs. Brown ingeniously created opportunities to make conversation with Peggy at recess, at lunch-time, before and after school. Gradually, she included, in the conversation, one or two other children, then small groups!

"A wise teacher never *forces* any child to speak, especially not in a large group like the entire class. He remembers that oral language does not 'come naturally' to all boys and girls, especially not to the culturally disadvantaged child. However, the teacher encourages this child's speaking and praises each small achievement, whether the pupil speaks up in a small group or even alone with the teacher. The teacher's approval gives the child confidence to try again. The teacher is very careful when and how he criticizes the child's speech. Criticism is never made before a group and, when given, is given constructively: for example, 'let's try saying it this way.'"

A panel member interposed. "Your emphasis on the importance of the teacher's role in encouraging culturally disadvantaged boys and girls to speak is 'taking the words out of our mouths.' The panel has prepared for new teachers a list of suggested *activities* which we thought useful in *encouraging* culturally disadvantaged *boys and girls to speak.* We begin by emphasizing that our first two suggestions — conversation with the teacher, and with a small group and the teacher — are basic. These two simple, though time-consuming activities, are the most effective methods of encouraging culturally disadvantaged boys and girls to begin to speak! Succeeding activities will be useful *after* these pupils have had satisfying experiences in the first two and thus gained confidence enough in themselves to want to speak. Again, an ingenious teacher will adapt our suggestions to any age group. We begin our list, then, as follows:

1. Although it sounds so simple, the most important oral language activity for the culturally disadvantaged boy or girl — especially upon his initial entrance into school — is conversation with the teacher (which may be very one-sided at first). The day begins with the teacher's greeting, "Good morning, Mary, I'm glad to see you this morning." (No response.) "Did you have a good breakfast?" "Yes." "What did you eat?" (No response.) "Did you have bread? Eggs? Beans? Coffee? Cereal?" The girl may repeat one word. You have made a beginning in conversation. It may take many beginnings before a boy or girl will respond freely — even more before he will initiate a conversation. However, when a pupil does begin to talk, the teacher will know that his efforts were worthwhile!

2. Another simple but effective method is discussion in a small group. It is

possible that all the culturally disadvantaged pupils may be in a low reading group. If so, the teacher again will have to take the initiative in conversation. He must be certain to keep his vocabulary within the range of the child's comprehension. He must also be on the alert to clarify and explain words signifying objects, even some in the classroom, which the teacher may take for granted, but whose names the children do not know. How can a pupil respond to your conversation if he hasn't the vaguest idea what you are talking about?

Response in this small group can often be initiated by reading a story, asking questions about it, and soliciting comparable experiences from the group. This situation also provides an opportunity to clarify word meanings. For example, words like *around* and *across,* previously mentioned, might occur naturally in a story about a chick who couldn't get *across* the puddle and found out how to go *around.* To encourage talking, a story could be both dramatized and discussed. Does discussion wander far afield from the story? Use it as a springboard for the boys and girls to talk about what interests them. If one pupil begins talking, others may gain enough confidence to contribute. Or the teacher may encourage a child to enter the conversation in a manner comparable to Mrs. Brown's. When her group was discussing pets, you remember, she said, "Peggy, do you have a dog?"

3. If, as suggested in a previous list, the teacher brings objects the boys and girls need to learn about, many speaking opportunities will arise; for example, "What is this?" A strawberry. "What color is it? What does it look like? How big is it? How does it feel? What are those things on the outside? Does it smell? How does it taste?" Have boys and girls bring things to a 'show and tell' period or to a discussion group.

4. Use a play telephone and have boys and girls dramatize answering it. Dramatic play helps these boys and girls gain confidence in themselves. Adolescents especially enjoy all forms of role-playing and dramatics—and puppetry.

5. Akin to dramatics is the use of puppets. Simple hand puppets can be made by boys and girls themselves. Their uses are infinite; you might begin as you help boys and girls learn to know one another through a "get-acquainted" game. A shy person may be encouraged to speak in a discussion or play—or to tell a story—if he can manipulate a puppet from behind the curtain of the puppet stage—and remain out of sight of the group as he talks. Shadow play is also useful with the boy or girl who is loath to speak. Young children will sometimes use a family of dolls and a dollhouse similarly. Both boys and girls may be willing to talk when it is the doll doing the talking. (And what you can learn about the child's family relationships in the process!)

6. A shy boy or girl, especially an adolescent, may be encouraged to take part in choral speaking—though he would not speak alone.

7. Use all kinds of toys, pictures, movies, and other visual aids to introduce boys and girls to new words, to carry on dramatic play and to encourage them to talk.

8. Let the boys and girls finish sentences started by the teacher, ones that

use action words which they can dramatize as well as speak: for example, a bird — (flies, hops, sings); a cow — (moos, eats, gives milk). Adapt your vocabulary to the social maturity of your group.

9. Collect and play a variety of singing games or folk songs, some of which feature rhymes and jingles, accompanied by action and word repetition. Boys and girls will often sing although they will not talk.

10. Use records or a rhythm band. You can teach poetry — or jingles in this manner. Let the boys and girls act out — or dance — whatever the words suggest to them. Children and adolescents who are loath to talk can often be persuaded to do so as they move around dancing or playing an instrument.

11. Let the children draw pictures of their families and identify everyone: This is my mother, father, sister, brother, grandmother, etc.

12. In small groups, play a variety of word games: this is especially important for preadolescents and adolescents who need a broadened base for language. They can gain it by giving and sharing information which will make words meaningful to them.

a) Finding opposites: if something is not hot, it must be --- (cold); if it is not hard, it must be --- (soft), etc.

b) Gaining abstract concepts: big, bigger, biggest; both, many, not so many; over, beyond, before, through, by, near, beside, behind, etc.

c) Incomplete sentences: use phrases like "let me, give me, I want to." The first person to complete the sentence is "it" and chooses the person to follow him.

d) Use synonyms: the boy I am thinking of is kind (nice, pleasant, good, etc.).

e) Categories: tell *where* something is or *when* something happened: *classify* words as something we can *see, hear, feel, taste,* etc.

f) Use picture cards and let each player find and say the names of words rhyming with the object pictured on the card.

g) Demonstrate what you discuss whenever possible; i.e., use concrete objects or draw pictures of objects to develop understandings foreign to these boys and girls.

h) As they read and talk, differentiate carefully between words of similar meaning or similar appearance; emphasize also that the same word may have different meanings.

"These boys and girls are frequently confronted, in their reading, with words which have no counterpart in their language or with concepts which, by nature of their background, are unintelligible to them — though they may be familiar to farm children or middle-class town and city children. Unless a teacher continuously, from kindergarten through high school, works at this problem of expanding a disadvantaged child's vocabulary by making words meaningful to him, such a boy or girl, year by year, will fall more hopelessly behind in his understanding of words and, therefore, in his school learning."

13. If possible, find an opportunity for family-style dining in small groups with all ages of boys and girls. Perhaps you can arrange to have five or six boys and girls at a time eat their lunch in the classroom while others go to the cafeteria. Thus you may find that some of them need to learn the words for certain foods, table coverings, napkins or silverware.

14. Provide opportunities for boys and girls of all ages to deliver messages for you to other teachers, the nurse, the librarian, or the office. Usually a boy or girl is delighted to be trusted with an errand; however, if he is shy, send a friend along.

15. Have many easy-to-read and colorful books available at your pupils' age and interest level. Encourage a boy or girl to find a story he likes and read it to you before or after school or whenever you can spare a few moments. Talk with the boy or girl about the story. Praise each one's interest and progress in reading. Arrange to have the boy or girl read the story to someone else—a friend, last year's teacher, the school nurse, librarian, dietitian, principal—anyone who understands what you are doing and who will encourage the boy's or girl's efforts.

16. Use the words "please," "thank you," and "excuse me" over and over and have the class imitate you so that, gradually, they learn to say the words "on their own."

"Now we have discussed and given you examples of *what you can do to teach culturally disadvantaged boys and girls to listen, to observe, and to speak.* We have talked about why it is important to work with them in this fashion: if we are to communicate with these boys and girls and have them understand what we say, we must help them to build concepts through meaningful experiences with words. *Only when a boy or girl can comprehend and use a language can he read it.* Obviously, then, it is necessary to teach these boys and girls first to listen, to observe, and to express themselves before we can hope to teach them to read.

"Let me end our discussion by emphasizing that our methods involve continuous, unending effort on the teacher's part. It will be difficult for you to find time in your crowded schedule to try out even some of these ideas. But you already knew it wouldn't be easy to help these boys and girls, didn't you?"

Several teachers in the audience smiled and nodded. One asked enthusiastically, "And if we do try to help—will these boys and girls become better readers for our effort?" A panel member replied seriously, "Would you like to find out? We can only say try."

Another added in an encouraging tone, "We're still trying because the greatest satisfaction in teaching is 'getting through' to a child — as the teachers who worked with Peggy, Juan, Victor, and Anthony know!" Mr. Jackson summarized — "Our 'focus and intent should be to work with the whole person . . . every phase of his experience should be evaluated in terms of helping him make a satisfactory and productive adjustment in school.'"[3]

---

[3] Robert L. Bennett, "Poverty — Its Effect on Indian Life," Intermountain School Workshop (Arizona, June 9, 1965), p. 4–5.